Chef Wan's Sweet Treats

*Chef Wan*

# Chef Wan's
# Sweet Treats

TIMES EDITIONS

# Chef Wan's Sweet Treats

Chef: Chef Wan Ismail
Chef's Assistant: Anne Rozario
Utensils and Crockery: Chef Wan Ismail

Project Editor/Editor of Malay Edition: Jamilah Mohd Hassan
Designer for Cover: Christopher Wong
Photographer: Jenhor Siow
Editors of English Edition: Juleen Shaw & Dinah Lee
Project Co-ordinator: Christine Chong
Production Co-ordinator: Nor Sidah Haron

The Publisher wishes to thank Metrojaya Berhad, Malaysia; Tangs Department Store Kuala Lumpur, Malaysia; Manja Restaurant, Bangsar Baru, Malaysia; Anne Rozario; and Christine Chong for the loan of their crockery and utensils.

First published (cased with jacket) November 1997, reprinted June 1998
Limp edition with gatefold December 1999, reprinted December 2000
This edition (limp with new cover design) April 2003, reprinted July 2004

© 1998 Times Editions Pte Ltd
© 2000 Times Media Private Limted
© 2004 Marshall Cavendish International (Asia) Pte Ltd

Published by Times Editions
An imprint of Marshall Cavendish International (Asia) Pte Ltd
A member of the Times Publishing Group

Times Centre, 1 New Industrial Road, Singapore 536196
Tel: (65) 6213 9288   Fax: (65) 6285 4871
E-mail: te@sg.marshallcavendish.com
Online Book Store: http://www.timesone.com.sg/te

Malaysian Office:
Federal Publications Sdn Berhad (General & Reference Publishing) (3024-D)
Times Subang, Lot 46, Persiaran Teknologi Subang, Subang Hi-Tech Industrial Park
Batu Tiga, 40000 Shah Alam, Selangor Darul Ehsan, Malaysia
Tel (603) 5635 2191   Fax: (603) 5635 2706
E-mail: cchong@tpg.com.my

All rights reserved. No part of this publication may be reproduced, stored in a retrieval system, or transmitted, in any form or by any means, electronic, mechanical, photocopying, recording or otherwise, without the prior permission of the copyright owner.

**National Library Board Singapore Cataloguing in Publication Data**

Wan, Chef, 1958-
Chef Wan's sweet treats. – Singapore: Times Editions, 2003.
p. cm
ISBN: 981-232-547-6

1. Pastry.  2. Cookies.  3. Desserts.  4. Cake.  I. Title.
TX773
641.86 — dc21                    SLS 20030006384

Printed by Times Offset (M) Sdn Bhd, Malaysia

# What's on the Plates?

8 Preface

10 Weights & Measures

12 Tarts & Pies

44 Muffins & Scones

60 Cheesecakes

88 Cookies

116 Bread

136 Cakes

170 Desserts

186 Index

# Preface

Baking has been one of my favourite pastimes since I was nine. I remember how I moulded and baked my first cookie at that young age. During the Hari Raya festive season, I was always proud and happy to tell all my friends and their mothers how many cookies my family had made so far.

My mother's kitchen was always like a *kilang* biscuit, or biscuit factory. There are seven of us in the family. I am the eldest and, of course, loved to boss my siblings around. It was like an assembly line in a cookie factory. My mother prepared the dough, two of my sisters took charge of cleaning, and the others took turns to mould the cookies, brush them with egg glaze and decorate them with glace cherries. My mother put the prepared cookies in the oven and, once they were baked and allowed time to cool, I gladly stored them in containers. Needless to say, some of the cookies found their way into my stomach!

On a normal day, we also helped our mother sell the *kuih kuih* (cakes and cookies) at the Royal Malaysian Air Force Camp. While most other children were out in the playground, I was usually in the kitchen trying to perfect the shape of my curry puff, of which we made hundreds each day. Pastry-making is unlike preparing a savoury dish. It takes time to master the skill and only practice can perfect it.

Although I love baking, I have never aspired to become a professional pastry chef. I have always been happy with being a "home chef". With a bit of reading, observing how things are put together and with a big heart and lots of practice, I am proud to be where I am today.

If you look at my recipes or have followed some of my baking shows on television, I have always projected a quick and easy style of baking. It fact, it has always been my contention that foods that have been fussed over too much before they are photographed come out looking a bit unreal. That is why some of my pastries may not look picture-perfect but I assure you they are easy to prepare and taste heavenly. It is my hope that the down-to-earth quality that I am projecting will encourage all those among you who are a little doubtful about your cooking abilities to get started; you can be just as successful as I am in turning out delicious sweet treats!

Many of my recipes have been gathered through the generosity of my wonderful friends worldwide and this book is dedicated in memory of Neil Monahan, San Francisco. My special thanks go to Mrs Maria Bischoff in Zurich and Evelyn in Melbourne. I also thank Christine Chong in Kuala Lumpur and Jamilah Mohd Hassan in Singapore for their efforts in seeing this project through even though there were times when I found it almost impossible to keep to editorial deadlines due to my hectic working schedule.

To Tuck Loong, I say a big "thank you" for his outstanding work on the creative aspects of this book, and I thank Jenhor Siow for his wonderful pictures. I also want to acknowledge the contribution put in by my loyal, faithful and kind-hearted assistant, Anne Rozario, who has given me so much of her time and life over the years. She is the best! Finally, I acknowledge my gratitude to all my fans who have made me what I am today.

# Weights & Measures

All measures are level unless otherwise stated. (All measurements given are approximations only.)

## MASS

| | | |
|---|---|---|
| 30 | grams | 1 ounce |
| 60 | grams | 2 ounces |
| 90 | grams | 3 ounces |
| 120 | grams | 4 ounces |
| 150 | grams | 5 ounces |
| 180 | grams | 6 ounces |
| 210 | grams | 7 ounces |
| 240 | grams | 8 ounces |
| 250 | grams | 8 1/3 ounces |
| 270 | grams | 9 ounces |
| 300 | grams | 10 ounces |
| 330 | grams | 11 ounces |
| 360 | grams | 12 ounces |
| 390 | grams | 13 ounces |
| 420 | grams | 14 ounces |
| 450 | grams | 15 ounces |
| 480 | grams | 16 ounces (1 pound) |
| 500 | grams | 1 pound 2/3 ounce |
| 600 | grams | 1 pound 4 ounces |
| 960 | grams | 2 pounds |
| 1 | kilogram | 2 pounds 1 1/3 ounces |

## LENGTH/WIDTH

| | | |
|---|---|---|
| 2.5 | cm | 1 inch |
| 5 | cm | 2 inches |
| 7.5 | cm | 3 inches |
| 10 | cm | 4 inches |
| 12.5 | cm | 5 inches |
| 15 | cm | 6 inches |
| 30 | cm | 12 inches (1 foot) |

## VOLUME

| | | |
|---|---|---|
| 30 | ml | 1 fl oz |
| 120 | ml | 4 fl oz |
| 240 | ml | 8 fl oz |
| 480 | ml | 16 fl oz |

## CUP EQUIVALENTS

| | |
|---|---|
| 1 cup liquid (12 tablespoons) | 250 ml |
| 1/2 cup liquid (6 tablespoons) | 125 ml |
| 1 cup flour | 120 grams |
| 1 cup sugar/rice | 240 grams |
| 1 tablespoon flour | 30 grams |
| 1 rounded tablespoon sugar | 30 grams |
| 1 rounded tablespoon butter | 30 grams |

## OVEN TEMPERATURE

Always preheat the oven 15 minutes before use.

| Description | °C | °F | Gas Regulo |
|---|---|---|---|
| Cool | 150 | 300 | 4 |
| | 160 | 325 | 5 |
| Moderate | 175 | 350 | 6 |
| Moderately hot | 190 | 375 | 7 |
| Hot | 205 | 400 | 8 |
| Very Hot | 220 | 425 | 9 |

# Tarts & Pies

The Art of Baking Tarts and Pies, p14  **1** Almond Apricot Tart, p16  **2** Flaming Heart, p16  **3** Lemon Custard Tart with Seasonal Fruit, p16  **4** All-American Apple Pie, p18  **5** Boston Peach Cream Pie, p18  **6** Clafoutis with Cherries, p20  **7** Custard Lime Tart, p20  **8** Apricot Tart, p20  **9** Cling Peaches and Almond Tart, p22  **10** Apple and Pear Tart with Butterscotch Sauce, p22  **11** Cointreau Pear Tart, p22  **12** Pear Pie, p24  **13** Lime Tart, p24  **14** Frangipane Pineapple Tart, p24  **15** Blueberry Custard Tart, p26  **16** Plum Tart, p26  **17** Black Cherry Pie, p26  **18** Date and Pecan Tartlet, p28  **19** Peanut Butter Chocolate Chip Pie, p28  **20** Mango and Banana Custard Tart, p28  **21** Honey Pumpkin Tart, p30  **22** Peach Cheese Pie, p30  **23** Tarte Danoise, p30  **24** Fruit Tartlets, p32  **25** Raspberry Lemon Tart, p32  **26** Walnut and Honey Tart, p32  **27** Lemon Meringue Pie, p34  **28** Lemon Tart, p34  **29** Linzer Torte, p34  **30** Pecan Pie with Chocolate Chips, p36  **31** Walnut Tart, p36  **32** Coconut Cream Pie, p36  **33** Tarte Alsacienne, p38  **34** Chocolate Mousse Tart, p38  **35** Almond Orange Tart, p38  **36** Dutch Country Pear Pie, p 40  **37** Strawberry Almond Tart, p 40  **38** Upside-Down Apple Tart, p 40  **39** Warm Chocolate Tart with Pistachio Sauce, p 42  **40** Chocolate and Pecan Pie, p 42

# The Art of Baking Tarts and Pies

Sweet tarts are irresistible … jewel bright fruit tarts decked with luscious berries and glazed with jam, or rich honeyed mixtures studded with nuts and thickly dusted with icing sugar. During my teen years, I enjoyed looking at the lovely tarts on sale at the pastry shops of the international hotel chains in town. I saved my pocket money during the week and as soon as the weekend came, I would buy some of the beautiful fruit tartlets I had admired and enjoy eating them down to the last crumb.

Good tarts and pies have a sweetness, tartness and freshness which distinguish them from other kinds of desserts. Over the years, I have developed my own variations of pastry crust and experimented with different custard and fruit fillings. In this book, I am sharing with you some of my delicious recipes that will not only tantalise your tastebuds but also introduce you to the art of baking tarts and pies.

To begin, we shall look at the difference between a pie and tart. In general, a pie uses a pastry crust as its base and is served in a dish with or without a top crust. A tart is generally not as deep and is customarily removed from the baking dish before being served. A tartlet is simply a small tart.

## PASTRY CRUSTS

Pastry used for tarts and pies is usually referred to as shortcrust pastry. Crisp, flaky and tender, it is made by combining fat (shortening, butter or even lard) with flour so that the fat coats the particles of flour. Different types of fat possess different qualities. For example, butter adds flavour to pastry dough but shortening makes it flakier. Margarine is an alternative to both. When deciding upon which type of fat to use, remember that you can combine the two (butter or shortening) to get the benefits of both. When moisture (usually water) is added, the fat prevents the moisture from activating the flour's gluten. The result is a sturdy yet tender and flaky crust.

The exact proportions of water or egg required for a perfect pastry dough depend on the dryness of the flour used; this varies according to age, country and even season. Some specialty doughs may call for cream cheese, sour cream or oil, which yields a less flaky crust.

Shortcrust pastry is the easiest and most versatile of all doughs. The ingredients are mixed as quickly as possible in a bowl, the fat lightly rubbed into the flour with the fingertips. Water is added together with egg yolk for a richer dough that should be soft but not sticky. Pastry crusts are usually made with sugar but this can be dispensed with for the more savoury tarts and quiches. Groundnuts may be substituted for half the flour but they have to be finely ground if the pastry has to be rolled Onto the tart pan. For more delicious types of pastry with a high content of fat and nuts, I usually press the pastry onto the pan using my fingertips while making sure that the pastry spreads out evenly.

## MAKING PASTRY

Pastry is simple to make but unless the dough is handled with care, uneven and shrunken pastry cases or hard, dense textures can arise. Such pitfalls can be avoided by observing the following guidelines:

1. Make sure that all the ingredients are cold.
2. The pastry must be made very quickly. A food processor may be used but take care not to overwork the mixture or it will form into a dough before the correct quantity of liquid has been added; this will produce pastry that is hard to handle..
3. Sift the flour into a bowl first; this adds air to the mixture and produces lighter results.
4. Use fat which is cold and cut into pieces. If the weather is warm, freeze the shortening and leave the flour in the refrigerator overnight. If you are using butter, there is no need to freeze it. Simply remove it from the fridge immediately before using. Make sure the liquid is cold so that it will not melt the fat.
5. Chill the pastry thoroughly before rolling it out. The crust should be rolled quickly, evenly and with a minimum of flour. A soft bristle brush can be used to remove excess flour. Once the pastry crust is in the baking dish, it is advisable to refrigerate it for at least 30 minutes to minimise shrinking and cracking during baking.
6. Fillings for tarts and pies taste best when freshly prepared. If fresh fruits are used, select quality ones that are in season.
7. Glazes are to be used as adornment and not as a cover-up for inferior fillings.
8. Do not stretch pastry when rolling it as it will shrink back during cooking, producing an uneven pastry case.

## Blind Baking

Blind baking is a term applied to crusts that are baked without a filling. As there is nothing to hold the crust in place, it must be weighted down during cooking so that it will not shrink or puff up too much. Crusts are pre-baked for several reasons:

1. They will be filled with an ingredient which has already been cooked or which does not need to be cooked, as in the example of fresh fruit.
2. The filling is so moist that unless the pastry is at least partially baked, it will become soggy.
3. The time needed to cook the filling is not long enough for the pastry to be thoroughly baked.

To blind bake, line the pastry with parchment, foil or wax paper. Fill the lined crust with commercially packaged aluminium pie weights, dried beans or rice. They should level with the top of the pastry to ensure that the pastry crusts do not shrink as they bake. The weights may be saved and reused. Sweet pastry cases will cook more quickly because of the sugar content. Egg in the dough will also help the pastry to keep its shape during cooking and will give the cooked case a golden colour.

## Tart Tins and Frames

When one thinks of a tart, a round pastry usually comes to mind, but tarts can come in all shapes and sizes, depending on the tin or frame used. These range in size from very large to tiny tartlet-size ones; there are square, oblong and decoratively shaped ones as well, such as those in the shape of a heart. A well-stocked shop that sells baking equipment will have a wide range of such tart tins.

Round tart tins with a removable base and plain or fluted edges are the most popular as they are easy to line with the pastry. When baked, the loose base can be removed to allow the easy removal of the tart from the mould.

## Using Ready-Made Pastry

In this fast-paced world, we often do not have too much time to spend on preparatory work in the kitchen. So it is helpful to know that convenient shortcuts are sometimes available. Where appropriate, ready-made frozen shortcrust and puff pastries can work well in place of the pastries suggested in the following recipes.

# TART AND PIE FILLINGS

It is the filling, rather than the type of pastry dough, that makes a tart or pie distinctive. This is where imagination and creativity come into play. Apples may be sliced, chopped or pureed. Most berries look best in an open tart with a shiny glaze. Fruits that tend to discolour, such as pears and peaches, are poached before being arranged in a baked pastry shell and glazed with the poaching syrup. Often, a layer of pastry cream is hidden beneath the fruit.

Fillings for tarts and pies are not limited to fruit but include a vast selection of nuts or custard. Pastry cream used in fillings can be heavy so it is often lightened with whipped cream and flavoured with a liqueur.

# Almond Apricot Tart

*Almond Crust*

    350 grams unsalted butter
    125 grams castor sugar
    2 eggs
    1 teaspoon vanilla essence
    a pinch of salt
    1/2 teaspoon almond essence
    2 tablespoons sliced almonds
    500 grams bread flour or
        all-purpose flour

*Method*

1. Cream butter and sugar until fairly smooth.
2. Add eggs, vanilla essence, salt and almond essence one at a time, followed by sliced almonds and flour. Form into a dough, wrap in cling wrap and leave in the refrigerator to chill for an hour before rolling out.
3. Roll out the almond pastry to fit a 22-cm tart pan. Prick the dough lightly with a fork. Cover the pastry with foil and place any type of beans or rice on top to bake blind for about 25 minutes at 190°C/375°F until golden. Discard foil and beans.

*Filling*

    4 eggs, separated
    200 grams castor sugar, divided equally
        into two parts
    200 grams almonds, finely ground
    200 grams unsalted butter, melted
    340 grams canned apricot, drained

    powdered sugar for dusting
    1/2 cup almond slices, toasted, to
        decorate

*Method*

1. Beat egg yolks and half of the castor sugar until creamy. Add ground almonds and melted butter.
2. In a separate bowl whisk egg whites and remaining castor sugar into a fluffy meringue. Gently fold meringue into the almond mixture.
3. Arrange half of the apricots in the base of the tart shell. Pour the almond mixture over. Top with remaining apricots. Bake at 175°C/350°F for about 30 minutes. If the top browns too quickly, cover the tart with foil. Cool before dusting with powdered sugar. Decorate with almond slices.

Chef's Note: You can also use two 10-cm tart pans instead of one 22-cm pan.

# Flaming Heart

*Crust*

    225 grams unsalted butter
    150 grams castor sugar
    3 eggs
    500 grams bread flour

*Method*

1. Cream butter and sugar until smooth. Add eggs one at a time followed by flour.
2. Roll the dough into balls and wrap in cling wrap. Leave to chill in the refrigerator for two hours before rolling out to line a 20-cm heart-shaped tart mould.
3. Bake blind, covered with foil and filled with beans, at 175°C/350°F for about 10 minutes until the crust is golden and the base dry. Discard foil and beans. Cool.

*Filling*

    1/2 cup whipping cream
    1 recipe pastry cream*
    2 tablespoons Grand Marnier

    20 large strawberries
    2 tablespoons raspberry jam, heated
        with 1 tablespoon water

*Method*

1. Prepare the tart shell.
2. With an electric mixer whip cream until stiff peaks form. Fold cream into pastry cream. Flavour with Grand Marnier. Pour into the tart shell and decorate with strawberries.
3. Warm jam together with water. Simmer until thick, then glaze fruits using a pastry brush.

\* See recipe for Fruit Tartlets on page 32.

# Lemon Custard Tart with Seasonal Fruit

*Crust*

    1 25-cm half-baked tart shell*

*Filling*

    3 whole eggs
    5 egg yolks
    grated zest and juice of 3 lemons
    1 1/4 cups castor sugar
    1 tablespoon dry vermouth
    1 tablespoon unsalted butter

    about 2 cups mixed seasonal fruit,
        chopped, to decorate

*Method*

1. Prepare the tart shell.
2. Combine all the ingredients, except butter and fruit, in a baine marie (a heatproof bowl set over a pot of simmering water). Cook for about 20 minutes, stirring constantly, until the custard is thick enough to coat the back of a spoon.
3. Add butter and stir until melted. Strain into the tart shell and top with fruit. Chill until custard sets. Serve at room temperature.

\* Refer to recipe for Flaming Heart on this page.

*Opposite: Almond Apricot Tart.*

# All-American Apple Pie

*Crust*

1 recipe for pie crust*

*Filling*

8 large, green apples, peeled and diced
1 cup brown sugar
1 tablespoon lemon juice
½ cup golden raisins
1 teaspoon ground cinnamon
½ teaspoon ground cloves
2 tablespoons cornstarch
50 grams butter, softened

a little milk or beaten egg to glaze
powdered sugar for dusting
vanilla ice-cream to serve

*Method*

1. Prepare the pie crust.
2. In a large bowl mix together all the ingredients for the filling except butter.
3. Roll out half of the pastry to cover a 22-cm pie pan. Spoon in apple filling, dot with butter and top with the remaining layer of pastry.
4. With a paring knife, make 5 cm-long slits on four sides. Glaze the top with a little milk. Bake at 180°C/360°F for about 40 minutes until golden. Cool before dusting with powdered sugar. Serve with vanilla ice-cream.

* Refer to recipe for Flaming Heart on page 16.

# Boston Peach Cream Pie

*Cake*

¾ cup unsalted butter, softened
1¼ cups castor sugar
1 teaspoon vanilla essence
2 large eggs
2 cups cake flour or all-purpose flour
1½ teaspoons double-acting baking powder
½ teaspoon salt
¾ cup milk

*Method*

1. Preheat oven to 175°C/350°F. Lightly grease and flour a 24-cm springform pan.
2. Beat butter, sugar and vanilla essence until light and fluffy. Beat in eggs one at a time.
3. Sift together flour, baking powder and salt. Alternately add flour and milk to the batter. Pour the batter into the pan and bake for 55 minutes until a skewer inserted in the centre comes away cleanly. Cool the cake before slicing in half horizontally.

*Filling*

3 tablespoons cornstarch
⅓ cup castor sugar
1 cup fresh milk
3 large eggs
½ cup heavy cream
a pinch of salt
¼ teaspoon vanilla essence
3 tablespoons unsalted butter

*Method*

1. In a saucepan whisk together cornstarch, sugar and milk. Add eggs, cream and salt. Whisk to a smooth custard. Add vanilla essence and bring to a boil over moderate heat, whisking constantly. Boil for two more minutes, remove from heat and add butter.
2. Let the custard cool completely, whisking occasionally.

*Chocolate Glaze*

150 grams bittersweet or unsweetened chocolate
3 tablespoons water
2 tablespoons unsalted butter
1½ tablespoons light corn syrup
¼ teaspoon salt

*Method*

Place all the ingredients for the glaze in a heatproof bowl and melt over a pan of simmering water.

*To Assemble Boston Cream Pie You Need:*

cake
filling
425 grams canned cling peaches
chocolate glaze

*Method*

1. Spread a layer of custard filling over the bottom layer of cake. Arrange peaches over the filling.
2. Cover with the top layer of cake and spread the glaze over the top, allowing it to drip over the edges.

*Opposite: All-American Apple Pie.*

# Clafoutis with Cherries

*Almond Crust*

    350 grams unsalted butter
    125 grams castor sugar
    2 eggs
    1 teaspoon vanilla essence
    a pinch of salt
    1/2 teaspoon almond essence
    2 tablespoons sliced almonds
    500 grams bread flour or all-purpose flour

*Method*

1. Cream butter and sugar until fairly smooth. Add eggs, vanilla essence, salt and almond essence one at a time, followed by sliced almonds and flour. Form into a dough, wrap in cling wrap and leave in the refrigerator to chill for an hour before rolling out.

2. Roll out the almond pastry to fit a 30-cm tart pan. Prick the dough lightly with a fork and bake blind, covered with foil and filled with beans, for about 25 minutes at 190°C/375°F until golden but not brown. Discard foil and beans.

*Filling*

    15 grams all-purpose flour
    170 grams castor sugar
    4 eggs
    1/2 cup heavy cream
    3/4 cup warm milk
    1 can pitted cherries, drained

    whipped cream to serve

*Method*

1. Combine flour and sugar. Add eggs and cream. Scald milk in a pan, then gradually whisk warm milk into the custard.

2. Arrange drained cherries on the crust, then pour the custard over the cherries. Bake at 175°C/350°F for approximately 30 minutes until the custard sets. Cool at room temperature, cut and serve with whipped cream.

Chef's Note: While the fruit most commonly used in clafoutis is cherries, other fruit such as apricots, blueberries and plums also go well with this tart.

# Custard Lime Tart

*Crust*

    350 grams unsalted butter
    125 grams castor sugar
    2 eggs
    1 teaspoon vanilla essence
    1 teaspoon almond essence, optional
    500 grams all-purpose flour
    125 grams almond slices, finely crushed

*Method*

1. Cream butter and sugar until smooth. Add eggs one at a time, then vanilla essence and almond essence.

2. Add flour and crushed almond. Form into a dough. Wrap in cling wrap and chill in the refrigerator for a few hours.

3. Roll out the pastry to fit a 30-cm tart pan. Bake blind, covered with foil and filled with beans, at 175°C/350°F for 20 minutes.

*Filling*

    1 cup whipped cream
    1/2 cup orange juice
    6 egg yolks
    1/4 cup castor sugar
    1 tablespoon grated lime zest
    juice of 1 lime

    3 limes, peeled and thinly sliced, to decorate

*Method*

1. Beat all the ingredients, except lime slices, until a smooth custard forms.

2. Pour the custard into the prepared pie crust and bake at 175°C/350°F for half an hour until the custard sets. Cool in the refrigerator before decorating with lime slices.

# Apricot Tart

*Crust*

    1 25-cm half-baked tart crust*

*Filling*

    1 kilogram apricots
    3/4 cup powdered almonds
    4 1/2 tablespoons icing sugar
    1 cup water
    4 1/2 tablespoons castor sugar

    1/3 cup apricot glaze

*Method*

1. Prepare the tart shell.

2. Preheat the oven to 200°C/390°F.

3. Separate the apricot halves, reserving half of the pits.

4. Sprinkle the bottom of the prepared pastry with powdered almonds.

5. Stand the apricot halves upright in concentric circles, starting on the outer rim and with the cut side facing the centre. Sprinkle with icing sugar.

6. Place the assembled tart in the oven and bake for 35 minutes.

7. Meanwhile crack open the apricot pits with a nutcracker and parboil the apricot "almonds" in boiling water for 30 seconds. Drain, cool under running water and peel.

8. Bring the water and sugar to a boil, add the peeled "almonds" and cook for 5 minutes.

9. When the tart is done, remove from the oven, sprinkle with the drained "almonds" and brush with apricot glaze. Allow to cool before serving.

* Refer to recipe for Flaming Heart on page 16.

*Opposite: Clafoutis with Cherries.*

## Cling Peaches and Almond Tart

*Almond Crust*

    350 grams unsalted butter
    125 grams castor sugar
    2 eggs
    1 teaspoon vanilla essence
    a pinch of salt
    ½ teaspoon almond essence
    125 grams sliced almonds
    500 grams bread flour or all-purpose flour

*Method*

1. Cream butter and sugar until fairly smooth. Add eggs, vanilla essence, salt and almond essence one ingredient at a time, followed by sliced almonds and flour.

2. Form into a dough, wrap in cling wrap and leave in the refrigerator to chill for an hour before rolling out.

3. Roll out the almond pastry to fit a 22-cm tart pan. Prick the dough lightly with a fork and bake blind, covered with foil and filled with beans, for about 25 minutes at 190°C/375°F until golden brown. Discard foil and beans.

*Filling*

    4 eggs, separated
    200 grams castor sugar, divided equally into two parts
    200 grams ground almonds
    200 grams unsalted butter, melted
    340 grams canned cling peaches, drained
    powdered sugar for dusting

*Method*

1. Whisk egg yolks with half of the sugar until light and fluffy. Add ground almonds and melted butter.

2. In another bowl beat egg whites, adding the remaining sugar until stiff peaks form. Gently fold egg whites into the almond mixture.

3. Pour half of the mixture into the prepared pie shell, arranging cling peaches over the filling. Top with remaining almond filling.

4. Bake at 180°C/360°F for 25 to 30 minutes. If the top browns too quickly, cover the tart with foil.

5. Dust with powdered sugar. This tart is best eaten lukewarm.

## Apple and Pear Tart with Butterscotch Sauce

*Cake*

    250 grams unsalted butter, at room temperature
    220 grams castor sugar
    5 eggs
    ½ teaspoon ground cinnamon
    1 teaspoon vanilla essence
    grated zest of ½ orange
    250 grams self-raising flour, sifted
    2 ripe pears, peeled and thinly sliced
    2 green apples, peeled and thinly sliced

*Method*

1. Cream butter and sugar. Gradually beat in eggs, cinnamon, vanilla essence and zest.

2. Fold in sifted flour. Pour into a 32-cm flan tin, or two small tins, and decorate with pear and apple slices.

3. Bake at 180°C/360°F for 45 minutes.

*Butterscotch Sauce*

    100 grams + 1 tablespoon butter
    100 grams brown sugar
    200 ml cream
    whipped cream to serve

*Method*

1. For the sauce, heat together 100 grams butter and brown sugar until the sugar starts to caramelise. Then add the cream. Stir constantly and bring the mixture to a simmer. Turn the heat off and whisk in 1 tablespoon cold butter. This gives the sauce a nice, shiny finish.

2. Serve tart in wedges with butterscotch sauce and a dollop of whipped cream.

## Cointreau Pear Tart

*Crust*

    4 10-cm blind-baked pie crusts*

*Filling*

    4 egg yolks
    100 grams castor sugar
    1½ cups heavy cream
    2 tablespoons Cointreau, or other orange liqueur
    3 semi-ripe pears, sliced thinly
    2 tablespoons castor sugar
    2 tablespoons apricot jam, heated with 1 tablespoon water, to glaze

*Method*

1. Prepare the tart shells.

2. Beat together egg yolks, sugar, cream and Cointreau. Pour the filling in the prepared tart shells. Arrange pears over the filling.

3. Sprinkle sugar over the pears. Bake at 175°C/350°F for 35 minutes until the custard sets.

4. Glaze the top of the cooled tart with apricot jam.

\* Refer to recipe for Flaming Heart on page 16.

# Pear Pie

*Crust*

    500 grams flour
    230 grams butter
    sufficient water to hold the crust together

*Method*

1. Mix all the pastry ingredients until a dough forms. Wrap the dough in cling wrap and chill in the refrigerator for 2 hours.
2. Roll out the dough, using half to line a 22-cm pie pan. Pinch the edges to decorate.

*Filling*

    3/4 cup brown sugar
    3 tablespoons cornflour
    a pinch of salt
    1/4 teaspoon ground nutmeg
    1/4 teaspoon ground cloves
    1/3 cup whipping cream
    7 pears, peeled, seeded and thinly sliced
    2 tablespoons lemon juice
    2 tablespoons butter, softened

    a little milk to glaze

*Method*

1. Mix all the filling ingredients except butter and milk and pour into the prepared pie crust.
2. Dot butter all over the pear filling.
3. Cut the remaining half of the pastry into strips to form a latticework.
4. Glaze the lattice with milk. Bake at 180°C/360°F for 40 minutes.

# Lime Tart

*Crust*

    1 1/4 cup all-purpose flour
    2 tablespoons castor sugar
    1/4 teaspoon salt
    250 grams butter, cut into small pieces
    1 egg yolk, beaten
    1 tablespoon cold water

*Method*

1. Mix flour, sugar and salt. Make a well in the flour and cut in cold butter so that the mixture resembles breadcrumbs.
2. Add beaten egg yolk and a little water to make a dough. Allow the dough to rest for half an hour before rolling out.
3. Roll out the dough to fit a 22-cm tart pan, then chill the pastry shell for an hour. Bake blind, covered with foil and filled with beans, at 175°C/350°F for 20 minutes until golden. Halfway through baking, discard the foil and beans.

*Filling*

    1/2 cup whipping cream
    2 tablespoons custard powder
    2 whole eggs
    2 egg yolks
    1/2 cup orange juice
    3/4 cup lime juice
    125 grams butter
    3/4 cup castor sugar

    lime slices
    mint leaves
    powdered sugar for dusting

*Method*

1. Whisk together cream and custard powder. Add eggs and egg yolks and continue whisking.
2. In a saucepan combine orange juice, lime juice, butter and sugar and heat until the butter melts and the sugar dissolves. Bring to a boil. Whisk into the egg mixture and boil for another minute.
3. Cool the filling slightly before pouring into the prepared tart shell. Chill overnight.
4. Decorate with lime slices and mint leaves. Dust the sides with powdered sugar.

# Frangipane Pineapple Tart

*Crust*

    1 22-cm blind-baked tart shell*

*Filling*

    3/4 cup raw almonds
    1/2 cup castor sugar, divided into two equal parts
    1/2 cup unsalted butter, softened
    1 large egg
    3/4 teaspoon almond essence
    1 tablespoon custard powder
    1/4 teaspoon salt
    1/4 cup brown sugar, melted with a little butter
    1 fresh pineapple, skinned, cut into rings and halved

    2 tablespoons dark rum, optional, to glaze

*Method*

1. Prepare the tart shell.
2. In a food processor grind almonds finely with 1/4 cup sugar.
3. In another bowl cream butter with remaining sugar. Beat in almond mixture, egg, almond essence, custard powder and salt.
4. Spread the filling evenly in the base of the tart shell and bake at 190°C/375°F for 25 minutes on the lowest oven shelf.
5. Melt a little butter with the brown sugar and stir. Cook pineapple slices in batches in the brown sugar until caramelised. At this point, do not crowd the pineapple slices too much or they will not caramelise easily. Work on 3 or 4 batches, separating the pineapple slices each time.
6. Decorate the tart with pineapples. Brush pineapples with rum reduced to a glaze. Bake on the lowest oven shelf at 190°C/375°F for 15 to 20 minutes.

\* Refer to recipe for Tarte Alsacienne on page 38.

*Opposite: Frangipane Pineapple Tart.*

# Blueberry Custard Tart

*Crust*

1½ cups bread flour
½ cup castor sugar
200 grams butter, chilled and cut into small pieces
1 egg yolk
1 tablespoon whipping cream
a little cold water to bind dough

*Method*

1. Combine flour and sugar in a food processor. Add butter and process using the pulse button until the mixture resembles coarse breadcrumbs.
2. Add egg yolk, whipping cream and a little water if the mixture is too dry. Blend together only until a dough forms. Gather the dough into a ball, wrap in cling wrap and refrigerate for at least one hour.
3. Preheat the oven to 170°C/340°F. Roll out the dough thinly on a lightly floured surface. Line a 22-cm tart pan, or smaller tartlet pans, with dough. Trim the edges. Bake blind, covered with foil and filled with beans, for 20 minutes while preparing the filling.

*Filling*

4 eggs
½ cup whipping cream
170 grams castor sugar
15 grams custard powder
¾ cup fresh milk, brought to a simmer
500 grams canned blueberries, drained

apricot jam, heated with a little water, to glaze

*Method*

1. Beat together eggs, whipping cream, sugar and custard powder. Slowly add warm milk.
2. Spread blueberries in the base of the prepared tart shell and pour the custard over. Bake for 40 minutes at 175°C/350°F until the custard sets. If baking in smaller tartlet pans, the baking time is half that of a larger tart. Glaze with apricot jam.

Chef's Note: As an option, add 1 tablespoon Creme de Cassis (fruit berry liqueur) in the custard for added flavour.

# Plum Tart

*Crust*

250 grams all-purpose flour
200 grams cold butter, cut into small pieces
100 grams powdered sugar
2 egg yolks
grated zest of 1 lemon

*Method*

In a food processor quickly mix all the pastry ingredients to form a ball of dough. Flatten the dough slightly and wrap in cling wrap. Refrigerate for several hours.

*Filling*

½ cup ground almonds
⅓ cup castor sugar
1½ tablespoons cornstarch
4 tablespoons butter, softened
1 egg
1 teaspoon vanilla essence
6 to 8 large, sweet, firm plums, halved and seeded
some melted butter

apricot jam, heated with a little water, to glaze

*Method*

1. Use electric mixer to combine almonds, sugar, cornstarch and butter. Increase the speed and whisk in the egg and vanilla essence.
2. Roll out the dough to form a circle 22 cm in diameter and 1 cm in thickness. Line a tart pan with the dough.
3. Spread the almond filling over the dough and arrange with plums. Brush with some melted butter and bake at 180°C/360°F for 35 minutes until the plums soften and the pastry is golden. Glaze with apricot jam.

# Black Cherry Pie

*Crust*

1 25-cm blind-baked pie crust*
100 grams fresh pie pastry*

*Filling*

2 cans dark, pitted cherries, with syrup drained and kept aside
½ cup castor sugar
1 tablespoon lemon juice
1 teaspoon vanilla essence
3 tablespoons cornstarch
1 egg, beaten

vanilla ice-cream to serve

*Method*

1. Prepare the pie shell.
2. Combine cherry, sugar, lemon juice, vanilla essence and cornstarch. Mix well and add a tablespoon of the cherry syrup if mixture is too sticky.
3. Pour batter into the prepared crust. Brush beaten egg around the rim of the crust.
4. Roll out the fresh pie pastry to about 6 mm thick and top the pie. Trim the edges and crimp decoratively with a fork.
5. Bake at 180°C/360°F for 10 minutes. Remove pie from the oven, brush the top with beaten egg and continue baking for another 30 minutes until golden. Serve warm with vanilla ice-cream.

*Refer to recipe for Flaming Heart on page 16.

*Opposite: Blueberry Custard Tart (left) and Plum Tart (right).*

## Date and Pecan Tartlet

*Crust*

- 200 grams unsalted butter, softened
- 3 tablespoons castor sugar
- 1 egg yolk
- 1/4 teaspoon salt
- 2 tablespoons water
- 1 1/3 cups all-purpose flour

*Method*

1. Cream butter and sugar until light and fluffy. Add egg yolk, salt and water.
2. Continue beating, slowly mixing in the flour until a dough forms. Chill the dough for an hour in the refrigerator before rolling out.
3. Roll out the pastry to fit tartlet shells or a large 22-cm tart pan. Let the shells rest in the refrigerator for half an hour before baking.

*Filling*

- 3 large eggs
- 3/4 cup packed brown sugar
- 1/2 cup light corn syrup
- 125 grams unsalted butter, melted and cooled
- 2 tablespoon unsulphured, or light, molasses
- 1 teaspoon vanilla essence
- 1 cup pecans, chopped
- 1/2 cup dates, chopped
- 10 dates, halved, to decorate

*Method*

1. Whisk together eggs, brown sugar, corn syrup, butter, molasses and vanilla essence. Stir in pecans and dates.
2. Pour the filling into the prepared tartlet shells. Arrange date halves over the filling and bake at 175°C/350°F for 15 to 20 minutes until the filling sets. Cool before serving.

Chef's Note: A combination of nuts such as hazelnuts, walnuts, peanuts and pinenuts may be used together with the dates if pecans are not available. If you are using a big tart pan instead of small tartlet pans, baking may take up to 40 minutes.

## Peanut Butter Chocolate Chip Pie

*Crust*

- 1 half-baked almond crust pastry*

*Filling*

- 4 eggs
- 1/2 cup heavy cream
- 3/4 cup milk
- 2/3 cup powdered sugar
- 1 teaspoon vanilla essence
- 1 cup creamy peanut butter
- 100 grams chocolate chips

apricot jam to glaze

*Method*

1. Prepare the almond pastry crust. Roll out to fit a 22-cm pie pan. Prick the base with a fork and bake blind, covered with foil and filled with beans, at 190°C/375°F for 15 minutes until golden. Discard foil and beans. Set aside.
2. Whisk eggs. Add cream, milk, powdered sugar, vanilla essence and peanut butter. Mix the ingredients well.
3. Scatter some chocolate chips evenly in the base of the pie crust before pouring in the peanut butter custard. Bake for 35 minutes at 175°C/350°F until the custard sets. Halfway through scatter the remaining chocolate chips over the custard. Glaze with apricot jam.

Chef's Note: If you like bananas, add 1/2 cup mashed bananas to the filling.

*Refer to recipe for Clafoutis with Cherries on page 20.

## Mango and Banana Custard Tart

*Crust*

- 1 recipe for sweet crust pastry*

*Method*

Prepare the pastry. Roll out to a thickness of 6 mm. Transfer to a 22-cm quiche pan. Pat the pastry into the corners of the pan, making sure the pan is evenly lined with the pastry before trimming off the excess. Bake blind, covered with foil and filled with beans, at 180°C/360°F for 15 minutes. Cool.

*Filling*

- 3 large eggs, beaten
- 80 grams castor sugar
- 1 teaspoon vanilla essence
- 45 grams all-purpose flour
- a pinch of salt
- grated zest of 1 lemon
- 450 ml thick coconut milk
- 300 grams or 2 mangoes, peeled and thinly sliced
- 300 grams or 2 big bananas, thickly sliced
- 1 teaspoon lemon juice
- 2 teaspoons brown sugar
- 30 grams almond flakes
- 30 grams butter, at room temperature

*Method*

1. Beat together eggs, sugar, vanilla essence, flour, salt and lemon zest.
2. Heat coconut milk until almost boiling and add to the batter.
3. Arrange mango and banana slices at the base of the prepared pastry and sprinkle with lemon juice, brown sugar and almond flakes. Pour the batter over the fruit and dot with butter.
4. Bake in a preheated 180°C/360°F oven for 35 to 40 minutes until the filling sets and the top is golden brown.

*Refer to recipe for Flaming Heart on page 16.

*Opposite: Date and Pecan Tartlet (above left), Peanut Butter Chocolate Chip Pie (above right) and Mango and Banana Custard Tart (below).*

## Honey Pumpkin Tart

*Crust*

- 1½ cups all-purpose flour
- ¼ teaspoon salt
- ½ cup vegetable shortening
- 3 to 4 tablespoons cold water

*Method*

1. Mix flour with salt. Gradually blend in shortening with a fork until the mixture resembles fine breadcrumbs.
2. Stir in water and mix well. Form the dough into a ball, wrap in cling wrap and chill in the refrigerator for an hour before rolling out. Cut the rolled-out pastry to fit a 22-cm pie pan.

Chef's Note: This is a delicious, crumbly crust. Sometimes, it is a bit too soft to roll out if it has not been chilled well. If this happens, use your fingers to press the pastry onto the tart pan.

*Filling*

- ½ cup castor sugar
- ½ teaspoon salt
- ½ cup honey
- 1½ teaspoons ground cinnamon
- ½ teaspoon ground ginger
- ½ teaspoon ground cloves
- 1½ cups pumpkin, boiled and mashed
- 1½ cups evaporated milk
- ½ cup milk
- 2 eggs, well beaten

*Method*

1. Mix together all the ingredients in the filling and beat well. Pour into the prepared pie crust and bake for 10 minutes in a preheated 220°C/425°F oven.
2. Lower the heat to 170°C/340°F and bake for another 45 minutes or until a skewer inserted in the centre comes away cleanly.

## Peach Cheese Pie

*Crust*

- 300 grams shortcrust pastry*

*Filling*

- 500 grams cream cheese, softened at room temperature
- ½ cup castor sugar
- 2 eggs
- 2 tablespoons all-purpose flour
- grated zest and juice of 1 lemon
- ½ cup sour cream
- 225 grams canned peaches, drained
- egg yolk to glaze
- powdered sugar for dusting

*Method*

1. Prepare the pastry. Roll out half of the pastry to line a greased, 22-cm pie pan. Line the pastry with aluminium foil and fill with beans. Blind bake at 175°C/350°F for 20 minutes. Discard foil and beans.
2. Beat the cream cheese until softened, add sugar and stir in the remaining ingredients except glaze and powdered sugar. Pour into the prepared pastry crust.
3. Roll out the remaining half of the pastry to top the pie, pinching the edges to seal. Make several holes on the top with a fork. Glaze with beaten egg yolk.
4. Bake at 190°C/375°F for 30 minutes or until golden. Dust with powdered sugar when cooled.

* Refer to recipe for Flaming Heart on page 16.

## Tarte Danoise

*Crust*

- 125 grams bread flour
- 60 grams cold butter
- 75 grams powdered sugar
- 1 teaspoon vanilla essence
- a pinch of salt
- 1 egg yolk
- 1 teaspoon water

*Method*

1. In a bowl mix together butter and powdered sugar and slowly add vanilla essence, salt, egg yolk, water and flour.
2. Wrap in cling wrap and chill for about an hour before rolling out to line a 22-cm tart pan.

*Filling*

- 80 grams sugar, divided into two equal parts
- 2 eggs, separated
- 100 grams ground almonds
- 100 grams unsalted butter, melted
- 1 can dark, pitted cherries, drained
- powdered sugar for dusting

*Method*

1. Whisk half of the sugar with the egg yolks until light and fluffy. Add ground almonds and slowly stir in melted butter.
2. In another bowl whisk egg whites, adding the remaining sugar to form a stiff meringue. Quickly fold the meringue into the almond mixture.
3. Arrange cherries at the base of the prepared tart shell and fill the shell with the almond mixture. Bake at 190°C/375°F for 25 to 30 minutes. Dust with powdered sugar.

*Opposite: Peach Cheese Pie (above left), Tarte Danoise (above right) and Honey Pumpkin Tart (below).*

# Fruit Tartlets

*Crust*

    225 grams unsalted butter
    150 grams castor sugar
    3 eggs
    500 grams bread flour

*Method*

1. Cream butter and sugar until smooth. Add eggs one at a time followed by flour.
2. Roll the dough into balls and wrap in cling wrap. Leave to chill in the refrigerator for two hours before rolling out thinly to line the tart moulds.
3. Bake blind, covered with foil and filled with beans, at 175°C/350°F for about 10 minutes until the crust is golden and the base dry. Discard foil and beans. Cool.

*Pastry Cream*

    2 cups fresh milk
    1 teaspoon vanilla essence
    4 egg yolks
    125 grams castor sugar
    50 grams cornstarch
    100 grams butter

*Method*

1. In a saucepan bring milk and vanilla essence to a simmer.
2. In another bowl beat egg yolks, sugar and cornstarch into a smooth custard. Slowly add hot milk.
3. Pour the custard back into the saucepan and continue cooking over low heat until thick and bubbly. Add butter and turn off the heat. Chill.

*To Assemble Fruit Tartlets You Need:*

    some melted chocolate
    crust
    pastry cream
    fruit of your choice
    apricot jam to glaze

*Method*

1. Brush melted chocolate at the base of the pastry shells. This keeps the pastry from becoming soggy when the pastry cream is added.
2. Pipe in the pastry cream and decorate with fruit. Brush with warm, melted apricot jam heated with a little water to keep the fruit fresh.

# Raspberry Lemon Tart

*Crust*

    1 3/4 cups all-purpose flour
    1/4 teaspoon salt
    2 teaspoons sugar
    120 grams unsalted butter, cut into cubes
    1 egg yolk
    4 tablespoons ice water

*Method*

1. Combine all ingredients in a food processor. Add water to form a dough. Cool in the refrigerator for a few hours before rolling the dough to line a 20-cm tart pan.
2. Prick the dough, line with aluminium, fill with beans and blind bake at 175°C/350°F for about 25 minutes until golden and thoroughly cooked. Remove foil and beans.

*Lemon Curd*

    grated zest of 2 lemons
    6 tablespoons lemon juice
    8 tablespoons butter
    3/4 cup castor sugar
    4 eggs

*Method*

1. Put zest, lemon juice, butter and sugar in a heatproof bowl set over a baine marie (a pot of simmering water). Stir occasionally until everything is well dissolved.
2. In a separate bowl beat eggs and slowly add the lemon mixture. Stir quickly and pour back into the baine marie bowl. Cook slowly until the custard begins to thicken. Remove and allow to cool.

*To Assemble Raspberry Lemon Tarts You Need:*

    crust
    lemon curd
    2 cups fresh raspberries
    2 tablespoons warm apricot jam
    1 tablespoon icing sugar

*Method*

1. Fill tart shell with lemon curd.
2. Arrange raspberries on top and glaze with warm apricot jam.
3. Dust with icing sugar around the tart shell.

# Walnut and Honey Tart

*Crust*

    1 recipe for pie crust*

*Filling*

    1 egg
    1/2 cup honey
    1/4 cup castor sugar
    1 tablespoon rum
    a pinch of salt
    1 1/2 cup walnuts, coarsely chopped

*Method*

1. Roll pastry crust onto a 20-cm tart pan. Blind bake the shell at 180°C/360°F for 12 minutes. Meanwhile beat eggs, honey and sugar in a bowl. Add rum and salt and stir in the walnut.
2. As soon as the crust starts to brown slightly, pour in the nut mixture. Continue baking until the nuts begin to turn brown. Cool on a rack (the filling will set as the tart cools) and serve with vanilla ice-cream.

\* Refer to recipe for Fruit Tartlets on this page.

*Opposite: Fruit Tartlets.*

# Lemon Meringue Pie

*Crust*

- 1 22-cm pie crust*, blind-baked until thoroughly cooked

*Filling*

- 1 cup milk
- 1 teaspoon vanilla essence
- 2 egg yolks
- 1/2 cup castor sugar
- 3 tablespoons cornstarch
- grated zest of 2 lemons
- juice of 3/4 lemon
- 3 egg whites, beaten with 2 tablespoons castor sugar
- 3/4 cup castor sugar
- 1/4 cup water

*Method*

1. Prepare the pie crust.
2. In a saucepan bring milk and vanilla essence to a simmer.
3. In a separate bowl beat egg yolks and castor sugar until creamy. Whisk in cornstarch. Whisk in the warm milk a little at a time and return to the saucepan. Add lemon zest and lemon juice. Bring to a simmer, whisking constantly to form a custard. Cool for a few hours.
4. In a saucepan bring 3/4 cup sugar and water to a simmer for 3 to 4 minutes. The resulting sugar syrup should be thick rather than runny.
5. Beat egg whites with two tablespoons sugar until soft peaks form. Slowly add the sugar syrup.
6. Fold one-third of the egg whites into the custard filling and pour into the prepared tart shell.
7. Fill a piping bag with the remaining egg whites and pipe over the pie. Place under a broiler for 2 to 3 minutes until golden brown.

\* Refer to recipe for Fruit Tartlets on page 32.

# Lemon Tart

*Crust*

- 142 grams butter
- 14 grams powdered sugar
- 1 egg white
- 255 grams bread flour
- 28 grams ground almonds

*Method*

1. In a food processor combine all the ingredients and blend quickly to form a soft dough. Chill for a few hours.
2. Roll out the dough to line a 22-cm pie dish. Bake blind, covered with foil and filled with beans, for 15 minutes at 170°C/340°F. Discard foil and beans and set aside.

*Filling*

- 9 eggs
- 380 grams castor sugar
- 1 1/4 cups cream
- juice and zest of 6 lemons
- lemon slices to decorate
- powdered sugar for dusting

*Method*

1. Mix together eggs and sugar. Add cream, lemon juice and lemon zest.
2. Pour the filling into the prepared pie crust. Bake for 45 minutes at 170°C/340°F. Decorate with lemon slices and dust with powdered sugar.

# Linzer Torte

*Crust*

- 708 grams butter
- 297 grams castor sugar
- 510 grams ground hazelnuts
- 297 grams cookie crumbs
- 3 eggs
- a pinch of ground cinnamon
- a pinch of salt
- a pinch of ground cloves
- 595 grams bread flour

*Method*

1. Cream butter. Mix together sugar, hazelnuts and cookie crumbs and add to the butter.
2. Add eggs and mix well. Add cinnamon, salt, cloves and bread flour, stirring only until the ingredients are just combined. Spread the dough on a baking sheet and refrigerate for an hour until firm.
3. Grease a rectangular tart pan. Roll out the dough between two sheets of parchment paper to a 5-mm thickness. Cut to fit the base of the tart pan, setting aside some dough for decoration. Refrigerate for until firm.

*To Assemble Linzer Torte You Need:*

- crust
- raspberry jam
- 1 egg, beaten, to glaze

*Method*

1. Brush a 1 cm-thick layer of raspberry jam at the base of the tart shell.
2. Roll out the remaining dough and cut into 1 cm-thick strips to make a latticework.
3. Glaze with beaten egg. Bake at 190°C/375°F until golden.

*Opposite: Lemon Meringue Pie (above right), Lemon Tart (above left) and Linzer Torte (below).*

## Pecan Pie with Chocolate Chips

*Crust*

1 recipe for pie crust*

*Method*

Prepare the pastry. Roll out to line 10 4-cm pie pans. Cover the pastry with foil and fill with beans or rice to bake blind. Bake at 175°C/350°F for 10 minutes until the base is cooked. Once the shells are baked, discard the foil and beans. Cool.

*Filling*

- 3 large eggs
- 3/4 cup packed brown sugar
- 1/2 cup light corn syrup
- 180 grams unsalted butter, melted and cooled
- 2 tablespoon unsulphured, or light, molasses
- 1 teaspoon vanilla essence
- 2 cups pecans, toasted and chopped
- 100 grams chocolate chips

whipped cream to serve

*Method*

1. Whisk eggs, brown sugar, corn syrup, melted butter, molasses and vanilla essence. Stir in pecans and chocolate chips.
2. Pour the filling into the blind-baked pastry shells. Bake at 175°C/350°F for about 20 minutes until the filling sets. If the top browns too quickly, cover the pie with foil.
3. Serve with whipped cream.

Chef's Note: As an option, use a teaspoon of rum or bourbon in the filling. Walnuts or hazelnuts may be used as a substitute for pecans, or a combination of all three types of nuts may be used.

* Refer to recipe for Fruits Tartlets on page 32.

## Walnut Tart

*Crust*

1 recipe for almond crust*

*Filling*

- 2 cups walnuts, coarsely chopped
- 1 cup brown sugar
- 1 tablespoon cornstarch
- 3 eggs
- 1 cup corn syrup
- 2 tablespoons butter, melted
- 1 teaspoon vanilla essence

*Method*

1. Line a 20 cm by 20 cm glass baking pan with the dough, allowing any excess to drape over the sides.
2. Spread the walnuts evenly at the base of tart shell. Set aside.
3. Beat together sugar, cornstarch and eggs. Add corn syrup, melted butter and vanilla essence. Pour the mixture over the walnuts. Bring dough up around the sides to flop over the filling.
4. Bake for 50 to 60 minutes at 170°C/340°F until the filling sets.

*Refer to recipe for Almond Apricot Tart on page 16.

## Coconut Cream Pie

*Crust*

1 22-cm pie shell, blind-baked*

*Meringue*

- 4 egg whites
- 1/4 teaspoon cream of tartar
- 1/4 teaspoon salt
- 1/2 cup castor sugar

*Method*

Whisk egg whites until stiff. Gradually add cream of tartar, salt and sugar.

*Filling*

- 2 cups fresh milk
- 1/2 cup castor sugar
- 1 1/4 cups grated coconut, toasted
- a pinch of salt
- 2 tablespoons custard powder
- 4 eggs
- 1 tablespoon butter
- 1 teaspoon vanilla essence

1/4 cup grated coconut to decorate

*Method*

1. Prepare the pie shell.
2. Boil milk, sugar, coconut and salt.
3. In a separate bowl dissolve the custard powder in some water and add to the eggs. Beat until mixed.
4. Add the milk mixture to the egg mixture and cook until thick. Stir in the butter and vanilla.
5. When slightly cooled, pour the custard into the prepared pie crust and top with meringue.
6. Bake at 170°C/340°F for 15 to 10 minutes. Top with grated coconut.

* Refer to recipe for Fruit Tartlets on page 32.

*Opposite: Pecan Pie with Chocolate Chips.*

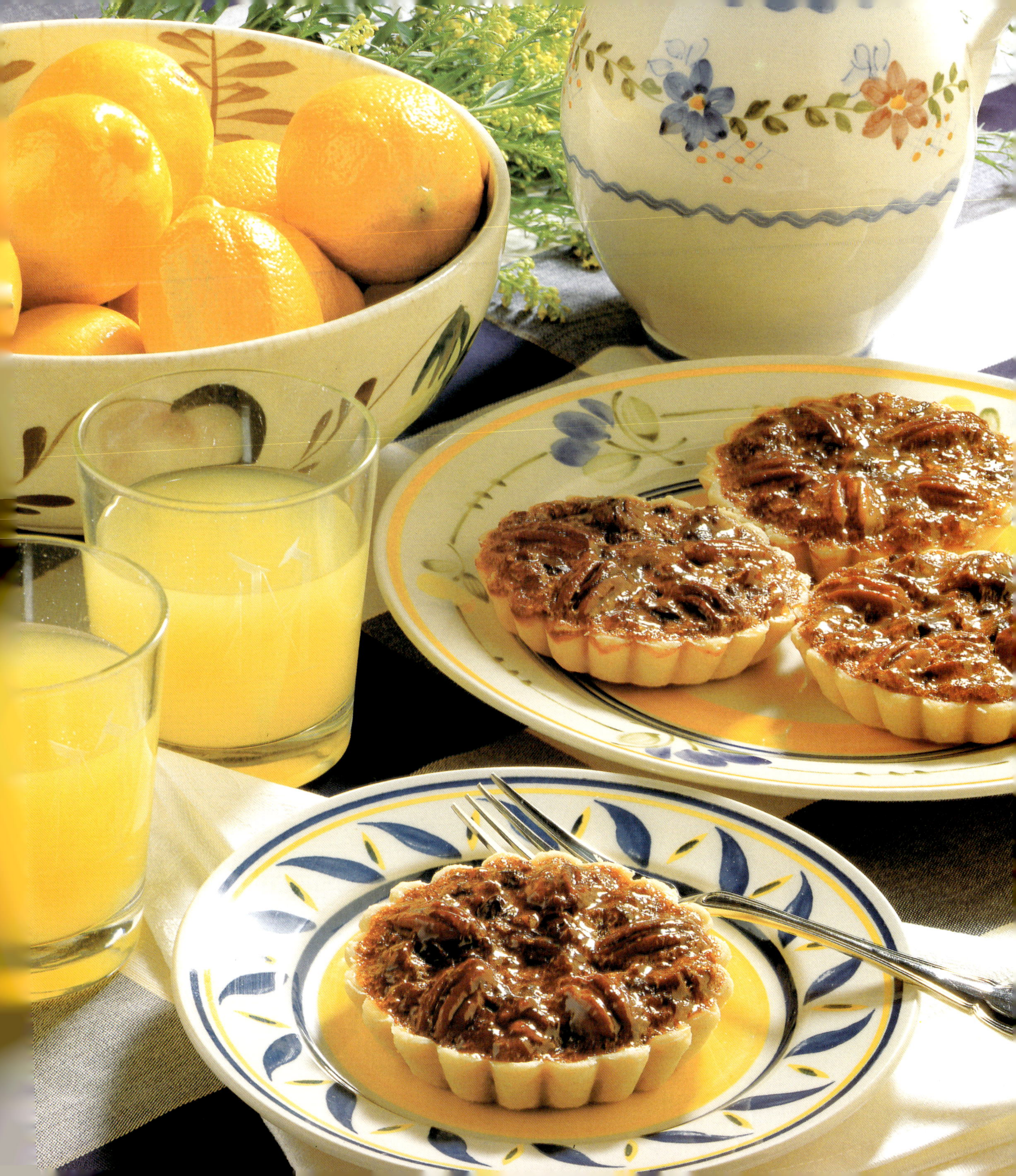

## Tarte Alsacienne

### Crust

- 500 grams bread flour, sifted
- 225 grams salted butter, cut into small pieces
- 1 teaspoon cold water

### Method

1. Mix sifted flour with butter until the mixture resembles breadcrumbs.
2. Add a little cold water to form a dough. Chill for an hour in the refrigerator to prevent shrinkage during baking.

Chef's Note: This pastry is also known as Pate Brisee or Savoury Dough. If preferred, Pate Sucre or Sweet Pie Dough (featured in the recipe for the Fruit Tartlet pie crust on page 32), can be substituted. Be careful not to overhandle while kneading the dough as this results in a less flaky pastry. Always use cold butter and let the dough rest an hour in the refrigerator before rolling out.

### Filling

- 6 red apples, peeled, cored, halved and sliced 3/4 of the way through
- 1 tablespoon castor sugar for sprinkling on the apples
- 2 eggs, beaten
- 1/2 cup castor sugar
- 1 cup cream
- 1 tablespoon lemon juice
- 1 teaspoon vanilla essence
- apricot jam, heated with a little water, to glaze
- a splash of brandy or Grand Marnier to serve

### Method

1. Roll out the chilled dough to line a 30-cm tart pan. Arrange semi-sliced apples on the tart shell and sprinkle with some sugar. The sugar will caramelise when heated. Bake uncovered at 205°C/400°F for 20 minutes.
2. When the apples are soft (test by pricking with a fork), remove the tart from the oven and drain the excess water from the pastry shell. (You can do this by placing a dinner plate on top and turning the shell upside down to drain the water.)
3. To prepare the custard, beat eggs, sugar and cream until well mixed. Add lemon juice and vanilla. Pour this into the pastry shell, lifting the apples a little (to let the custard flow beneath them) and bake uncovered for another 20 minutes or until the custard sets.
4. Glaze with apricot jam and serve slightly warm with a splash of brandy or Grand Marnier.

Chef's Note: Pouring a little warm Calvados on the tart turns it into Tart Normande Flambee.

## Chocolate Mousse Tart

### Crust

- 3/4 cup all-purpose flour
- 3 tablespoons unsalted butter, cold
- 1 tablespoon sugar
- 2 tablespoons ice water

### Method

1. Process all ingredients in a food processor until a dough is formed. Cover dough with cling wrap and refrigerate for an hour.
2. Roll out dough to fit 22-cm quiche pan and bake blind for 25 minutes at 180°C/360°F until thoroughly cooked.

### Filling

- 200 grams bittersweet chocolate, chopped into small pieces
- 2 tablespoons Cointreau (orange liqueur)
- 4 tablespoons heavy cream
- 3 eggs, separated
- segments from 2 oranges for decoration
- 1 tablespoon cocoa powder for dusting

### Method

1. Melt the chocolate, Cointreau and heavy cream until smooth over a baine marie (heatproof bowl set over a pot of simmering water). Stir in egg yolks and use whisk to beat the mixture until well blended and thick. Remove from the heat.
2. In another bowl whisk egg whites until fluffy and fold slowly into the chocolate mixture.
3. Pour the mixture into the prepared crust and refrigerate for a few hours to firm it up. Just before serving, dust cocoa powder around the tart rim and garnish with orange segments.

## Almond Orange Tart

### Crust

- 1 22-cm half-cooked almond crust, cooled*

### Filling

- 4 eggs, lightly beaten
- 1 cup castor sugar
- 1 cup freshly squeezed orange juice
- grated zest of 1 orange
- 1/4 cup heavy cream
- 6 oranges, peeled and thinly sliced
- 3 tablespoons orange marmalade, heated with 2 tablespoons water until thick for glaze

### Method

1. Prepare the tart shell.
2. Beat eggs and sugar. Add in orange juice, orange zest and cream.
3. Pour the custard into the prepared crust. Bake at 180°C/360°F for about 35 minutes until the custard is set and slightly browned. Cool.
4. Arrange orange slices on top of the custard, overlapping each other in symmetrical order. Glaze with orange marmalade.

*Refer to recipe for Almond Apricot Tart on page 16.

*Opposite: Tarte Alsacienne.*

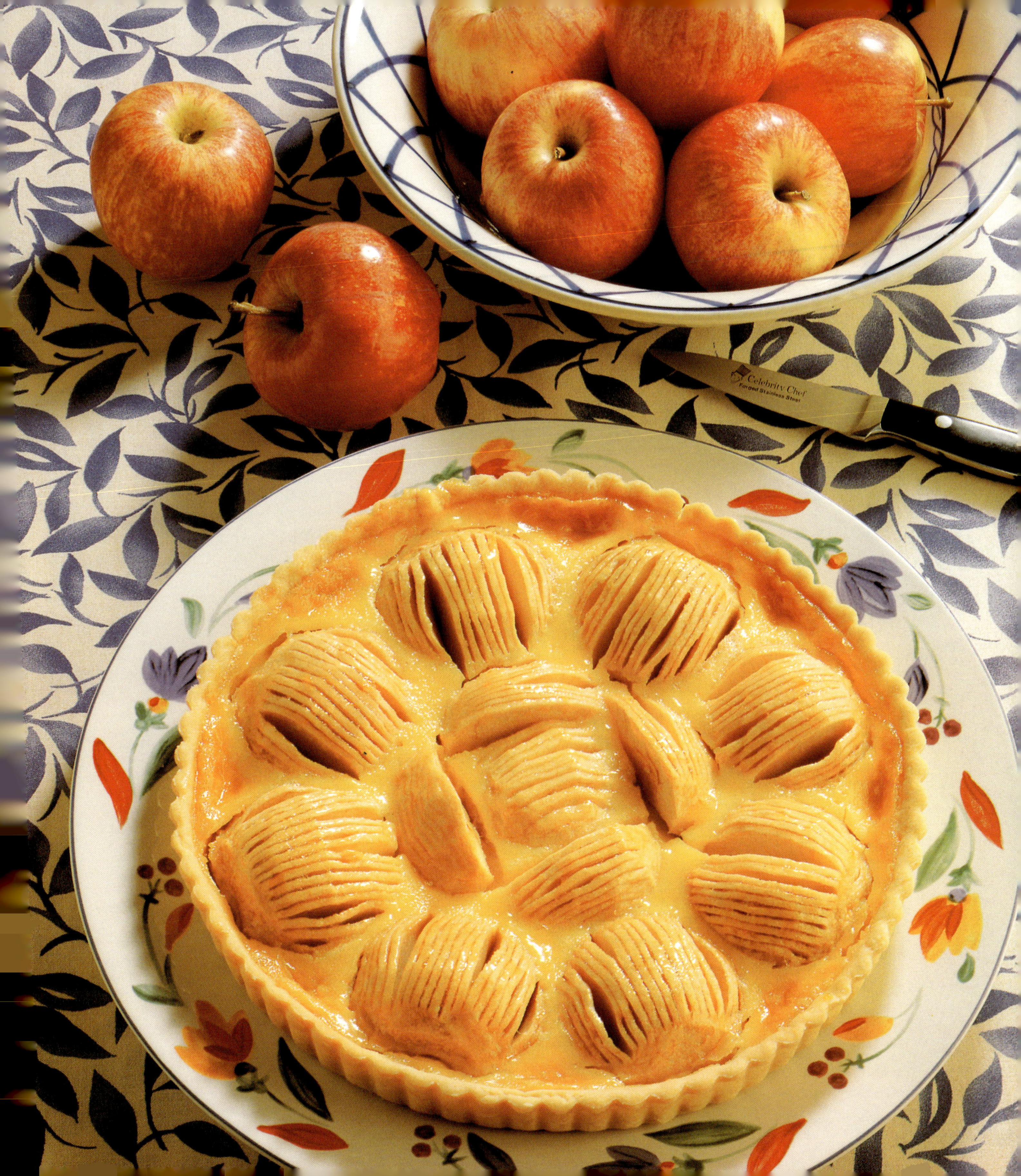
Celebrity Chef
Forged Stainless Steel

## Dutch Country Pear Pie

*Crust*

- 3 cups all-purpose flour
- ½ cup castor sugar
- 1 cup cold unsalted butter, cut into small pieces
- 1 egg, beaten

*Method*

1. Combine flour and sugar. Cut in butter until the mixture resembles breadcrumbs.
2. Add the beaten egg and mix the ingredients by hand until the dough is smooth and uniformly coloured. Refrigerate while preparing the filling.

*Filling*

- 5 ripe pears, peeled, seeded and diced
- ¾ cup currants
- ¾ cup raisins
- zest of 1 lemon
- ½ cup brown sugar
- 1 teaspoon powdered cinnamon
- ½ teaspoon allspice
- 1 tablespoon lemon juice

*Method*

1. Mix pear with all the remaining ingredients except egg.
2. Line a large, greased a 22-cm springform pan with the chilled dough to a depth of 2.5 cm in the base and a little thicker on the sides.
3. Spoon the filling into the pastry shell and bake at 180°C/360°F for about an hour until golden.

## Strawberry Almond Tart

*Crust*

- 1¼ cups all-purpose flour
- 6 tablespoons unsalted butter, diced
- 2 tablespoons vegetable shortening
- ¼ teaspoon salt
- some iced water

*Method*

1. Mix together all the pastry ingredients as quickly as possible. Add a few tablespoons of iced water to form a dough. Wrap in cling wrap and chill in the refrigerator for a few hours.
2. Roll out the pastry thinly to line a 22-cm tart pan. Prick the base with a fork. Cover with foil and fill with beans. Bake blind for 15 minutes at 180°C/360°F. Remove the foil and beans.

*Filling*

- 1 cup almonds, skinned
- ⅔ cup castor sugar
- 2 eggs, lightly beaten
- a drop of almond essence

- 30 strawberries to decorate
- strawberry jam, heated with a little water, to glaze

*Method*

1. Finely grind almonds and castor sugar. Add beaten eggs and almond essence. Beat until smooth. Pour into the prepared tart shell.
2. Bake for 20 minutes at 180°C/360°F until cooked and golden brown.
3. Remove the tart from the oven and cool. Decorate with strawberries and glaze with strawberry jam heated with a little water until thick.

## Upside-Down Apple Tart

*Crust*

- 1 recipe for sweet crust pastry*

*Filling*

- 6 tablespoons butter
- ½ cup sugar
- 1½ kilograms apples, peeled, cored and cut into wedges

*Method*

1. Preheat the oven to 220°C/425°F.
2. Thickly butter a 22-cm high-sided pie pan and sprinkle with half of the sugar. Cover the bottom of the pan with the apples and sprinkle with the remaining sugar.
3. Place the pan directly over a stove and cook the contents for about 15 minutes or until the sugar starts to caramelise. Remove the pan, place in the oven and bake for about 25 minutes.
4. Meanwhile roll out the dough into a circle larger than the pie pan. Remove the pan from the oven, lay the dough over the apples and tuck it in around them.
5. Return the pan to the oven and bake for another 15 minutes or until the dough is nicely browned. Remove and leave to cool for 20 minutes before turning out.
6. Just before serving, place the pan back over the stove just long enough to melt the caramel. Turn out and serve warm.

Chef's Note: This tart can be baked ahead of time and reheated just before serving.

* Refer to recipe for Fruit Tartlets on page 32.

*Opposite: Dutch Country Pear Pie.*

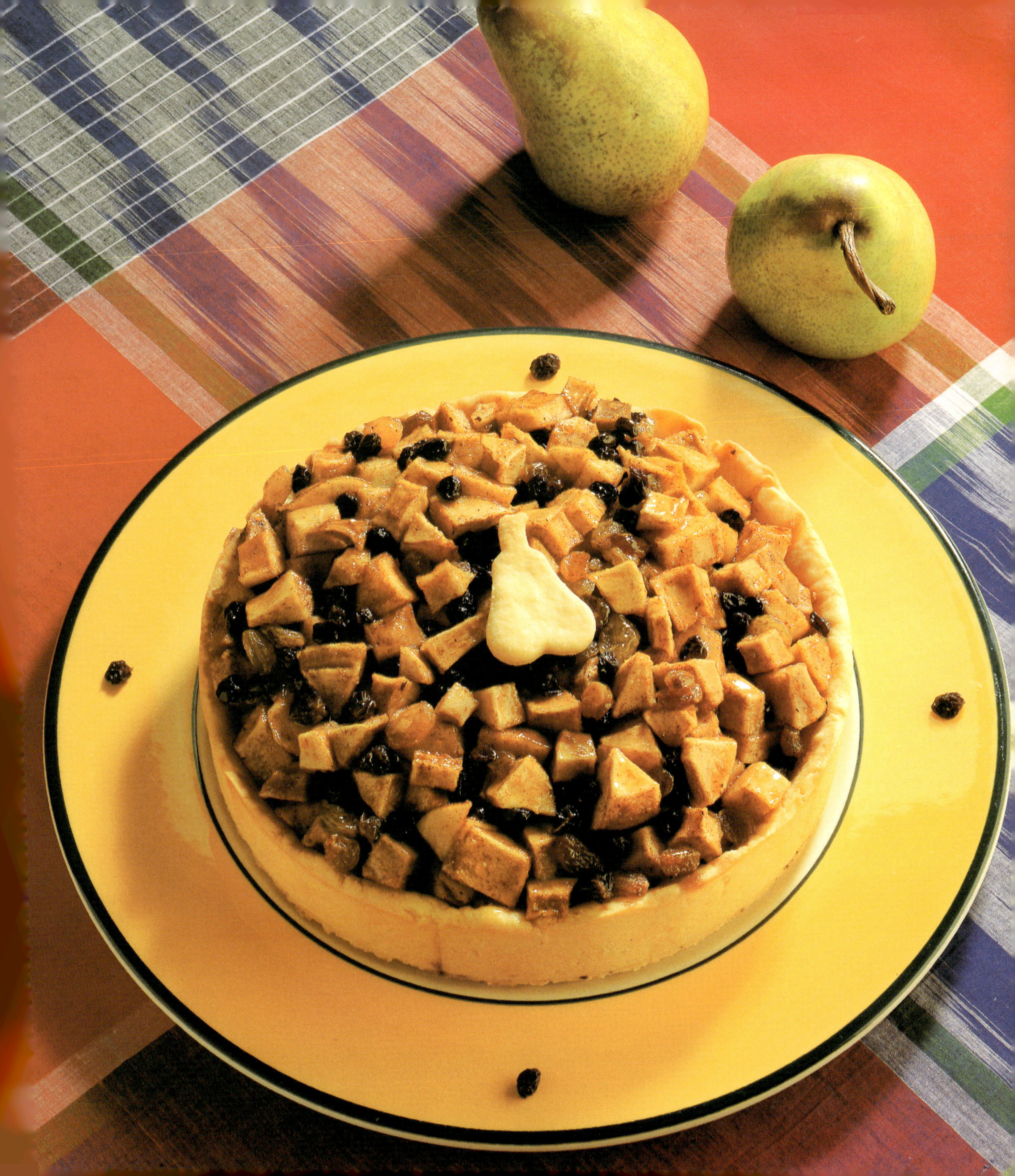

## Warm Chocolate Tart with Pistachio Sauce

*Pistachio Sauce*

- 3 egg yolks
- 1/3 cup castor sugar
- 1 cup fresh milk, scalded
- 1/4 cup pistachios, ground

*Method*

1. Gradually whisk egg yolks and sugar in a small saucepan over low heat. Whisk in scalded milk. Continue whisking over low heat for about 2 minutes or until the sauce coats the back of a spoon. Stir in pistachios.
2. Place a sheet of cling wrap directly on the surface of the sauce to prevent a skin from forming. Cool to room temperature.

*Warm Chocolate Tart*

- 130 grams bittersweet chocolate, chopped into small pieces
- 1/4 cup brewed espresso or other strong coffee
- 7 tablespoons butter
- 1/4 cup unsweetened cocoa
- 4 eggs, separated
- 2/3 cup castor sugar, divided into two equal parts

*Method*

1. Butter a 22-cm springform tart pan. Line the base with parchment paper.
2. Wrap and secure a 10-cm wide parchment paper collar around the outside of the pan to prevent batter from seeping through during baking.
3. Stir chocolate, espresso and butter in a heatproof bowl set over a saucepan of hot water until the chocolate melts. Stir in cocoa. Cool to room temperature.
4. In a medium bowl beat egg yolks and one-third cup of the sugar until pale yellow. Stir into cooled chocolate.
5. In a separate bowl whip egg whites. Gradually add remaining 1/3 cup sugar and whip into stiff peaks. Fold into the chocolate.
6. Adjust the oven rack to the middle position and heat the oven to 205°C/400°F. Place the tart pan on a baking tray. Pour one-third of the batter into the pan. Bake for about 8 minutes until dry but not firm. Cool to room temperature.
7. Lower the oven heat to 170°C/340°F. Pour the remaining batter over the cooled layer in the pan. Resume baking for about 15 minutes until the filling rises like a souffle. Cool slightly. The tart will deflate upon cooling. To serve, remove the warm tart from the pan and cut into wedges. Serve immediately with pistachio sauce.

Chef's Notes: (1) If you prefer to use smaller 10-cm tart pans, this recipe yields 6 small tarts.
(2) Sometimes, the sauce may curdle if you are not careful about controlling the heat. To save it, put into a blender and blend until smooth, then strain. Or start all over again.
(3) Pistachios may be substituted with one of the following to give the sauce a different flavour:

- Orange zest, concentrated juice
- Ground almond and essence
- Melted chocolate
- Whipped cream, ice-cream

## Chocolate and Pecan Pie

*Crust*

- 1 recipe of pastry crust*

*Method*

Roll out pastry crust and line a 25-cm springform pie pan. Refrigerate for half an hour to avoid shrinkage during baking.

*Filling*

- 8 eggs
- 400 grams golden syrup
- 110 grams unsalted butter, melted
- 350 grams semisweet cooking chocolate, chopped and melted
- 1 tablespoon rum, optional
- 350 grams pecans, coarsely chopped

*Method*

1. Beat eggs and golden syrup until well blended. Add melted butter, chocolate and rum.
2. Spread pecans at the base of pie crust. Gently pour in the chocolate filling.
3. Bake at 175°C/350°F for an hour until the custard sets.

* Refer to recipe for Fruit Tartlets on page 32.

*Opposite: Warm Chocolate Tart with Pistachio Sauce.*

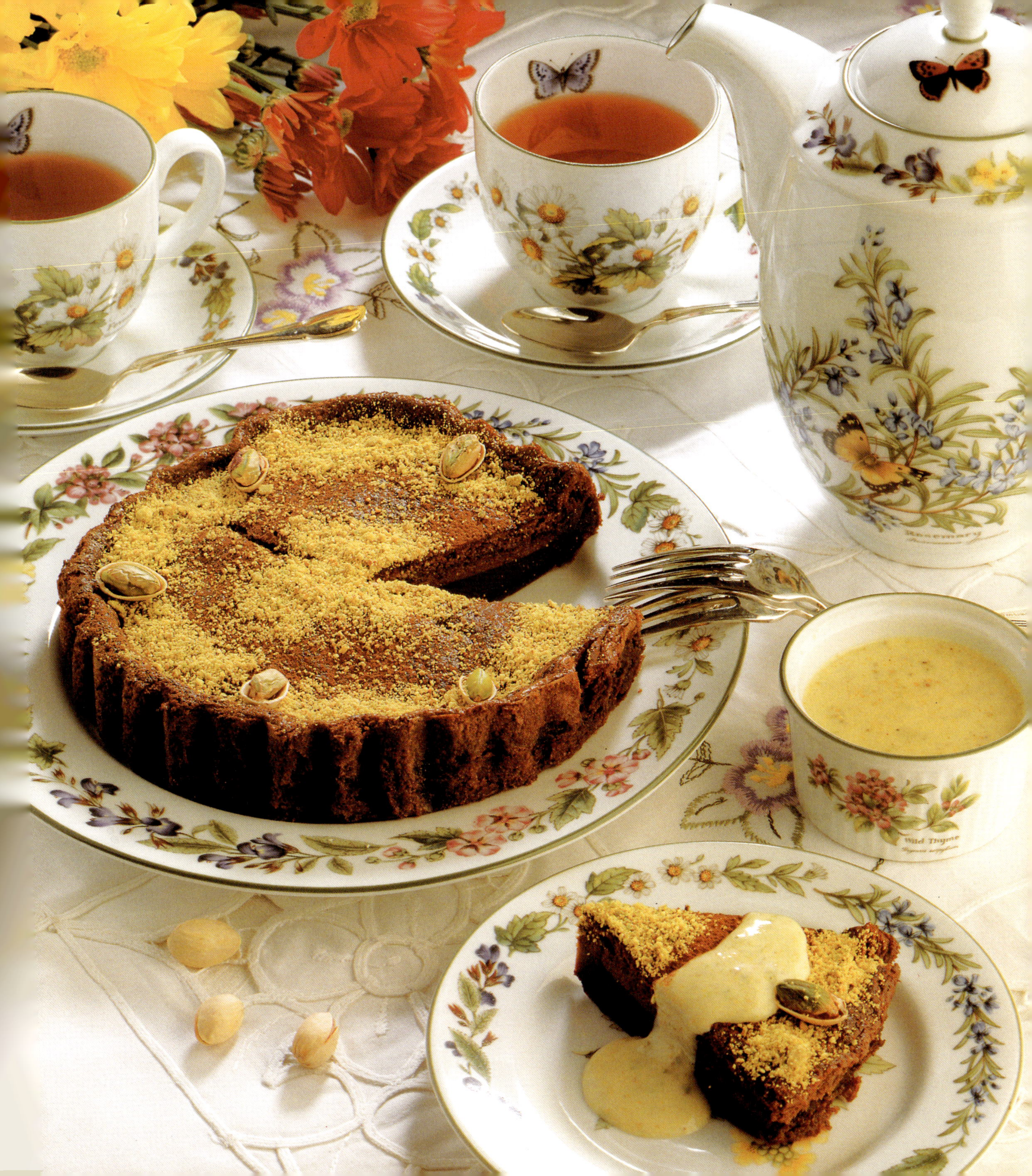

# Muffins & Scones

The Art of Baking Muffins & Scones, p46 & 47  1 Apple Pecan Muffins, p48  2 Apple Raisin Muffins, p48  3 Coconut Pineapple Muffins, p48  4 Oatmeal Date Scones, p48  5 Blueberry Muffins, p50  6 Fruitcake Muffins, p50  7 Raisin Pear Muffins, p50  8 Gingerbread Raisin Scones, p50  9 Honey Corn Muffins, p52  10 Apple and Macadamia Nut Muffins, p52  11 Cheddar Cheese and Onion Scones, p52  12 Crumpets, p52  13 Cheddar Cheese Scones, p54  14 Currant Oat Scones, p54  15 Orange Cream Scones, p54  16 Date, Honey and Carrot Muffins, p56  17 Oat Bran and Fruit Muffins, p56  18 Blueberry and Oats Muffins, p56  19 Spiced Pumpkin Muffins, p58  20 Banana Chocolate Chip Muffins, p58  21 Apricot and Almond Muffins, p58  22 Miniature Herb Cream Biscuits, p58

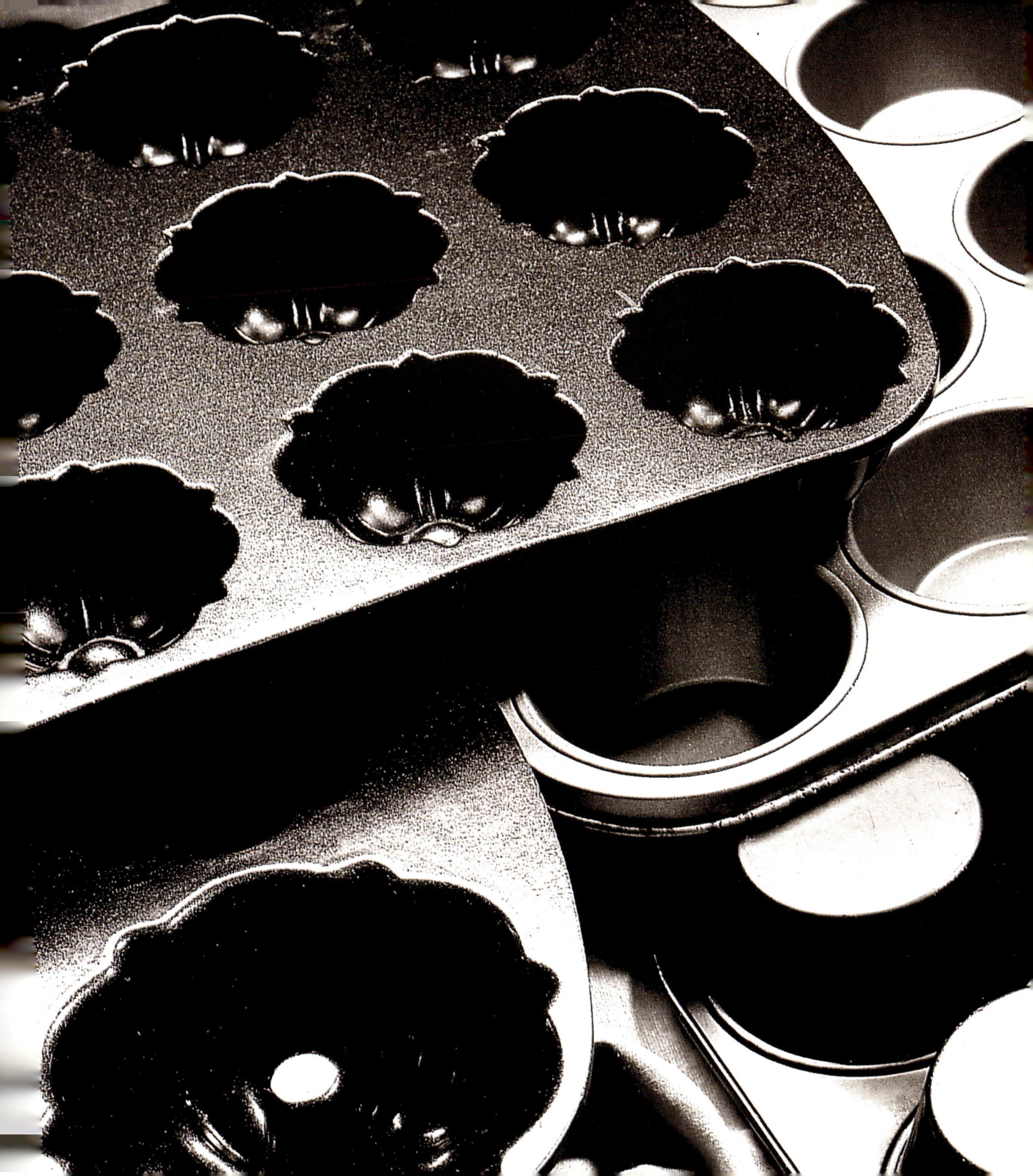

# The Art of Baking Muffins

Muffins are quick and easy to make. A batch of fresh, aromatic muffins can be prepared, baked and served well within an hour.

The basic muffin-making technique is simple. Wet ingredients are mixed in one bowl and dry ingredients in another so as to evenly distribute the leavening. Some oil or melted butter is added to achieve the coarse, crumbly texture typical of most muffins. In some muffin recipes the butter and sugar are creamed for a finer texture. Adding liquids such as buttermilk, yoghurt, molasses and citrus juices also adds moisture and tenderness. Grains and brans are soaked and softened in liquid before being added to the batter.

Liquid and dry ingredients are combined just until the batter holds together; mixing should take no more than 15 seconds. Lumps and clumps are natural. The less the batter is handled the better. An overbeaten muffin is tough, flat and overrun with tunnels. I like to mix my batter by hand because I can exercise better control over it. There is less risk of overmixing compared with using a food processor, which tends to run too fast.

Use all-purpose flour except when a recipe specifies otherwise. Pastry and cake flour produce muffins that are too soft to hold their shape. The classic formula for a tender muffin is two parts flour to one part liquid.

Fill muffin cups about three-quarters full for thin batters. For thick batters fill the muffin cups to the rim. Use a small ladle, large spoon, or ice-cream scoop to fill the cups. Take heed: insufficient batter, or oven heat that is too low, can result in flat muffins. Too much batter, on the other hand, will cause the batter to spill over during baking and you may end up with lopsided muffins.

Muffin batters made only with baking powder can be mixed and kept in the refrigerator for up to three days. After that the leavening and flour break down.

Muffins should be baked in the centre of a preheated oven. Baking them on the lower rack browns the bottoms too much and baking them on the higher rack cooks the tops too quickly. The middle rack is your best choice for an evenly baked muffin.

Muffins are done when the tops are domed and dry to the touch and the sides have pulled away from the pan slightly. Alternatively if a tester inserted in the centre of a muffin comes away cleanly, it is cooked. Muffins are best eaten the day they are baked, but they also freeze well.

The variety of muffins to choose from is staggering. They can be either sweet or savoury and you can take your pick of ingredients: bran, oats, blueberries, carrots, apples, bananas, yoghurt, chocolate or cheese. Grated cheddar has always been a favourite ingredient of mine in scones, cookies, breads and muffins. The kids love it as well.

# The Art of Baking Scones

Scones are the highlight of afternoon high tea. I first tasted scones 15 years ago at a hillside resort in Australia's Blue Mountains. I was studying in Sydney then. My friend and I ordered tea and scones. Our meal came complete with linen, silver and fine china. We were served teacakes and scones straight out of the oven. The scones were of the melt-in-the-mouth variety and were delicious with jam and a dollop of cream. I have never forgotten the experience.

Today I have learnt to make more than 50 different kinds of scones, some recipes of which I am sharing with you in this section of the book.

Scones began as simple nourishment for harvesters and farmers who needed some form of midday sustenance. These simple scones were made only with white or wholewheat flour, baking soda and either milk or buttermilk. They were known as "harvest scones" and were served in thick wedges along with jars of jam and strong, black tea.

Eventually more elaborate scones were concocted. These were made with cane sugar, raisins, spices, fresh fruit, eggs and cheese. They were richer and daintier than the original scones and were served at teatime when farmers and their wives dropped by to discuss the produce or harvest.

Today scones are still perfect for breakfast or at high tea.

## INGREDIENTS
### Flour
Whole grain flours such as barley, rye or oat make a nutritious and scrumptious base for scones when combined with all-purpose flour. However be careful not to overbake scones made from wholegrain flour as the scones will end up dry and crumbly.

### Fat
Use butter or margarine or a combination of the two for tender, flaky scones. Make sure the fat is cold. Vegetable shortening or olive oil may be used for savoury scones.

### Leavening
Most scones use baking powder as leavening. Double-acting baking powder starts the dough rising when liquid is added and again when warmed by oven heat.

Baking powder gradually loses its effectiveness once the box or can is opened, so take note of the expiry date. Discard the baking powder after a year.

Baking soda may be required to neutralize acidic ingredients such as buttermilk, brown sugar or molasses.

### Liquid
For tender, moist scones use milk, buttermilk or plain yoghurt. But when making substitutes, keep in mind that the taste of all the ingredients should blend well with each other. For extra-rich scones replace the milk with cream.

### Baking
Do not to overmix your scones, especially after the butter and liquid are combined, as scones will not rise properly when the dough has been overhandled.

Make sure your oven is preheated before baking.

## Apple Pecan Muffins

*Ingredients*

1¼ cups all-purpose flour
1 teaspoon baking soda
½ teaspoon ground cinnamon
a pinch of salt
1 egg
1 cup castor sugar
½ cup corn oil
2 tablespoons lemon juice
1½ teaspoons vanilla essence
¾ teaspoon grated orange zest
3 apples, peeled and diced
½ cup pecans, toasted and chopped
20 whole pecans to decorate

*Method*

1. Sift flour, baking soda, cinnamon and salt into a bowl.
2. In a separate bowl beat egg, sugar, oil, lemon juice, vanilla essence and orange zest. Fold in the dry ingredients and mix well. Add apples and toasted pecans.
3. Spoon the batter into greased muffin cups and top each muffin with a whole pecan. Bake at 175°C/350°F for half an hour.

## Apple Raisin Muffins

*Ingredients*

2 cups all-purpose flour
1 tablespoon baking powder
¾ teaspoon baking soda
1 teaspoon ground cinnamon
¼ teaspoon allspice
¼ teaspoon salt
¾ cup castor sugar
1½ cups sour cream
4 tablespoons butter, melted
2 green apples, peeled and diced
½ cup dark raisins
½ cup walnuts, chopped

*Topping*

½ cup brown sugar
⅓ cup all-purpose flour
4 tablespoons butter

*Method*

1. Sift together flour, baking powder, baking soda, cinnamon, allspice and salt.
2. In another bowl mix sugar, sour cream and butter until combined. Add the sifted ingredients to the butter mixture. Add apples, raisins and walnuts.
3. Combine all ingredients for the topping and mix well.
4. Spoon batter into a greased muffin pan and sprinkle the topping on it.
5. Bake at 175°C/350°F for 20 to 25 minutes until cooked all the way through.

## Coconut Pineapple Muffins

*Ingredients*

¼ cup brown sugar
¼ cup vegetable oil
1 egg white
½ cup fresh milk
1 cup all-purpose flour
1½ teaspoons double-acting baking powder
½ teaspoon ground cinnamon
¼ teaspoon salt
¾ cup sweetened coconut flakes, toasted lightly
1 cup canned pineapple rings, sliced

*Method*

1. Whisk together brown sugar, oil, egg white and milk.
2. Sift together flour, baking powder, cinnamon and salt. Fold the sifted ingredients into the batter. Add coconut flakes and sliced pineapples. Stir until just combined.
3. Divide the batter among paper cups set in a muffin tray and bake at 180°C/360°F for about 25 minutes.

## Oatmeal Date Scones

*Ingredients*

¾ cup milk
1 large egg
3 tablespoons brown sugar
1 teaspoon vanilla essence
2½ cups all-purpose flour
1 cup rolled oats
1 tablespoon double-acting baking powder
½ teaspoon baking soda
½ teaspoon salt
6 tablespoons cold, unsalted butter, cut into small pieces
½ cup chopped dates

*Method*

1. Whisk together milk, egg, brown sugar and vanilla essence. Set aside.
2. In another bowl mix together flour, oats, baking powder, baking soda and salt. Transfer the dry ingredients to a food processor and blend in butter until the mixture resembles coarse breadcrumbs.
3. Stir dates and milk mixture into the flour mixture until a sticky dough forms.
4. Spoon scones out onto an ungreased baking sheet and shape as desired. Bake at 200°C/390°F for 15 to 18 minutes until golden.

*Opposite: Coconut Pineapple Muffins (above) and Apple Pecan Muffins (below).*

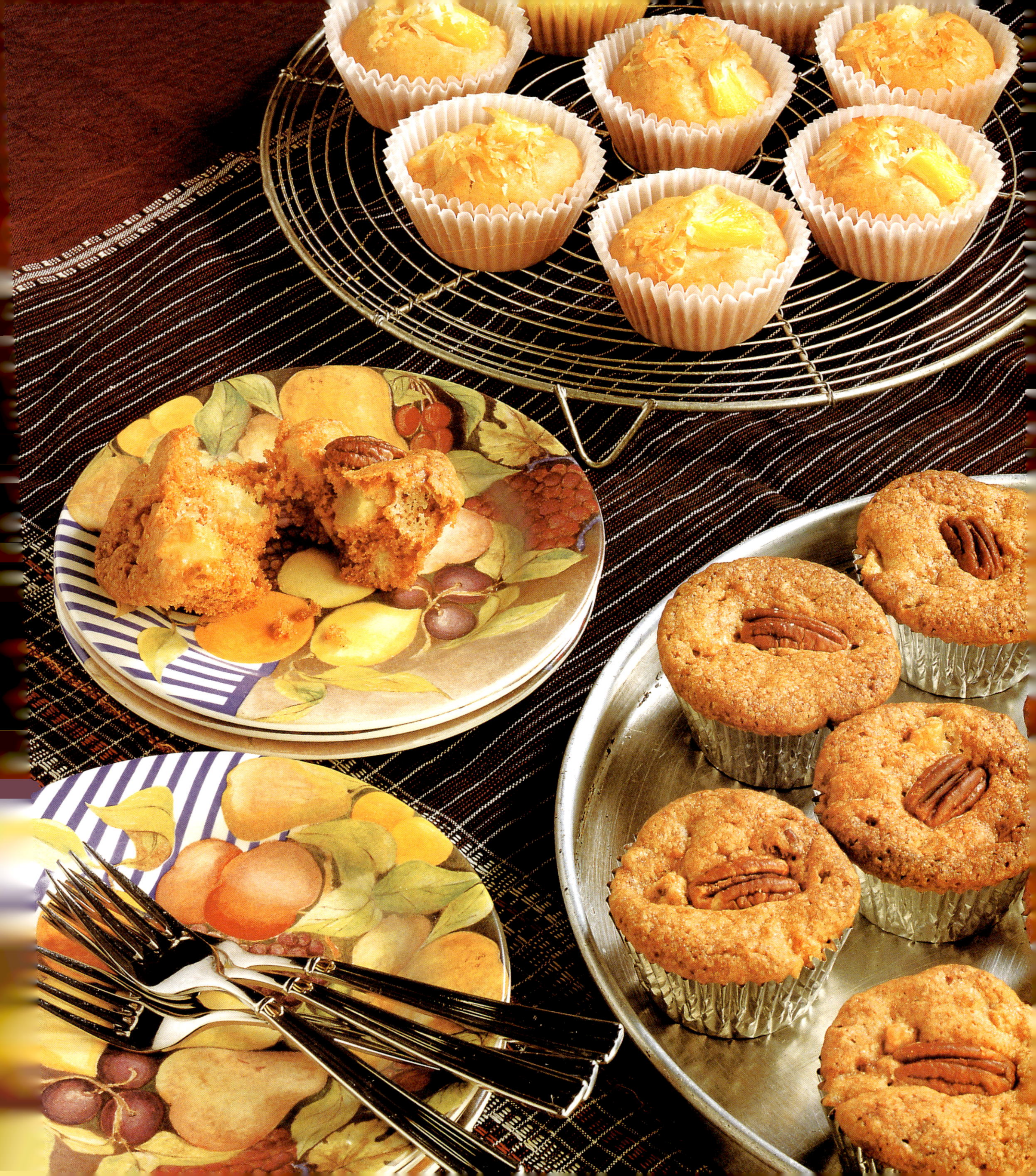

# Blueberry Muffins

### Ingredients

- 2 cups all-purpose flour
- 1 tablespoon baking powder
- ½ teaspoon salt
- 6 tablespoons butter, softened at room temperature
- ¼ cup brown sugar
- 2 eggs
- 1 cup canned blueberries, drained
- ½ cup milk
- ½ cup cream
- 4 tablespoons almond slices

### Method

1. Sift together flour, baking powder and salt.
2. In another bowl cream butter and sugar. Add eggs one at a time. Alternately fold in blueberries, sifted ingredients, milk and cream.
3. Spoon the batter into greased muffin cups and sprinkle with almond slices.
4. Bake at 180°C/360°F for 25 minutes.

# Fruitcake Muffins

### Ingredients

- 2½ cups all-purpose flour
- 1 teaspoon baking soda
- ½ teaspoon salt
- 1 cup raisins
- ½ cup currants
- grated zest of 1 orange
- grated zest of 1 lemon
- ½ cup red glace cherries, coarsely chopped
- ⅓ cup castor sugar
- ¼ cup lime juice
- 3 eggs
- ½ cup corn oil
- 1 tablespoon brown sugar
- 1 tablespoon fresh milk
- ½ teaspoon ground nutmeg
- ¼ teaspoon ground cloves

### Method

1. Sift together flour, baking soda and salt.
2. Soak raisins, currants, orange and lemon zest, cherries and sugar in lime juice for about half an hour.
3. Whisk eggs and corn oil until well mixed. Add brown sugar, milk, nutmeg and cloves. Follow with flour and soaked fruit.
4. Spoon the batter into greased muffin cups and bake for 25 minutes at 170°C/340°F.

# Raisin Pear Muffins

### Ingredients

- 4 large pears, peeled, cored and diced
- 1 cup castor sugar
- ½ cup vegetable oil
- 2 large eggs, beaten
- 2 teaspoons vanilla essence
- 2 cups all-purpose flour
- 2 teaspoons baking soda
- 2 teaspoons ground cinnamon
- 1 teaspoon ground nutmeg
- 1 teaspoon salt
- 1 cup raisins
- 1 cup walnuts, chopped

whole walnuts to decorate

### Method

1. Preheat the oven to 170°C/340°F. Butter 18 muffin cups.
2. Mix together pears and sugar.
3. In a large bowl blend together oil, eggs and vanilla essence.
4. In a medium bowl combine flour, baking soda, cinnamon, nutmeg and salt, and sift together.
5. Stir pears into the egg mixture and slowly add the dry ingredients.
6. Fold in raisins and walnuts without overmixing. Divide the batter among the greased muffin cups. Decorate with whole walnuts. Bake for 30 minutes until a skewer inserted in the centre of a muffin comes away cleanly. Serve warm or at room temperature.

# Gingerbread Raisin Scones

### Ingredients

- 2 cups all-purpose flour
- ⅓ cup packed, dark brown sugar
- 1 tablespoon baking powder
- ¾ teaspoon ground cinnamon
- ½ teaspoon ground ginger
- ⅛ teaspoon ground cloves
- 6 tablespoons chilled butter, cut into small pieces
- ¼ cup milk
- 1 large egg
- 3 tablespoon unsulphured, or light, molasses
- 1 teaspoon vanilla essence
- ⅔ cup raisins

butter and marmalade to serve

### Method

1. In a food processor blend first six ingredients. Add butter and process until the mixture resembles coarse breadcrumbs.
2. Beat together milk, egg, molasses and vanilla essence. Add the flour mixture and raisins. Stir until a dough forms. Roll out on a lightly floured surface and cut with a cookie cutter. Place on a lightly greased baking tray and bake for 25 minutes at 175°C/350°F. Serve with butter and marmalade.

*Opposite: Raisin Pear Muffins (left), Blueberry Muffins (centre) and Fruitcake Muffins (right).*

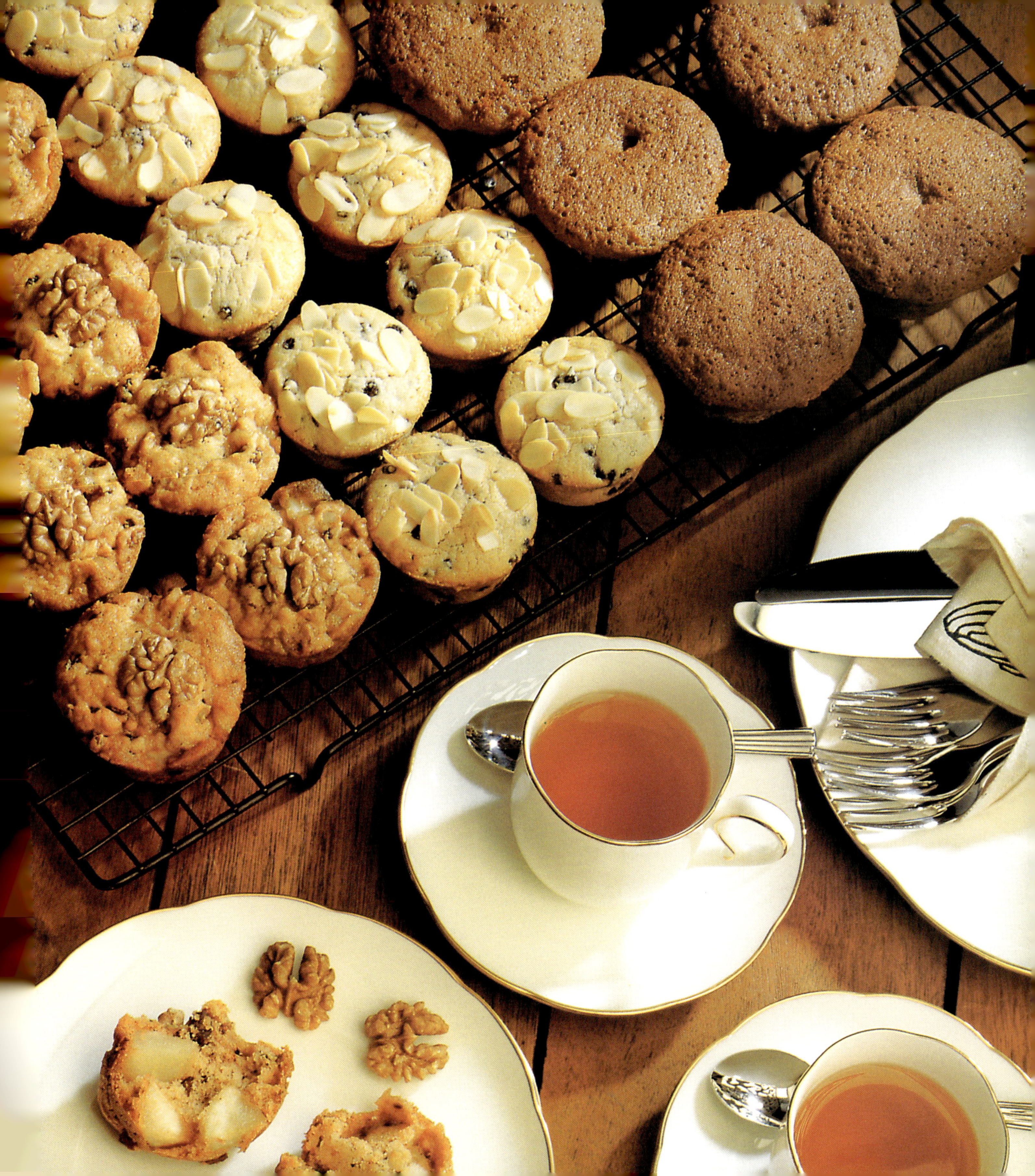

## Honey Corn Muffins

*Ingredients*

- 100 grams all-purpose flour
- 1 tablespoon baking powder
- a pinch of salt
- 100 grams cornmeal
- 3 tablespoons honey
- 50 grams dark raisins
- 4 tablespoons corn oil
- 225 grams creamed corn
- 1/3 cup water

- butter for serving

*Method*

1. Sift together flour, baking powder and salt. Stir in cornmeal. Add honey, raisins, oil, creamed corn and water.
2. Spoon the batter into greased muffin cups.
3. Bake at 180°C/360°F for 15 to 20 minutes until risen and golden. Serve warm with butter.

## Apple and Macadamia Nut Muffins

*Ingredients*

- 1 1/4 cups all-purpose flour
- 1 teaspoon baking soda
- 1/2 teaspoon ground cinnamon
- a pinch of salt
- 1 cup castor sugar
- 1/2 cup vegetable oil
- 1 egg
- 2 tablespoons lemon juice
- 1 tablespoon vanilla essence
- grated zest of 1 lemon
- 2 green apples, peeled and diced
- 1/2 cup coarsely chopped macadamia nuts

*Method*

1. Sift together flour, baking soda, cinnamon and salt.
2. Beat together sugar, oil, egg, lemon juice, vanilla essence and lemon zest.
3. Combine egg mixture with the sifted ingredients. Stir in apples and nuts.
4. Spoon batter into greased muffin cups and bake at 175°C/ 350°F for 20 minutes.

## Cheddar Cheese and Onion Scones

*Ingredients*

- 1 egg
- 1/2 cup fresh milk
- 1 teaspoon powdered English mustard
- 1 onion, chopped and fried golden in butter
- 1 1/2 cups all-purpose flour
- 1 1/2 teaspoons cream of tartar
- 1/2 teaspoon baking soda
- 1/2 teaspoon salt
- 4 tablespoons cold butter, cut into small pieces
- 1 cup cheddar cheese, grated
- 2 tablespoons parmesan cheese

*Method*

1. Combine egg, milk, mustard and fried onion.
2. Sift together flour, cream of tartar baking soda and salt. Cut cold butter into the flour until the mixture resembles coarse breadcrumbs. Add the egg mixture and both kinds of cheese.
3. Mix into a dough and roll out. Cut into desired shapes and bake for 20 minutes at 180°C/360°F until golden brown.

## Crumpets

*Ingredients*

- 1 1/2 teaspoons dry yeast
- 1/4 cup warm water
- 1 teaspoon castor sugar
- 1 1/2 cups warm milk
- 2 cups all-purpose flour
- 1 teaspoon salt
- 1/2 teaspoon baking soda
- 1/4 cup warm water

*Method*

1. Sprinkle the yeast into 1/4 cup warm water. Stir in sugar and let the mixture sit for 5 minutes, allowing the yeast to dissolve. Add milk, flour and salt. Beat until smooth. Cover the bowl with cling wrap and leave to rest for an hour.
2. Dissolve the baking soda in 1/4 cup warm water and pour into the yeast mixture. Cover and set aside for another 30 minutes.
3. Remove the top and bottom from a few 8-cm tin cans, such as a tuna cans. Heat a griddle, brush it with vegetable oil and place the rings on the griddle.
4. Pour 3 tablespoonfuls of the batter into each ring. Lower the heat and cook until holes appear on the surface.
5. Remove the rings and serve the crumpets warm.

*Opposite: Honey Corn Muffins.*

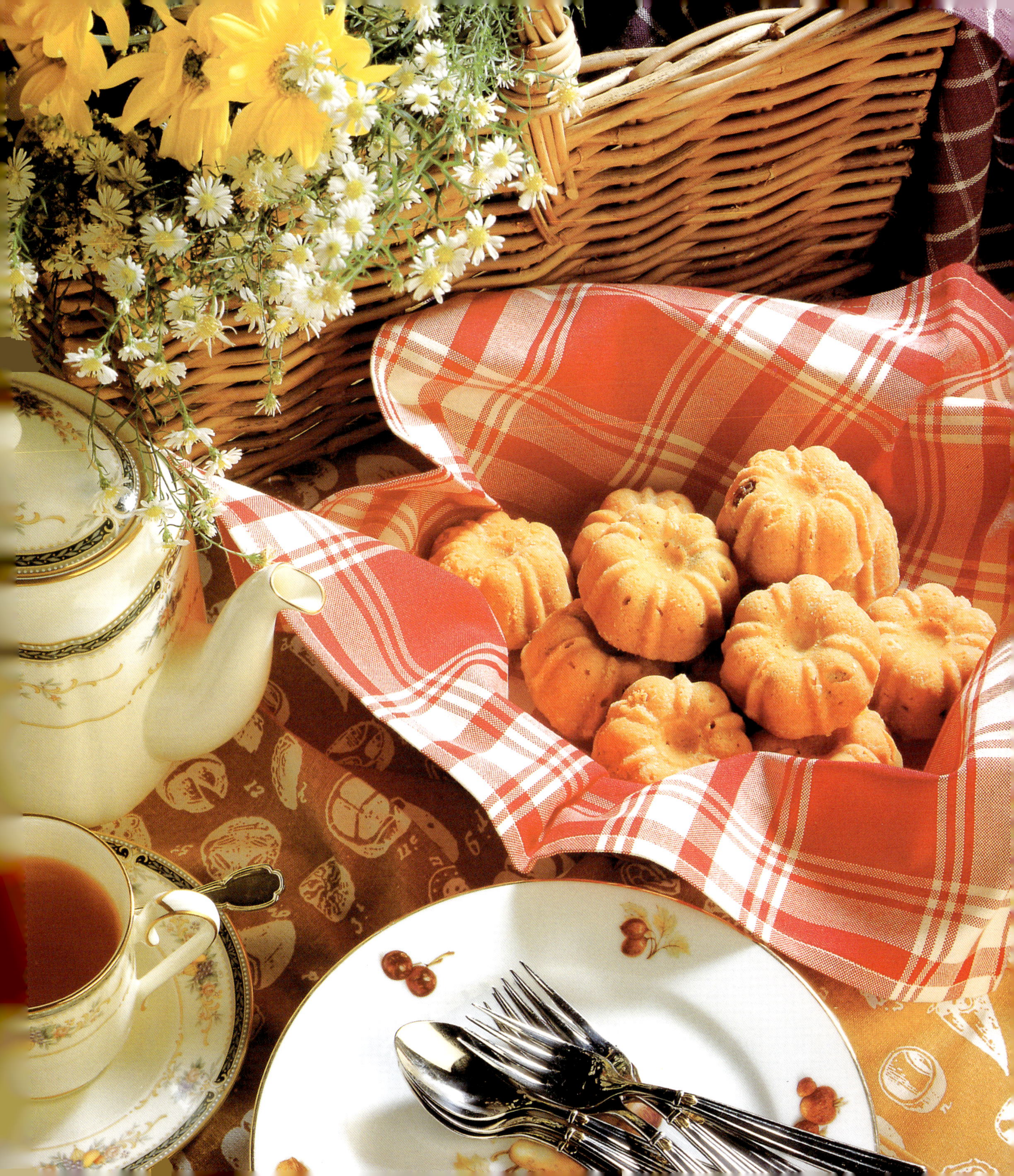

## Cheddar Cheese Scones

### Ingredients

- 1½ cups all-purpose flour
- 1½ teaspoons baking powder
- 1 teaspoon dry mustard
- ½ teaspoon salt
- 2 tablespoons chopped parsley
- 125 grams cold, unsalted butter, cut into small pieces
- 1 cup shredded cheddar cheese
- 1 large egg and ¼ cup fresh milk, beaten together
- 1 egg yolk, beaten, to glaze
- 2 tablespoons whole cumin seeds to decorate

### Method

1. Sift together flour, baking powder, mustard and salt. Add chopped parsley and mix well.

2. Cut cold butter into the flour until the mixture resembles coarse breadcrumbs.

3. Add cheese and toss to mix. Add the egg-and-milk mixture and mix the dough briefly by hand.

4. Turn the dough out onto a lightly floured surface and roll out to a thickness of 1.5 cm. Use a cookie cutter to cut as many shapes as possible. Place on a floured baking tray. Brush with beaten egg yolk before sprinkling with cumin seeds. Bake at 190°C/375°F for 12 to 15 minutes until golden brown.

## Currant Oat Scones

### Ingredients

- 1½ cups all-purpose flour
- ¾ cup rolled oats
- 1 tablespoon baking powder
- ¼ cup sugar
- ¼ teaspoon salt
- ¼ cup cold butter, cut into pieces
- ¼ cup heavy cream
- 2 eggs, well beaten
- ½ cup currants

butter and fruit preserves to serve

### Method

1. In a food processor blend together flour, oats, baking powder, sugar and salt. Process briefly. With the motor running add butter and process until the mixture resembles coarse breadcrumbs. Leave in the food processor.

2. Mix together cream and eggs. Add to the butter mixture in the food processor with the motor running. Process until a dough forms.

3. On a lightly floured surface, knead currants into the dough, making sure they are evenly distributed. Pat the dough into circles about 2.5 cm thick. Score into wedges. Bake on an ungreased baking sheet at 180°C/360°F for 15 minutes until golden brown. Serve with butter and fruit preserves.

Chef's Note: The dough may be sticky if the eggs are unusually large, the flour is moist or the kitchen is humid. Should this happen just add a few additional tablespoons of flour to the dough.

## Orange Cream Scones

### Ingredients

- 2½ cups all-purpose flour
- 5 teaspoons baking powder
- 5 tablespoons castor sugar
- 5 tablespoons cold, unsalted butter, cut into small pieces
- ½ cup milk
- ¼ cup cream
- 1 egg yolk
- 1 teaspoon orange essence
- grated zest of 2 oranges
- 1 egg, beaten, to glaze

### Method

1. Sift together the flour and baking powder. Add sugar. Cut in cold butter so that the mixture resembles coarse breadcrumbs.

2. In a separate bowl beat milk, cream, egg yolk, orange essence and orange zest. Add sifted ingredients, working quickly to form a dough. Do not overmix. If the dough feels sticky, add a little more flour.

3. Roll the dough out on a floured surface to a thickness of 1 cm. Cut out circles with an 8-cm round cookie cutter.

4. Arrange the scones on a greased baking tray. Brush with beaten egg and bake at 200°C/390°F for 15 to 18 minutes until golden brown.

*Opposite: Cheddar Cheese Scones (top left), Orange Cream Scones (top right) and Currant Oat Scones (below).*

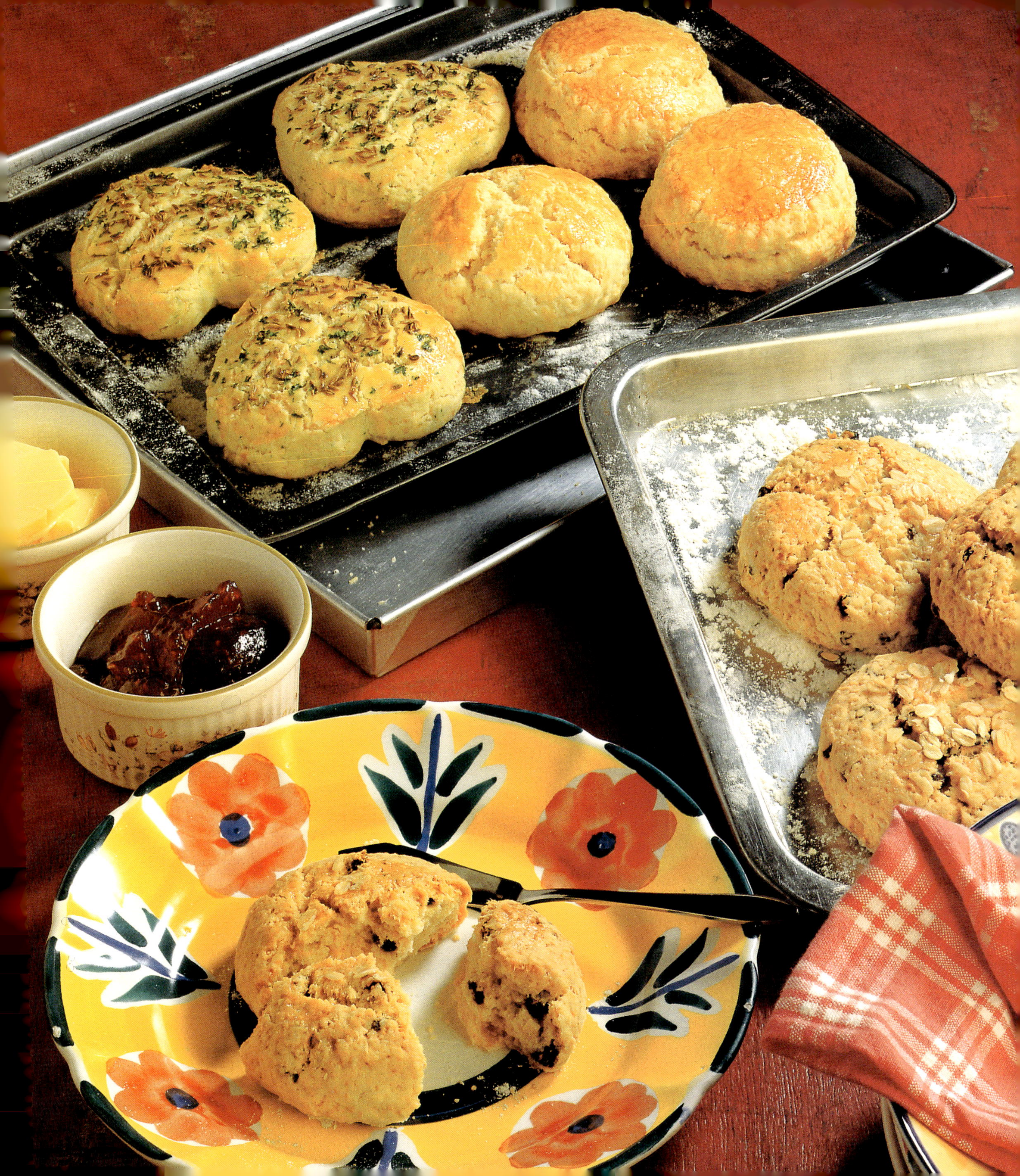

## Date, Honey and Carrot Muffins

*Ingredients*

- ¼ cup butter
- ½ cup honey
- ½ cup fresh milk
- 2 eggs
- 1 tablespoon lime zest
- 1 cup wholewheat flour
- 1 tablespoon all-purpose flour
- 1 tablespoon baking powder
- 1 teaspoon salt
- 1 cup grated carrots
- 1 cup chopped dates

*Method*

1. Melt butter and honey. Cool. Add milk, eggs and lime zest.
2. Sift together both types of flour, baking powder and salt. Add to the butter mixture. Add carrots and dates and stir until just combined.
3. Spoon the batter into greased muffin cups and bake at 180°C/360°F for 20 minutes until cooked all the way through.

## Oat Bran and Fruit Muffins

*Ingredients*

- 150 grams assorted dried fruit such as apple, pear, apricot and mango, coarsely chopped
- 115 grams oat bran
- 85 grams rolled oats
- 70 grams all-purpose flour
- 40 grams brown sugar
- 20 grams baking soda
- 1 teaspoon ground cinnamon
- 140 grams or 3 ripe bananas, mashed
- grated zest of 1 orange
- 60 ml orange juice
- 30 ml corn oil
- 2 eggs
- 240 ml low-fat or skimmed milk

*Method*

1. Combine dried fruit, oat bran, rolled oats, flour, brown sugar, baking soda, cinnamon and mashed bananas in a food processor and process until evenly mixed. Transfer to a large bowl and make a well in the centre.
2. Combine orange zest, orange juice, corn oil, eggs and milk and pour into the well. Mix thoroughly.
3. Drop the batter into a muffin tray lined with paper cups. Bake at 180°C/360°F for 20 to 30 minutes. Remove the muffins from the muffin tray and cool.

## Blueberry and Oats Muffins

*Ingredients*

- 1 cup fresh yoghurt
- 1 egg yolk
- 1 teaspoon baking soda
- 4 tablespoons butter, melted
- ½ cup sugar
- a pinch of nutmeg
- ⅓ cup oats
- 1⅔ cups all-purpose flour
- 1 cup canned blueberries, drained

*Method*

1. Combine yoghurt, egg yolk, baking soda, melted butter, sugar and nutmeg in a food processor. Blend to mix well.
2. Add the oats and flour before folding in the blueberries.
3. Spoon into a muffin tray with well-greased paper cups and bake at 175°C/350°F for 20 minutes until the muffins are cooked through.

*Opposite: Date, Honey and Carrot Muffins.*

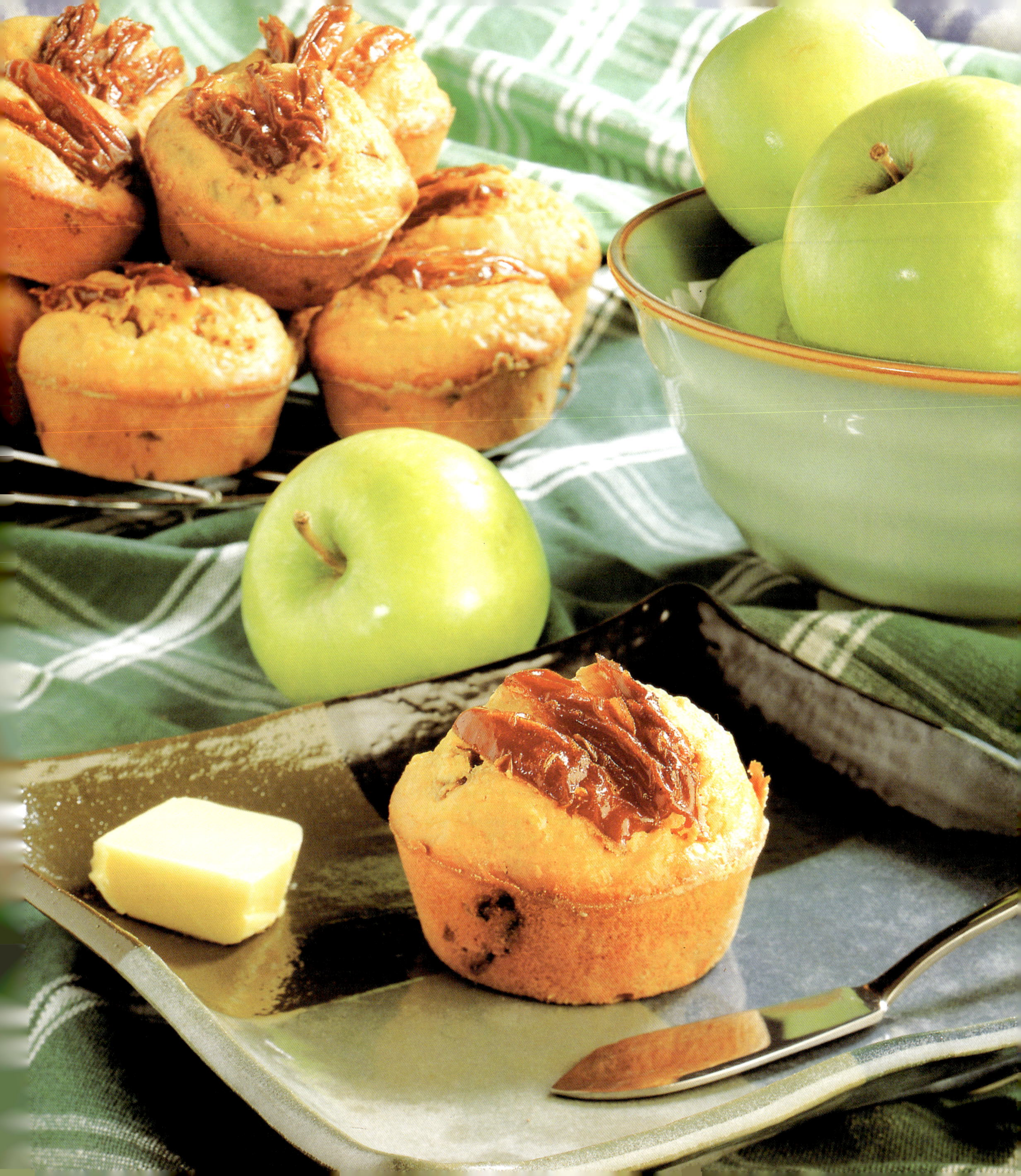

# Spiced Pumpkin Muffins

*Ingredients*

1½ cups castor sugar
1⅔ cups all-purpose flour
¼ teaspoon baking powder
1 teaspoon baking soda
¾ teaspoon salt
1 teaspoon ground cinnamon
½ teaspoon ground cloves
½ teaspoon ground nutmeg
2 eggs, beaten
½ cup vegetable oil
½ cup water
1 cup pumpkin, baked and mashed
½ cup walnuts, chopped

*Method*

1. Sift together the first eight ingredients.
2. In a separate bowl mix together the eggs, oil and water. Add the sifted ingredients. Add mashed pumpkin and walnuts. Stir.
3. Spoon into greased muffin cups and bake at 175°C/350° for 25 minutes until cooked.

# Banana Chocolate Chip Muffins

*Ingredients*

½ cup butter
1 cup brown sugar
1 egg
1 cup ripe bananas, mashed
1 teaspoon baking soda
2 tablespoons hot water
1½ cups all-purpose flour
½ teaspoon salt
¼ cup chocolate chips

bananas, cut into chunks, and chocolate chips, to decorate

*Method*

1. Cream butter and sugar until fluffy. Add egg and bananas.
2. Mix baking soda with hot water and pour into the butter mixture.
3. Fold in flour and salt. Stir in chocolate chips.
4. Spoon the batter into greased muffin cups. Top each muffin with two chunks of banana and sprinkle with chocolate chips. Bake at 180°C/360°F for about 20 minutes.

# Apricot and Almond Muffins

*Ingredients*

1 cup apricot, chopped
1 cup boiling water
1 tablespoon baking soda
½ cup butter
1 cup sugar
2 eggs
2 cups fresh yoghurt
2½ cups all-purpose flour
1¼ cups bran flakes
½ teaspoon salt
½ teaspoon almond essence
½ cup almond, blanched and chopped

*Method*

1. Combine apricot, boiling water and baking soda. Leave to soak for a few hours.
2. Cream butter and sugar until smooth. Add in eggs one at a time. Add the soaked apricot.
3. Gradually add in yoghurt, flour, bran flakes, salt, almond essence and almond. Stir quickly until just mixed.
4. Spoon batter into greased muffin cups and bake for 20 minutes at 175°C/350°F until a skewer inserted in the centre of the muffins comes away cleanly.

# Miniature Herb Cream Biscuits

*Ingredients*

4 cups all-purpose flour
2 tablespoons baking powder
1 teaspoon salt
1 teaspoon thyme
1 teaspoon basil
2 tablespoons parsley, chopped
grated zest of 1 lemon
200 grams cold, unsalted butter, cut into pieces
1 cup milk, combined with 1 cup cream

*Method*

1. Sift together flour, baking powder and salt. Add in herbs and lemon zest. Rub in cold butter until the mixture resembles coarse breadcrumbs.
2. Add the milk to form a soft dough. Do not overmix. Roll out the dough on a floured surface to a thickness of about 6 mm. Cut with cookie cutter and transfer onto floured baking sheet.
3. Bake at 200°C/390°F for 10 to 12 minutes until golden. (Note: you may also brush the top of the biscuits with milk or dust some flour over it.) Serve warm.

Chef's Note: This is a scone recipe but is called biscuit in the southern states of America.

*Opposite: Spiced Pumpkin Muffins (left) and Banana Chocolate Chip Muffins (right).*

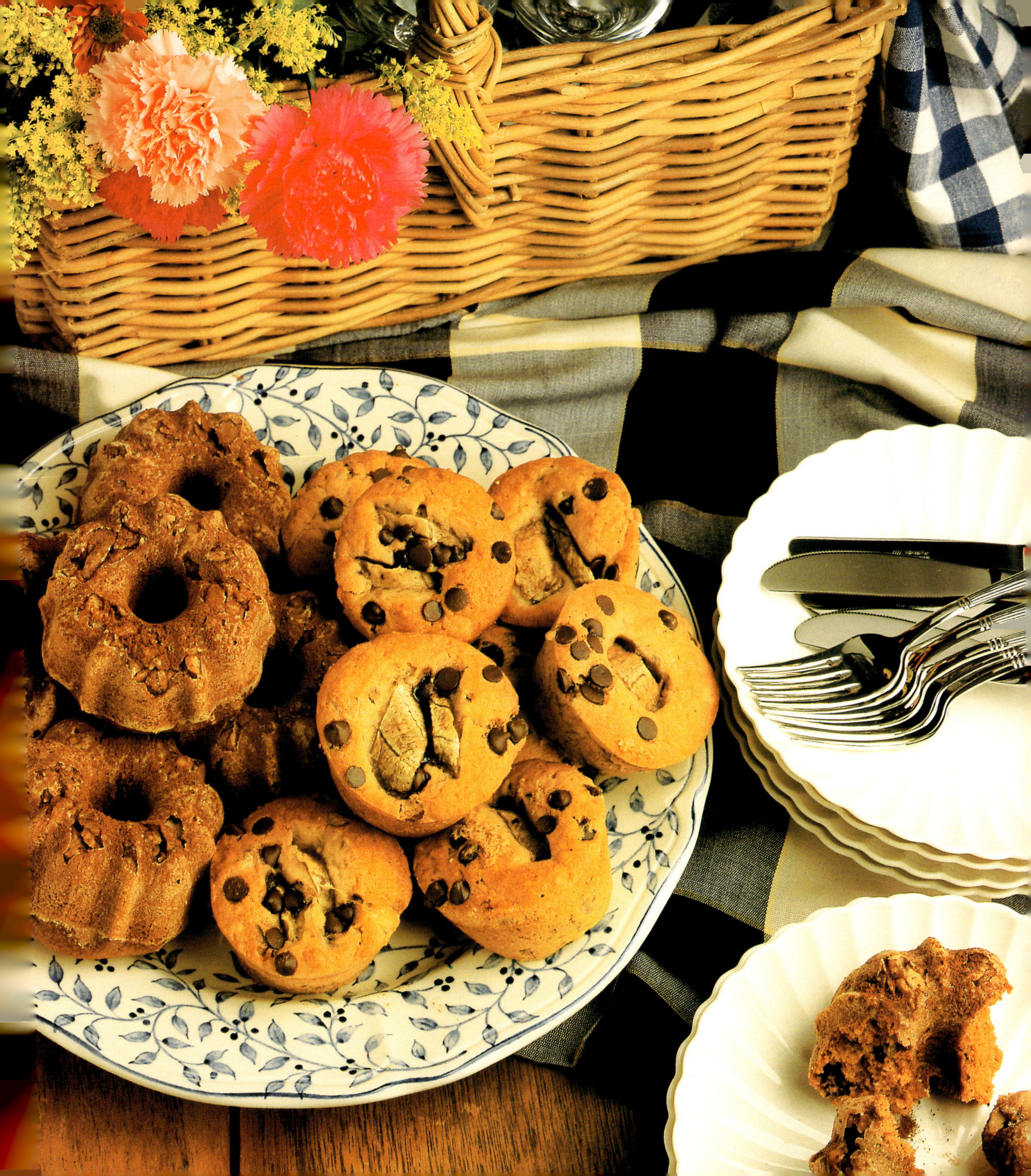

# Cheesecakes

The Art of Baking Cheesecakes, p62　1 Plain Baked Cheesecake, p64　2 Papaya Orange Cheesecake, p64　3 Nougat Cheesecake, p64　4 Cappuccino Chocolate Cheesecake, p66　5 Citrus Cheesecake, p66　6 Durian Delight Cheesecake, p68　7 Orange Sultana Cheesecake, p68　8 Greek Honey Citrus Cheesecake, p70　9 Chocolate and Orange Cheesecake, p70　10 Coconut Peach Cheesecake, p72　11 Chocolate Hazelnut Cheesecake, p72　12 New York Cheesecake, p74　13 Chocolate Swirl Espresso Cheesecake, p74　14 Peanut Butter Chocolate Chip Cheesecake, p76　15 Chocolate Mousse Cheesecake, p76　16 Pina Colada Cheesecake, p78　17 Nestum Cheesecake, p78　18 Honey and Mango Chilled Cheesecake, p78　19 Sunshine Cheesecake, p80　20 Apricot Walnut Cheesecake, p80　21 Orange Ginger Cheesecake, p80　22 Caramelised Apple Cheesecake, p82　23 Pumpkin Cheesecake with Pecan Topping, p82　24 Fresh Strawberries and Cream Cheesecake, p84　25 Brownie Cheesecake, p84　26 Coffee Cheesecake, p84　27 Fresh Strawberries and White Chocolate Cheesecake, p86　28 Marble Cheesecake, p86　29 Plain Chocolate Cheesecake, p86

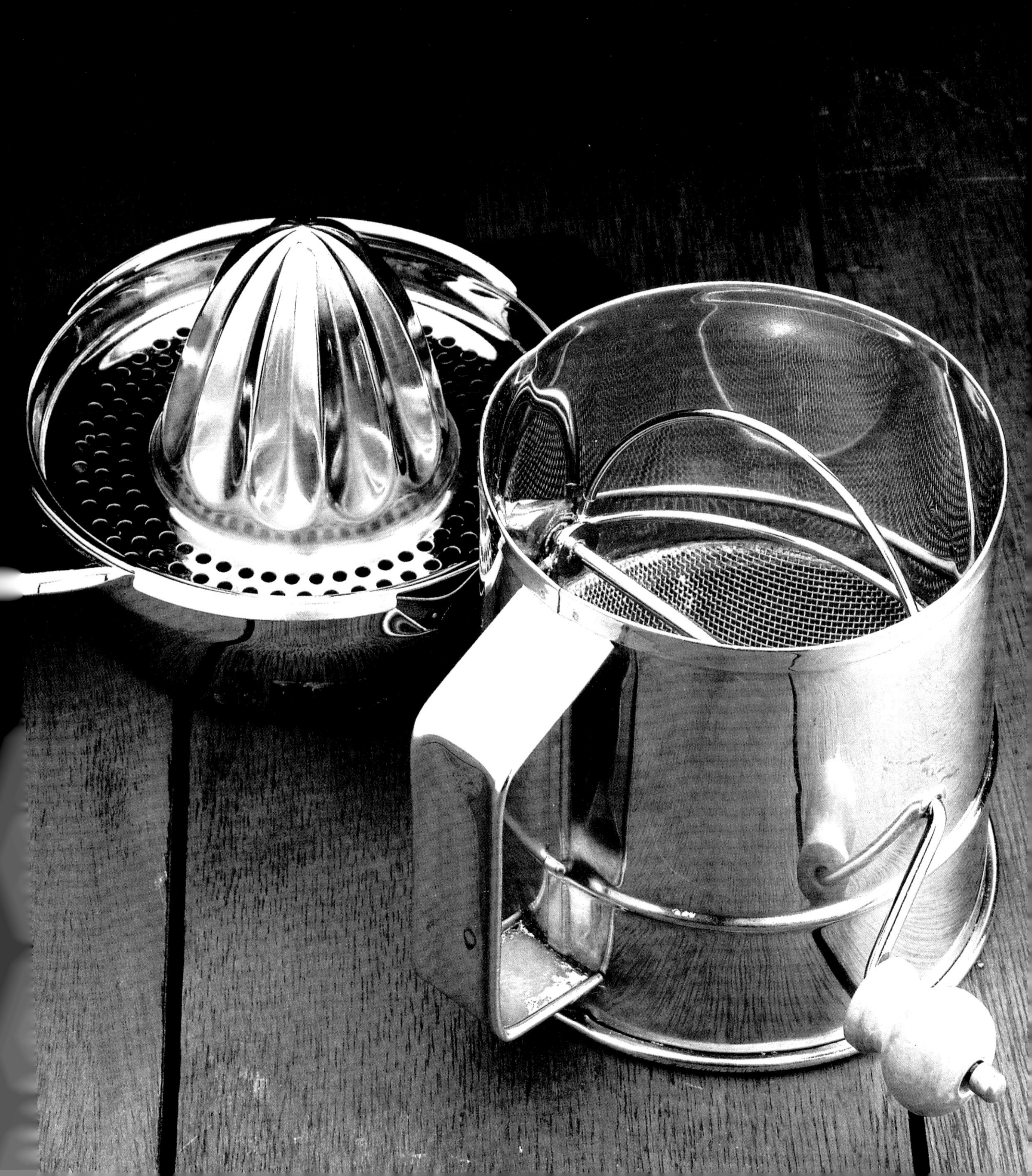

# The Art of Baking Cheesecakes

Cheesecakes are the most sensuous of desserts. There is something almost sinful in the richness of a well-made cheesecake.

According to my personal poll, cheesecakes rank only second in popularity to chocolate desserts. Cheesecakes are wonderful for parties as one cake serves a whole crowd. They can be refrigerated for several days before serving and frozen when there are leftovers.

Each cheesecake recipe has its own personality so no one rule applies across the board. However a common feature is that they appear a little undercooked when first removed from the oven. Home cooks are often confused by a cooked cheesecake that still jiggles in its pan. Once the cheesecake cools it does solidify.

Most cheesecakes are really quite easy to make and even a novice baker can turn out a superb cheesecake at first attempt.

You can get really creative with cheesecakes. By varying the ingredients, proportions or baking time you can produce a cheesecake that is heavy or light, moist or dry, cake-like or smooth according to your mood.

Over the years I have developed my own baking technique for cheesecake. I begin by baking the cheesecake in a 200°C/390°F oven for 10 to 15 minutes, then reducing the temperature to 160°C/325°F and baking the cake for an additional 45 minutes or so. This technique results in an incredibly creamy cake with a very smooth top.

Be sure to let the cake cool completely in a draft-free spot when you remove it from the oven. If a cheesecake cools too quickly, it tends to crack.

All my recipes use cream cheese rather than other cheeses like cottage or ricotta. Cream cheese produces the richest, creamiest cakes.

## INGREDIENTS

### Cheese
Cream cheese contains at least 33 per cent butterfat and a water content of 50 per cent, so its texture is smooth and its flavour delicate. Allow cream cheese to be at room temperature before use. Be sure to check the expiry date when you buy cheese.

### Cream
Cream is used to lighten a cake or provide a richer flavour. It comes in several different grades according to fat content and is most often whipped before use in order to double its volume. For best results use a chilled bowl and chilled beaters when whipping cream.

### Sweeteners
When using honey remember that it will make your cheesecake darker. Also, as it is less soluble than sugar, care must be taken to blend the batter well. Honey is sweeter and has a higher moisture content than castor sugar. So when possible reduce the volume of other liquids by $1/4$ cup for each cup of honey used.

### Thickening Agents
Eggs, flour and cornstarch are good thickening agents. In many store-bought cheesecakes, however, too much flour and not enough cheese is used. The result is tough cheesecake. Cornstarch is much finer in texture and the cheesecake does not get tough. If you use gelatine sheets rather than

granules, soften the sheets by soaking them in cold water before dissolving them in hot water. Be careful not to use too much gelatine or you will end up with rubbery cheesecake.

### Fruit and Nuts

The zest and juice of lemons and oranges are delicious in cheesecakes. If you are not baking the cheesecake, make sure you toast the nuts before they are ground in order to release their aroma.

### Spices and Flavouring

Spices such as cinnamon, cloves, ginger, nutmeg and cardamom contrast well with the mildness of the cheese. Instant coffee, chocolate, liqueur, fruit puree and flavoured yoghurt also give an interesting flavour.

## THE PERFECT CRUST

Some cheesecake purists insist that the crust is an unnecessary distraction, hence the creation of the Bare Bottom Cheesecake! Even if you are a Bare Bottom Cheesecake purist, you will find that a light dusting of graham cracker crumbs on a lightly buttered baking pan will greatly facilitate the removal of the finished cheesecake.

The most popular crust is the basic crumb crust, simply because it is quickest and easiest to make. Nearly all kinds of crackers, biscuits, cookies and even some cereals can be used in a cheesecake crust.

Graham crackers are the standard biscuits used, but you can also consider digestive biscuits, oatmeal cookies, ginger snaps, vanilla wafers and chocolate chips for chocolate cheesecakes. I save my stale cookies and scones in the freezer and occasionally use them in my cheesecake base. I sometimes use ground cinnamon and ginger in my pumpkin cheesecake, and lemon or orange zest in my New York Cheesecake. Toasted hazelnuts, almonds and walnuts are great in chocolate-based cheesecakes.

Sponge cake or a jelly roll are options for a chilled cheesecake.

Pie crust is delicious as a base in fruity cheesecakes. The secret to a good pie crust is not to overhandle the ingredients. You can flavour the pie crust with instant coffee, cocoa, spices or the zest of citrus fruits.

## TROUBLESHOOTING

The most common problem that novice cheesecake bakers encounter is cracking. The problem lies in either the baking or cooling. As a cheesecake bakes it gives off a considerable amount of moisture. Too much moisture released too quickly will cause the cheesecake to crack.

Some commercial bakeries have steam injection systems designed to counter cracking. At home the same result can be obtained by placing your cake pan in a water bath or by placing a pan of water on the bottom shelf of the oven. As springform pans are not watertight, place a skirt of aluminium foil around the entire external bottom of the pan before placing it in a water bath.

Deep concentric cracks and a dark brown top indicate that the cake has been baked for too long or at too high a temperature.

"Grand Canyon" crevices across the centre of the cheesecake are caused by drafts during the cooling process. I recommend that you do not open the oven door any more or any longer than is absolutely necessary. Never open the oven door during the first 30 minutes of baking unless the recipe specifically calls for it.

To prevent cracking run a knife or spatula along the edge of the pan so that the cake can pull away freely as it contracts. Here's a tip: unsightly cracks can be hidden with judicious use of a topping!

The best test of doneness is in a cheesecake's appearance. The sides should be raised and just barely beginning to brown. The centre may still be a little soft, but it will harden as the cake cools. Turn the oven off at this stage. If possible allow the cheesecake to cool in the oven for a few hours with the oven door slightly ajar. Once the cake has reached room temperature, refrigerate it for at least four hours before serving. Cover the cheesecake to prevent it from drying out in the refrigerator.

Generally the best cheesecakes are balanced in flavour and texture. A crisp crust offsets creamy custard and the tartness of lemon juice balances the sweetness of sugar. Vanilla, almond or other fruit liqueur and extracts add subtly to the flavour, as will grated orange or lemon zest.

I would not recommend anchovies or chillies in a cheesecake, but beyond that the possibilities are as rich as your imagination!

# Plain Baked Cheesecake

*Base*

- 4 cups Marie biscuit crumbs
- 1/2 cup powdered sugar
- 1 cup walnuts, coarsely chopped
- 1/2 cup butter, melted

*Method*

Mix all the ingredients and press into the base of a 22-cm springform pan. Bake for 15 minutes at 175°C/350°F and cool.

*Filling*

- 3 tablespoons custard powder
- 3 tablespoons water
- 455 grams cream cheese
- 1 1/2 cups castor sugar
- a pinch of salt
- 1 teaspoon vanilla essence
- 1 tablespoon lemon juice
- 2 cups sour cream
- 6 eggs, separated
- 1 teaspoon grated lemon zest

lemon slices to decorate

*Method*

1. Dissolve custard powder in water. Beat in cream cheese and sugar until fluffy. Add salt, vanilla essence and lemon juice and beat until smooth.
2. Add sour cream, egg yolks and lemon zest. In a separate bowl whip egg whites until stiff and gradually fold into the batter. Pour into the prepared crust. Bake for an hour at 170°C/340°F.
3. Leave the cheesecake to cool in the oven, with the door ajar, for at least one hour. Decorate with lemon slices.

# Papaya Orange Cheesecake

*Base*

- 1 1/2 cups orange shortbread biscuit crumbs or Marie biscuit crumbs
- 1/3 cup butter, melted
- 2 tablespoons sliced almonds, toasted

*Method*

Combine all the ingredients for the crust. Press onto the base of a 20-cm springform pan. Chill.

*Filling*

- 500 grams cream cheese
- 3/4 cup castor sugar
- 1 1/2 tablespoons gelatine, dissolved in 1/3 cup hot water
- 1/4 cup orange juice
- 1/2 cup ripe papaya, mashed
- 2 teaspoons grated orange zest
- 1/2 cup heavy cream, lightly whipped
- 1 cup diced papaya
- 2 tablespoons orange marmalade, heated with a little water, to glaze

papaya balls to decorate

*Method*

1. With an electric mixer beat cream cheese until smooth. Add sugar and continue beating until well blended.
2. Slowly add gelatine, orange juice, mashed papaya and orange zest. Gradually fold in the whipped cream.
3. Arrange diced papaya at the base of the prepared crust and slowly pour in the filling. Chill overnight until firm.
4. Glaze with marmalade and decorate with papaya balls.

# Nougat Cheesecake

*Sponge Cake*

- 8 eggs
- 200 grams castor sugar
- 85 grams Nestum cereal
- 100 grams all-purpose flour
- 105 grams cornflour
- a pinch of baking powder
- 65 grams butter, melted

*Method*

1. Beat eggs and sugar until fluffy. Gradually stir in cereal, flour, cornflour and baking powder. Add melted butter.
2. Pour into a cake pan and bake in a preheated 180°C/360°F oven for 25 minutes.

*Filling*

- 200 grams cream cheese
- 100 grams powdered sugar
- 2 egg yolks
- grated zest of 1 lemon
- 60 grams gelatine, dissolved in 3 tablespoon of water over a low fire
- 400 grams whipping cream
- 20 red glace cherries, quartered
- 40 grams peanut-flavoured nougat

almonds to decorate

*Method*

1. Beat cream cheese and sugar. Add egg yolks and lemon zest. Add gelatine and whipping cream, followed by cherries and nougat.
2. To assemble the cheesecake, slice the cooled sponge cake into three layers horizontally. Place the first layer in the base of a cake pan. Spread with one-third of the filling. Repeat the layering process with the remaining cake and filling, ending with a nougat layer. Chill until the filling sets. Unmould and decorate with almonds as desired.

*Opposite: Plain Baked Cheesecake.*

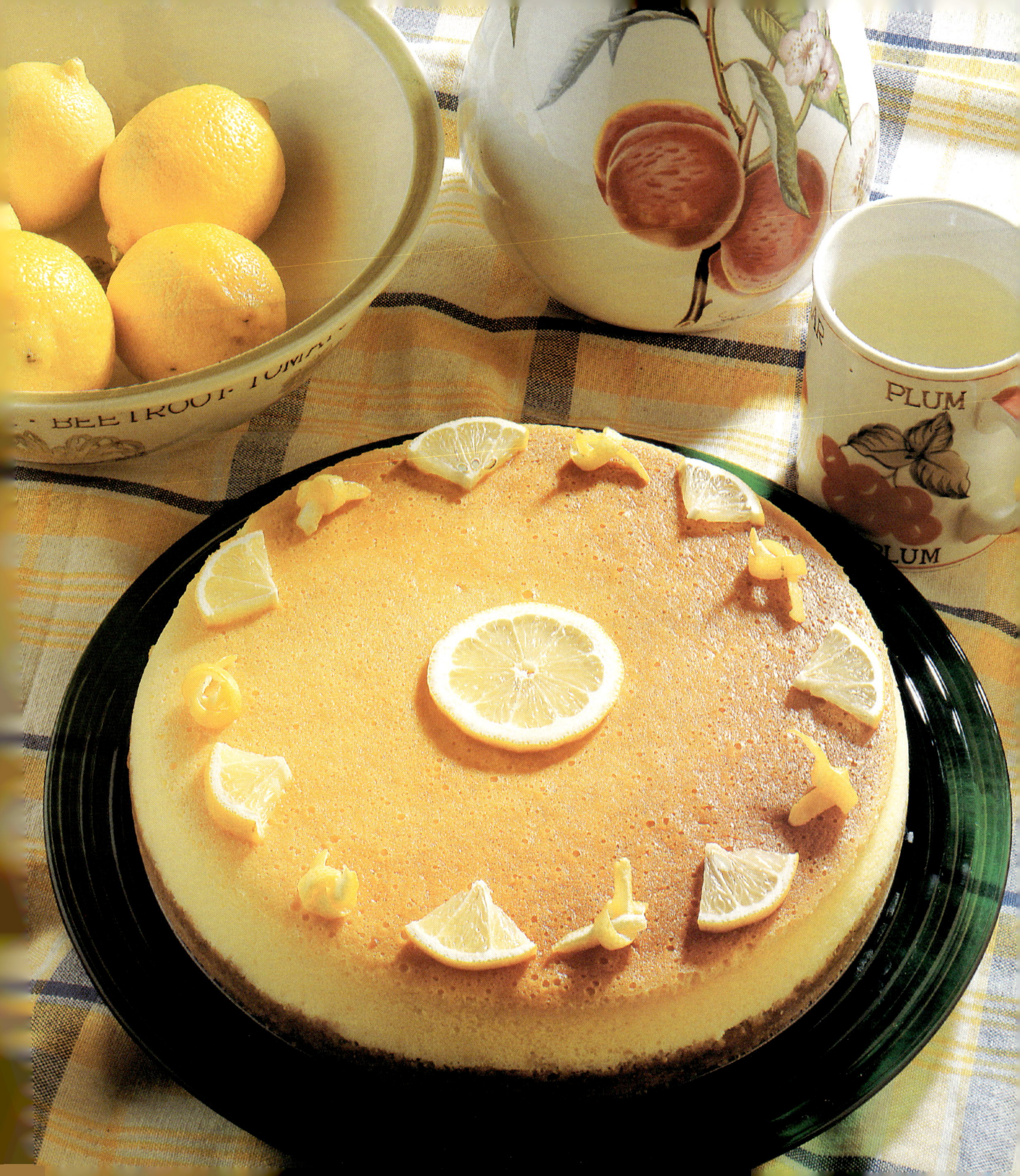
BEETROOT
PLUM

# Cappuccino Chocolate Cheesecake

## Base

- 2 cups chocolate chip cookie crumbs
- 1/2 cup hazelnuts, toasted and ground
- 1/4 cup brown sugar
- 1 teaspoon ground cinnamon
- 1/2 cup unsalted butter, melted

## Method

Mix all the ingredients and press onto the base of a 22-cm springform pan. Set aside.

## Filling

- 750 grams cream cheese, softened at room temperature
- 1 1/2 cups castor sugar
- 4 eggs
- 1/3 cup instant coffee, made by dissolving 1 tablespoon coffee in 1/3 cup hot water
- 1/2 teaspoon ground cinnamon
- 150 grams couverture chocolate, chopped and melted over a pan of boiling water

## Method

1. With an electric mixer beat cream cheese and sugar until smooth. Beat in eggs one at a time.
2. Add coffee and cinnamon and continue beating until smooth.
3. Pour the filling into the prepared crust and spoon over the melted chocolate, dotting it all over. Bake at 175°C/350°F for 40 minutes. Turn off the oven, leaving the door ajar, and allow the cake to cool inside for a few hours. Cover with cling wrap and chill in the refrigerator for another few hours.

## Topping

- 200 grams couverture chocolate, finely chopped
- 4 tablespoons whipping cream
- 100 grams butter
- 1 tablespoon cocoa powder for dusting
- chopped hazelnuts and coffee beans to decorate
- 1/2 cup whipped cream to serve

## Method

1. Melt the chocolate, whipping cream and butter. Pour over the cake before dusting with cocoa powder. Sprinkle with chopped hazelnuts and coffee beans.
2. Beat whipped cream until fluffy and serve with the cheesecake.

*Chef's Note: If couverture chocolate is not available, use semisweet or bittersweet cooking chocolate.*

# Citrus Cheesecake

## Base

- 250 grams sweet pastry crust*

## Method

1. Prepare the pastry crust. Roll out to a thickness of 1/2 cm. Place a 20-cm springform pan on the rolled-out dough and cut a circle of pastry to fit the base.
2. Lay the pastry dough in the base and prick with a fork. Cover with foil and fill with beans. Blind bake for 15 minutes at 180°C/360°F. Discard foil and beans. Cool.

## Filling

- 375 grams cream cheese
- grated zest of 1 lemon
- juice of 2 lemons
- juice of 1 orange
- 1/2 cup + 1 tablespoon castor sugar
- 2 tablespoons cornflour
- 1 teaspoon vanilla essence
- 1 cup sour cream
- 4 eggs, separated

powdered sugar for dusting

## Method

1. Beat cream cheese with citrus zest and juice. Add 1/2 cup sugar, cornflour, vanilla essence, sour cream and egg yolks and blend until smooth.
2. In a separate bowl beat egg whites with the remaining 1 tablespoon of sugar until stiff peaks form. Fold into cream cheese. Pour into the prepared crust.
3. Bake at 170°C/340°F for about 1 hour 20 minutes until the cheesecake sets. Cool for a few hours in the oven, with the door ajar, before removing the cheesecake from the pan. When cool, dust with powdered sugar.

*Chef's Note: To achieve a smoother and creamier texture, I recommend that you bake this cheesecake in a hot water bath. To do so, wrap the base of the springform pan with aluminium foil almost three-quarter way up the sides of the pan so that no water will leak through.*

*Refer to recipe for Tarte Alsacienne on page 38.

*Opposite: Cappuccino Chocolate Cheesecake.*

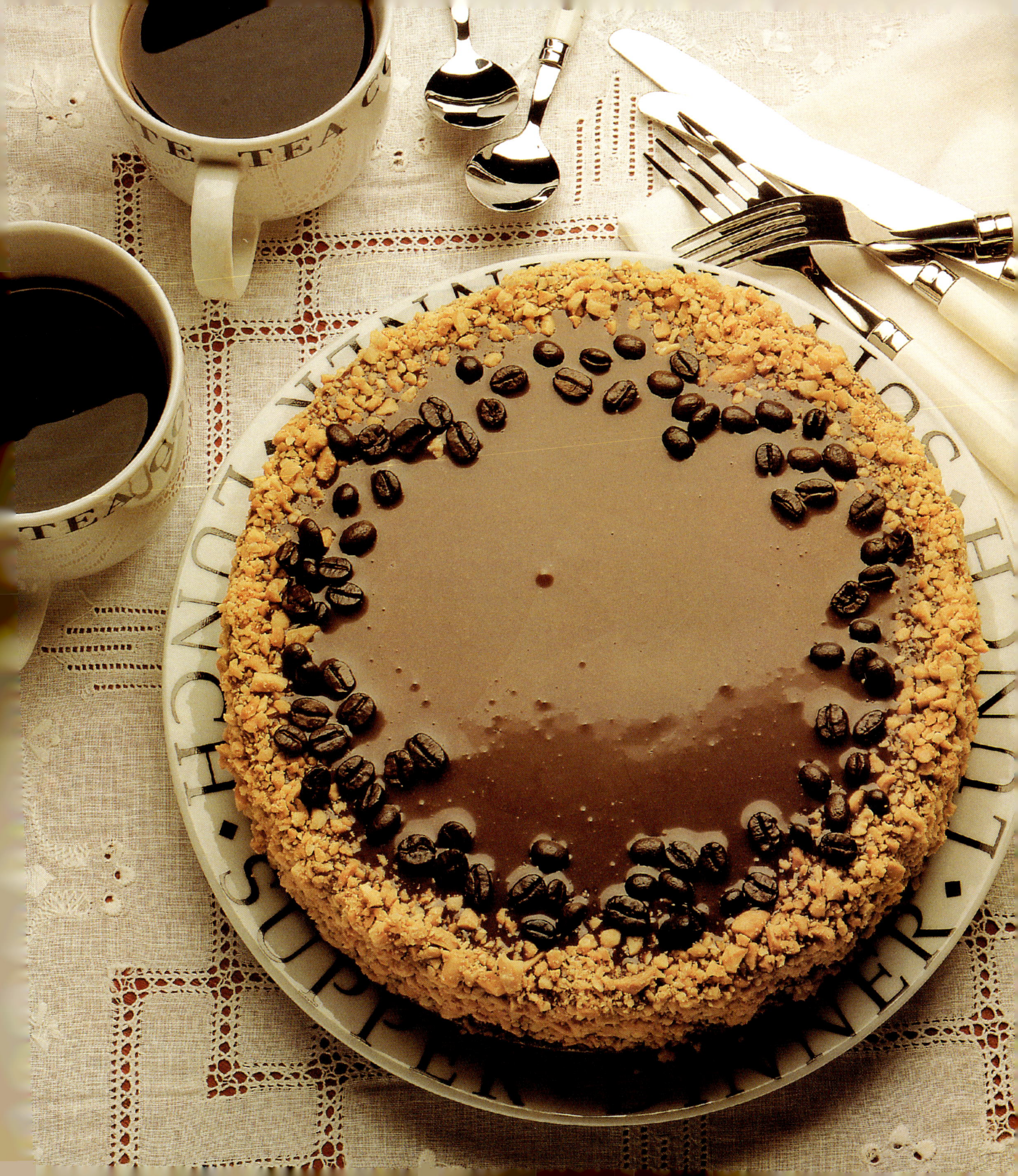
TEA
LUNCH
SUPPER

## Durian Delight Cheesecake

*Base*

    150 grams butter
    1/4 cup castor sugar
    1 egg
    1 1/2 cups all-purpose flour
    1/2 cup sliced almonds, toasted

*Method*

1. Beat butter and sugar until creamy. Add egg, flour and almonds. Chill for half an hour.
2. Press the dough onto the base of a 22-cm springform pan. Bake blind, covered with foil and filled with beans, for 20 minutes at 180°C/360°F. Set aside.

*Filling*

    900 grams cream cheese
    1/2 cup sour cream or natural yoghurt
    3/4 cup honey
    1 tablespoon castor sugar
    4 large eggs, separated
    1/2 cup fresh milk
    1 1/2 cups durian flesh
    1 tablespoon vanilla essence

powdered sugar for dusting

*Method*

1. With an electric mixer blend cream cheese and sour cream until smooth. Add honey and sugar.
2. Add egg yolks one at a time, mixing well with each addition. Occasionally use a plastic spatula to scrape the sides of the bowl.
3. Add milk, durian flesh and vanilla essence. Mix well.
4. In a separate bowl beat egg whites until stiff peaks form and fold into the batter.
5. Pour into the prepared crust and bake for 45 minutes at 175°C/350°F. Turn the oven off, leaving the door ajar, and allow the cheesecake to cool in the oven for an hour or two.
6. Once the cheesecake has cooled, dust the top lightly with powdered sugar.

Chef's Note: The durian flesh can be very sweet at times. If this is the case, reduce the honey to only 1/2 cup.

## Orange Sultana Cheesecake

*Base*

    1 1/2 cups Marie biscuit crumbs
    1/2 cup butter, melted

*Method*

Mix together the biscuit crumbs and butter and press onto the base of a 22-cm springform pan. Chill.

*Filling*

    500 grams cream cheese
    3/4 cup castor sugar
    3 eggs, separated
    1/3 cup cream
    2 tablespoons lemon juice
    1/2 cup custard powder
    1 teaspoon baking powder
    3/4 cup sultanas, soaked in 1/4 cup orange juice

*Method*

1. Beat together cream cheese and castor sugar until smooth. Add egg yolks and the rest of the ingredients except egg whites.
2. Whisk egg whites until stiff peaks form and fold it into the batter.
3. Pour the batter into the prepared crust and bake at 170°C/340°F for an hour.

*Opposite: Durian Delight Cheesecake.*

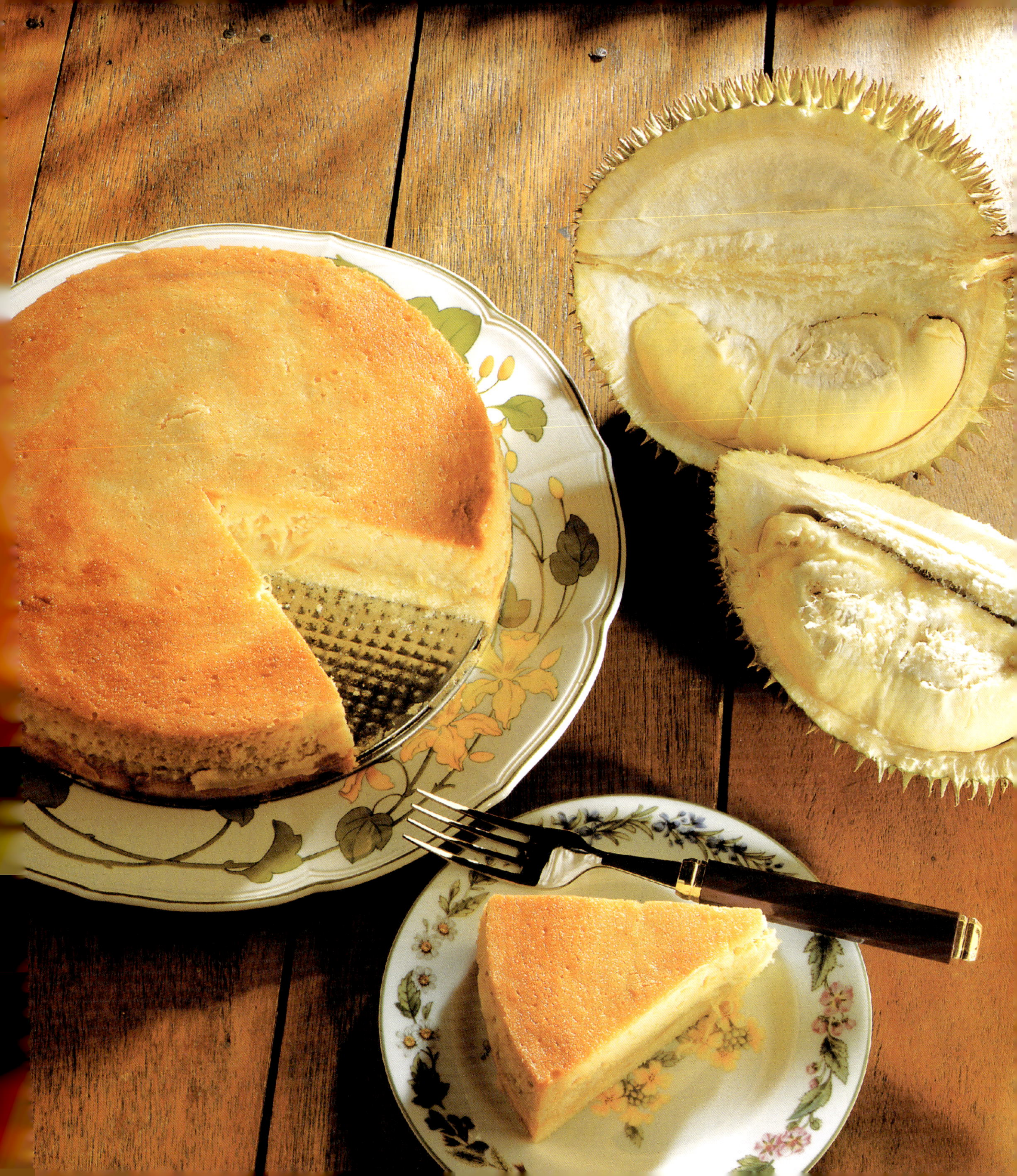

## Greek Honey Citrus Cheesecake

*Base*

    2 cups walnuts, toasted, cooled and finely ground
    1/4 cup castor sugar
    1/2 teaspoon ground cinnamon
    1 cup graham cracker crumbs
    a little melted butter

*Method*

1. Grease a 22-cm springform pan and wrap a collar of foil around the outside of the pan.
2. Combine walnuts, sugar, cinnamon and cracker crumbs with melted butter. Press onto the base of the pan and set aside.

*Filling*

    900 grams cream cheese
    1/2 cup sour cream or yoghurt
    3/4 cup honey
    1 tablespoon castor sugar
    4 large eggs
    grated zest of 1 orange
    grated zest of 1 lemon
    1 teaspoon vanilla essence
    juice of 1 orange and lemon, reduced to 1 tablespoon by cooking it
    1/4 teaspoon ground cinnamon
    200 grams dried figs or dates, chopped
    dates, dried figs and chopped walnuts to decorate

*Method*

1. With an electric mixer blend cream cheese and sour cream at medium speed, occasionally scraping the sides of the bowl.
2. Add honey, sugar and eggs one at the time. Add zest, vanilla essence, reduced juice, cinnamon and figs.
3. Pour the filling over the prepared crust. Place in a large baking dish and add enough boiling water to come halfway up the sides of the springform pan.
4. Bake in a preheated oven at 180°C/360°F for about 50 minutes. Turn the oven off and, leaving the door ajar, allow the cake to cool in the oven for one to two hours. This prevents the cake from cracking.
5. Wrap the cheesecake in cling wrap and refrigerate overnight to allow it to set. Decorate with dates, dried figs and chopped walnuts.

Chef's Note: The citrus juice is optional but will appeal to those who like their cheesecakes tart.

## Chocolate and Orange Cheesecake

*Base*

    200 grams chocolate cookie crumbs
    50 grams toasted hazelnuts, chopped
    80 grams melted butter

*Method*

Mix all ingredients and press onto the base of a 22-cm springform pan. Bake in a preheated oven at 175°C/350°F for 15 minutes until the biscuit base is just beginning to change its colour.

*Filling*

    400 grams cream cheese, at room temperature
    150 grams castor sugar
    60 ml whipping cream
    juice of 2 oranges
    grated zest of 1 orange
    1 large egg, beaten with a fork

*Method*

1. Put cream cheese, sugar, whipping cream, orange juice and orange zest into a food processor and blend until smooth. Add the beaten egg and blend for 30 seconds.
2. Pour the smooth cheese mixture into the warm biscuit base. Bake in a preheated oven at 175°C/350°F for 35 to 40 minutes or until just set. Cool in the oven with the door ajar.
3. Loosen edges with a knife and remove cake from tin.

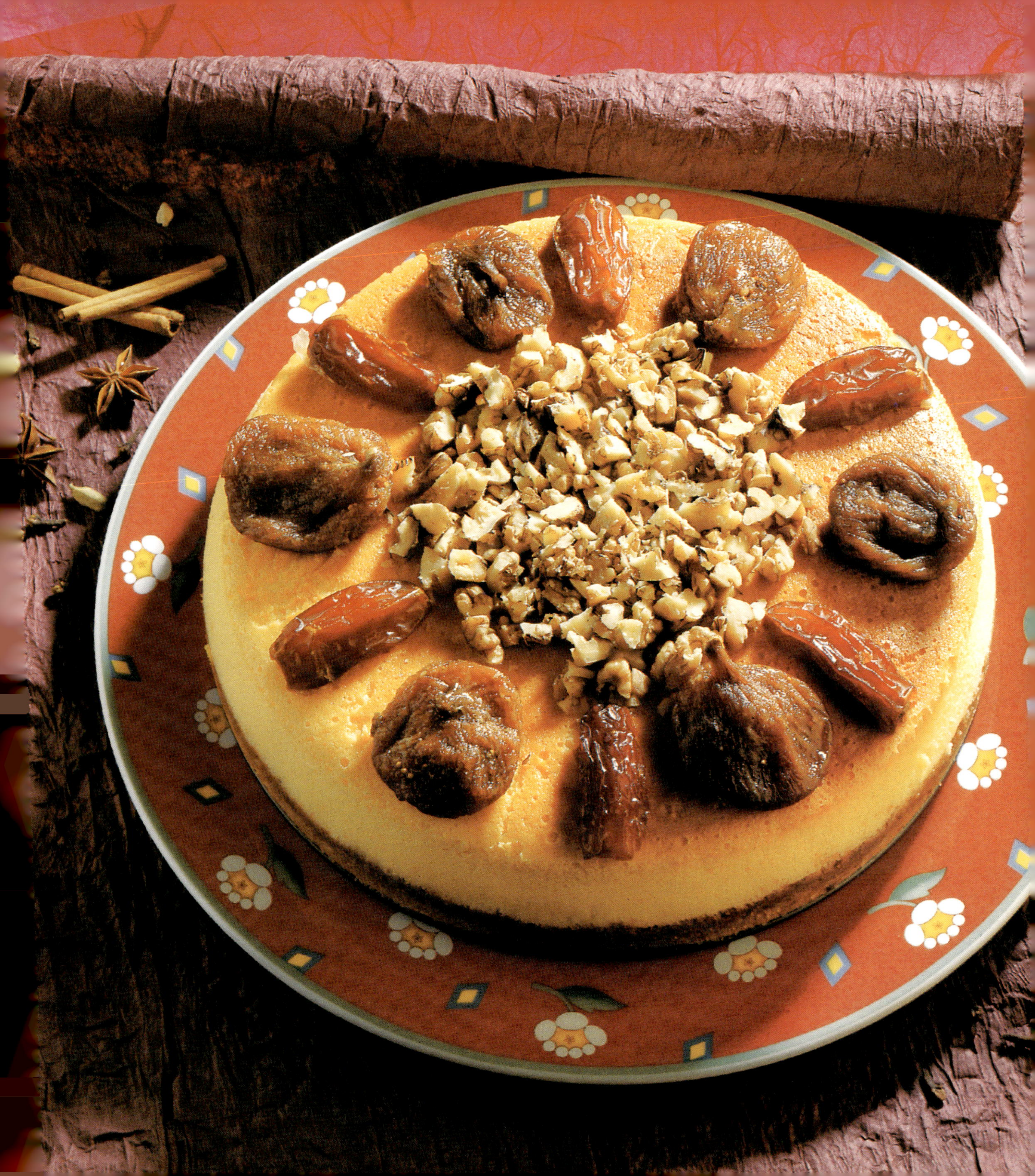

## Coconut Peach Cheesecake

*Base*

- 1 cup Nestum cereal
- ½ cup pecans, chopped
- 100 grams butter, melted
- ¼ cup brown sugar

*Method*

Combine all the ingredients for the crust and press onto the base of a 20-cm springform pan. Bake for 15 minutes at 175°C/350°F. Set aside.

*Filling*

- 750 grams cream cheese
- ¾ cup castor sugar
- 3 tablespoons all-purpose flour
- 3 eggs
- 454 grams canned peaches, drained and pureed
- ¼ cup thick coconut milk
- 1 cup sweetened coconut flakes
- 15 whole pecans
- 1 peach half

*Method*

1. Combine cream cheese, sugar and flour and mix well. Add eggs one at a time, mixing well after each addition.
2. Add peaches and coconut milk and mix well. Pour in the prepared crust.
3. Bake at 170°C/340°F for 10 minutes. Reduce the oven temperature to 160°C/320°F and continue baking for another 1 hour 5 minutes. Turn the oven off and, leaving the oven door ajar, allow the cheesecake to cool inside for several hours.
4. Decorate with coconut flakes, pecans and peach half.

## Chocolate Hazelnut Cheesecake

*Base*

- ¾ cup chocolate chip cookie crumbs
- ¼ cup melted butter
- ½ cup toasted ground hazelnuts

*Method*

Butter a 22-cm springform pan. Combine all the ingredients and press onto the base of the pan. Chill for half an hour.

*Filling*

- 680 grams cream cheese
- 1 cup castor sugar
- 2 large eggs
- 2 tablespoons heavy cream
- ¾ cup sour cream
- 1 tablespoon instant coffee, dissolved in hot water
- 225 grams semisweet chocolate, melted

*Method*

1. In a food processor mix cream cheese, sugar and eggs until well blended.
2. Add cream, sour cream, coffee and melted chocolate. Mix again until smooth before pouring into the prepared crust. Bake at 190°C/375°F for 50 minutes.

*Topping*

- 125 grams semisweet chocolate, finely chopped
- ¼ cup heavy cream
- ¼ teaspoon vanilla essence
- 1 egg, beaten
- ½ cup ground hazelnuts
- 3 strawberries, halved
- 12 hazelnuts

*Method*

1. Place a heatproof bowl over a pot of simmering water. In the bowl stir together the chocolate, cream and vanilla essence until melted. Add the egg and ground hazelnuts and stir vigorously. Mix well and pour over the cheesecake. Let the topping set in the refrigerator.
2. Decorate with strawberry halves and hazelnuts.

Chef's Note: As an option add 2 tablespoons of rum in the filling just before baking.

*Opposite: Chocolate Hazelnut Cheesecake (above) and Coconut Peach Cheesecake (below).*

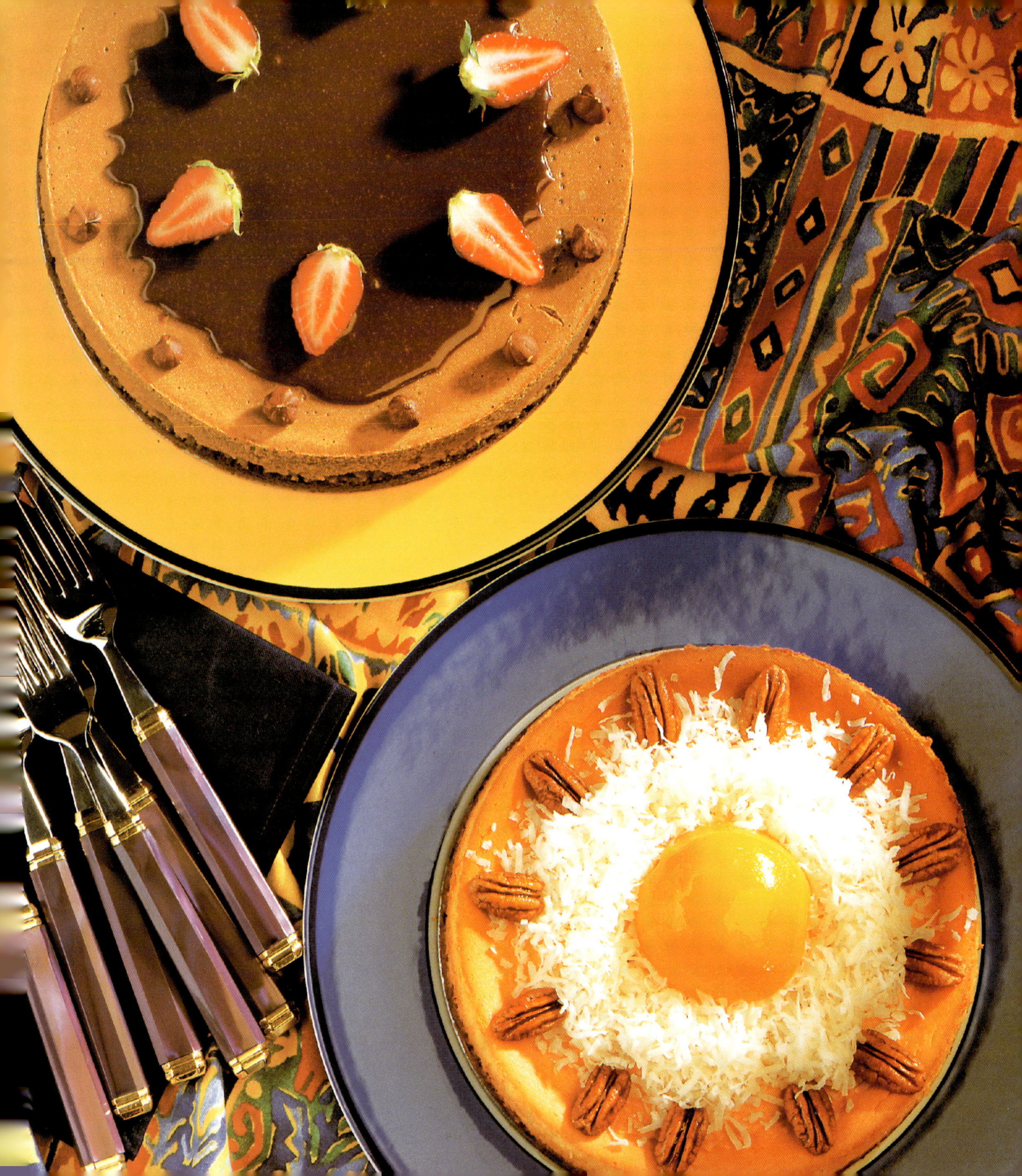

# New York Cheesecake

## Base

- 3 cups graham cracker crumbs
- 6 tablespoons castor sugar
- 2 tablespoons ground cinnamon
- 226 grams butter, melted and cooled

## Method

1. Grease a 22-cm springform pan.
2. Using a wooden spoon mix together all the ingredients for the crust. Press the crumbs onto the base and partly up the sides of the pan.
3. Refrigerate for 30 minutes.

## Filling

- 680 grams cream cheese
- 1¼ cups castor sugar
- 6 eggs, separated
- 2 cups sour cream
- ⅓ cup cornflour
- 2 teaspoons vanilla essence
- grated zest and juice of 2 lemons

## Method

1. Beat cream cheese until smooth. Gradually add sugar and continue beating until light and fluffy. Add egg yolks one at a time. Fold in sour cream, flour, vanilla essence, lemon juice and zest.
2. In a separate bowl whip egg whites until stiff peaks form. Fold into the cream cheese lightly.
3. Pour the batter into the prepared crust and bake at 165°C/330°F for 1 hour 15 minutes.

## Cherry Sauce

- 1 tablespoon cornflour
- 1 large can pitted dark cherries with syrup
- 1 tablespoon Kirsch, or other cherry liqueur
- 1 tablespoon butter

## Method

1. Mix cornflour with cherries and bring to a simmer.
2. As soon as the mixture thickens remove from the heat, add Kirsch and butter. Stir and cool. Pour over the cheesecake.

# Chocolate Swirl Espresso Cheesecake

## Base

- 1½ cups chocolate wafer cookies
- 6 tablespoons unsalted butter, melted
- ½ cup walnuts, chopped

## Method

1. Place the oven rack in the central position and preheat the oven to 200°C/390°F.
2. Grind cookies in a food processor to make crumbs. Add butter and walnuts and process using the pulse button until the mixture is moist.
3. Transfer the wafer crust into a 22-cm springform pan and press hard to make it compact. Bake in the oven for 15 minutes before filling it.

## Filling

- 2 tablespoons instant espresso
- 1 tablespoon water
- 750 grams cream cheese, at room temperature
- 1 cup castor sugar
- 3 large eggs
- ¼ cup unsalted butter, melted and cooled
- 170 grams bittersweet chocolate, chopped
- ¼ cup whipping cream

## Method

1. Dissolve instant espresso in the water.
2. With an electric mixer beat cream cheese until smooth. Add sugar and continue beating until light and fluffy. Add eggs one at a time, beating well after each addition. Add the espresso and melted butter.
3. In a small saucepan combine chocolate and whipping cream. Stir over low heat until melted.
4. Pour half of the espresso batter into the prepared crust. Drop 5 tablespoons melted chocolate evenly around the edge of the filling. Dip a small, sharp knife in the chocolate and make swirling patterns all around the filling. Carefully pour the remaining filling over the first layer. Drop the remaining melted chocolate around the edge of the second layer of filling and repeat the swirling.
5. Bake the cheesecake in the preheated oven at 200°C/390°F for about 40 minutes or until the edges are puffed and beginning to crack and the top is golden brown. Cool on a wire rack in a draft-free area.

*Opposite: New York Cheesecake.*

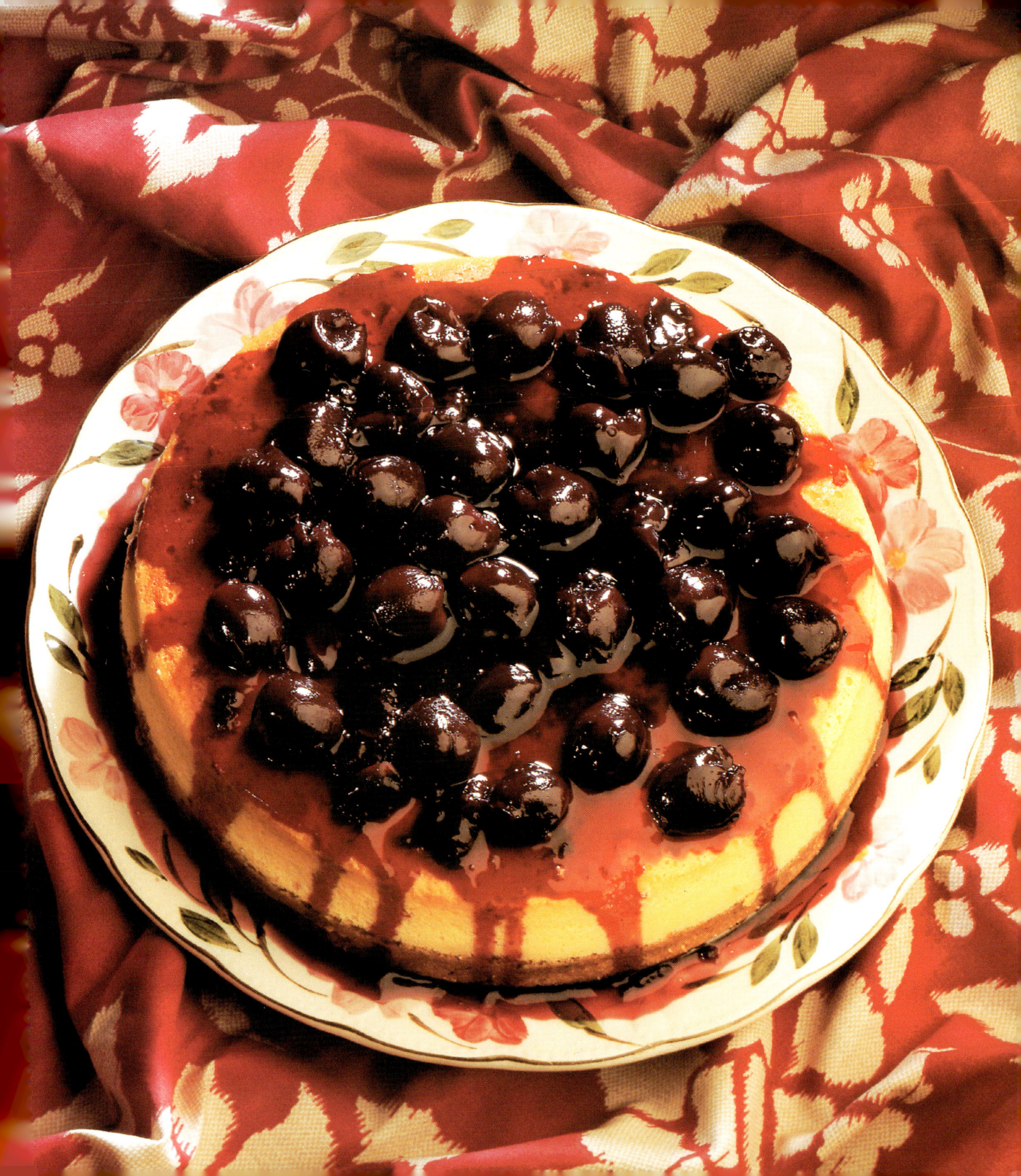

## Peanut Butter Chocolate Chip Cheesecake

*Base*

- 2 cups chocolate wafer crumbs
- 250 grams unsalted butter, melted

*Method*

Grease a 22-cm springform pan. Mix crumbs with melted butter. Press evenly onto the base and two-thirds up the sides of the pan. Refrigerate while preparing the filling.

*Filling*

- 340 grams cream cheese, at room temperature
- 1 cup castor sugar
- 1 cup creamy or chunky peanut butter
- 5 large eggs
- 1/2 cup sour cream
- 2 teaspoons lemon juice
- 1 cup chocolate chips

cocoa powder for dusting

*Method*

1. Preheat the oven to 160°C/320°F.
2. Beat cream cheese and sugar until light and fluffy. Add peanut butter and mix well. Beat in eggs one at a time, add sour cream, lemon juice and half of the chocolate chips and mix well. Pour into the prepared crust.
3. Place the springform pan on a baking sheet and bake for 55 to 65 minutes until the sides are firm. Halfway through, sprinkle the cheesecake with the remaining chocolate chips and resume baking. When the cheesecake is done, remove the pan to a wire rack and cool in a draft-free place for 15 minutes.
4. To decorate sprinkle the warm cheesecake with the remaining chocolate chips. Dust with cocoa powder.

Chef's Note: You may decorate the cheesecake with chopped peanuts as an alternative to chocolate chips.

## Chocolate Mousse Cheesecake

*Base*

- 1/4 cup butter, melted
- 3/4 cup chocolate chip cookie crumbs
- 1/2 cup hazelnuts, toasted and coarsely ground

*Method*

Grease a 25-cm springform pan. Combine all the ingredients and mix well. Press the crumbs onto the base of the springform pan and chill for half an hour.

*Filling*

- 680 grams cream cheese
- 1 cup castor sugar
- 2 large eggs
- 2 tablespoons heavy cream
- 2 tablespoons instant coffee
- 3/4 cup sour cream
- 225 grams semisweet chocolate, melted

*Method*

1. In a food processor mix cream cheese, sugar and eggs until well blended.
2. Add cream, coffee, sour cream and melted chocolate. Mix until smooth before pouring into the prepared crust. Bake at 190°C/375°F for about 50 minutes. Cool.

*Topping*

- 125 grams semisweet chocolate, finely chopped
- 1/4 cup heavy cream
- 15 grams castor sugar
- 1/4 teaspoon vanilla essence
- 1 egg yolk, beaten

*Method*

1. In a heatproof bowl placed over a pot of simmering water, stir together chocolate, cream, sugar and vanilla essence until the mixture melts.
2. Add egg yolk and stir vigorously. Mix well and pour over the cheesecake. Allow the topping to set in the refrigerator.

Chef's Note: As an option add 2 tablespoons of rum to the filling just before baking.

*Opposite: Peanut Butter Chocolate Chip Cheesecake.*

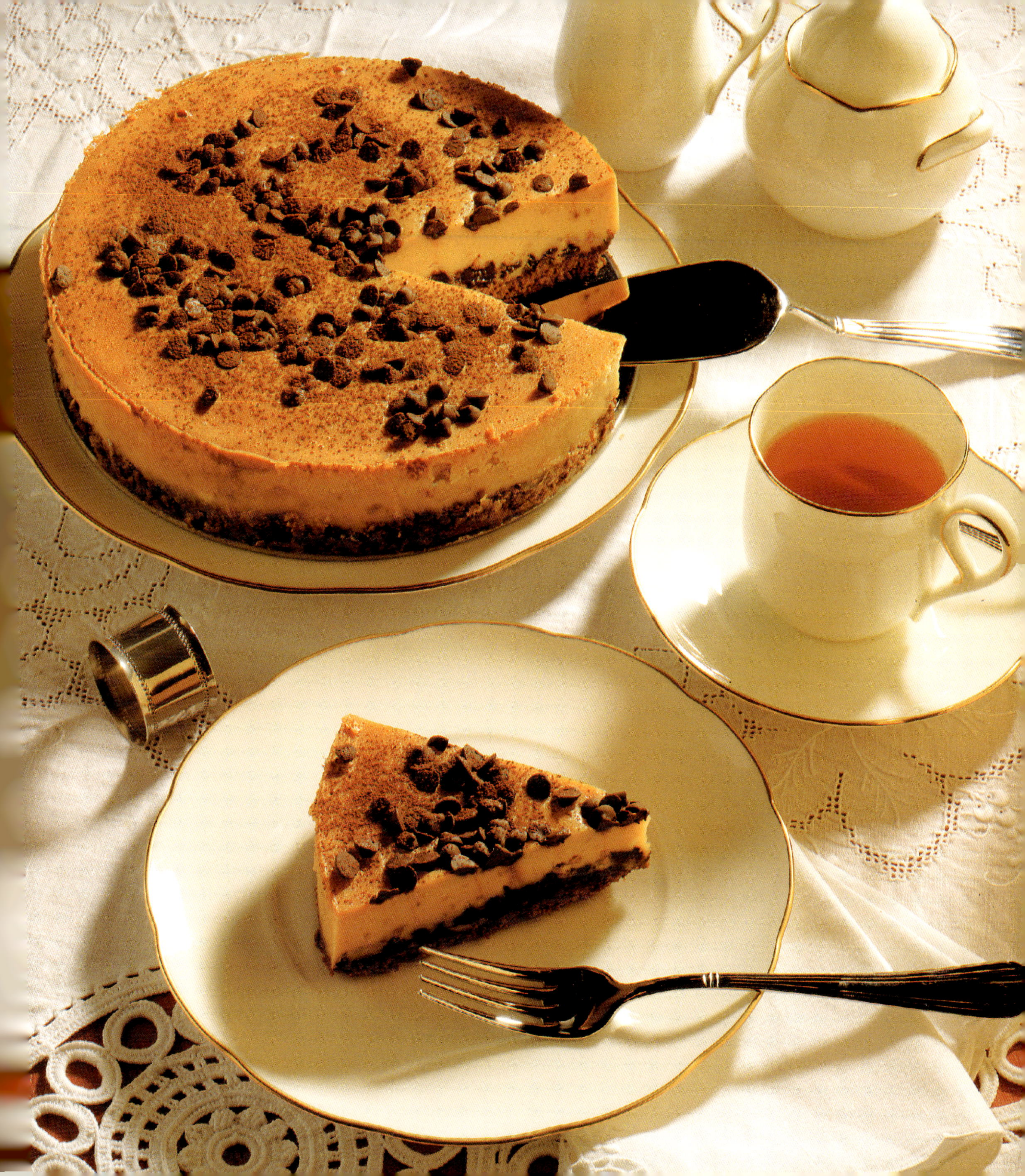

## Pina Colada Cheesecake

*Base*

- 2 cups Marie biscuits, crushed
- ½ cup melted butter
- ¼ cup toasted almond, sliced and crushed

*Method*

Combine all the ingredients and press onto the base of a 20-cm springform pan. Chill in the refrigerator.

*Filling*

- ¼ cup canned pineapple juice
- 1 tablespoon gelatine powder
- 500 grams cream cheese, softened at room temperature
- 400 grams condensed milk
- 1 cup lemon juice
- 1½ cups canned grated pineapple, drained
- 2 tablespoons marmalade to glaze
- 10 pineapple rings and 1 cup grated coconut to decorate

*Method*

1. Heat the pineapple juice and dissolve gelatine in it.
2. Beat cream cheese until smooth. Add condensed milk, gelatine, lemon juice and grated pineapple. Stir well.
3. Pour into the prepared crust and chill for at least 5 hours.
4. Remove the cheesecake from the pan by running a hot knife around the sides. Glaze with marmalade heated with a little water and decorate with pineapple rings and grated coconut.

Chef's Note: It is important not to substitute canned pineapple juice with fresh pineapple juice unless you cook the fresh juice first. This is because the presence of bromelin enzyme in the fresh pineapple can destroy the gelatine and prevent it from coagulating.

## Nestum Cheesecake

*Base*

- 150 grams butter
- 200 grams castor sugar
- 4 eggs
- 250 grams Nestum cereal
- 100 grams all-purpose flour
- a pinch of ground cloves

*Method*

Beat butter and sugar until soft. Add eggs and beat until fluffy. Fold in Nestum, flour and cloves. Mix well.

*Filling*

- 200 grams cream cheese
- 2 egg yolks
- grated zest of ½ lemon
- 80 grams powdered sugar

*Method*

1. Beat cream cheese until soft. Add egg yolks, lemon zest and powdered sugar. Beat until well mixed.
2. Layer a cake pan alternately with the Nestum mixture and the cream cheese mixture. Bake in a preheated 200°C/390°F oven for 45 minutes.

## Honey and Mango Chilled Cheesecake

*Base*

- 2 pieces of plain swiss roll sliced about 1 cm thick and arranged closely at the bottom of a 22-cm springform pan. (The swiss roll can be bought ready-made.)

*Filling*

- 1 tablespoon powdered gelatine
- ¼ cup water
- 500 grams cream cheese
- 1 tablespoon honey
- 1 400-gram can of condensed milk
- ½ cup lemon juice
- 1 cup ripe mango puree

*Method*

1. Combine gelatine and water and dissolve over heat until smooth.
2. Beat cream cheese and honey until smooth. Add condensed milk, lemon juice and mango puree. Combine well.
3. Add the warm gelatine and mix until smooth.
4. Pour into the prepared base in a springform pan and chill in the refrigerator overnight before serving.

*Opposite: Pina Colada Cheesecake.*

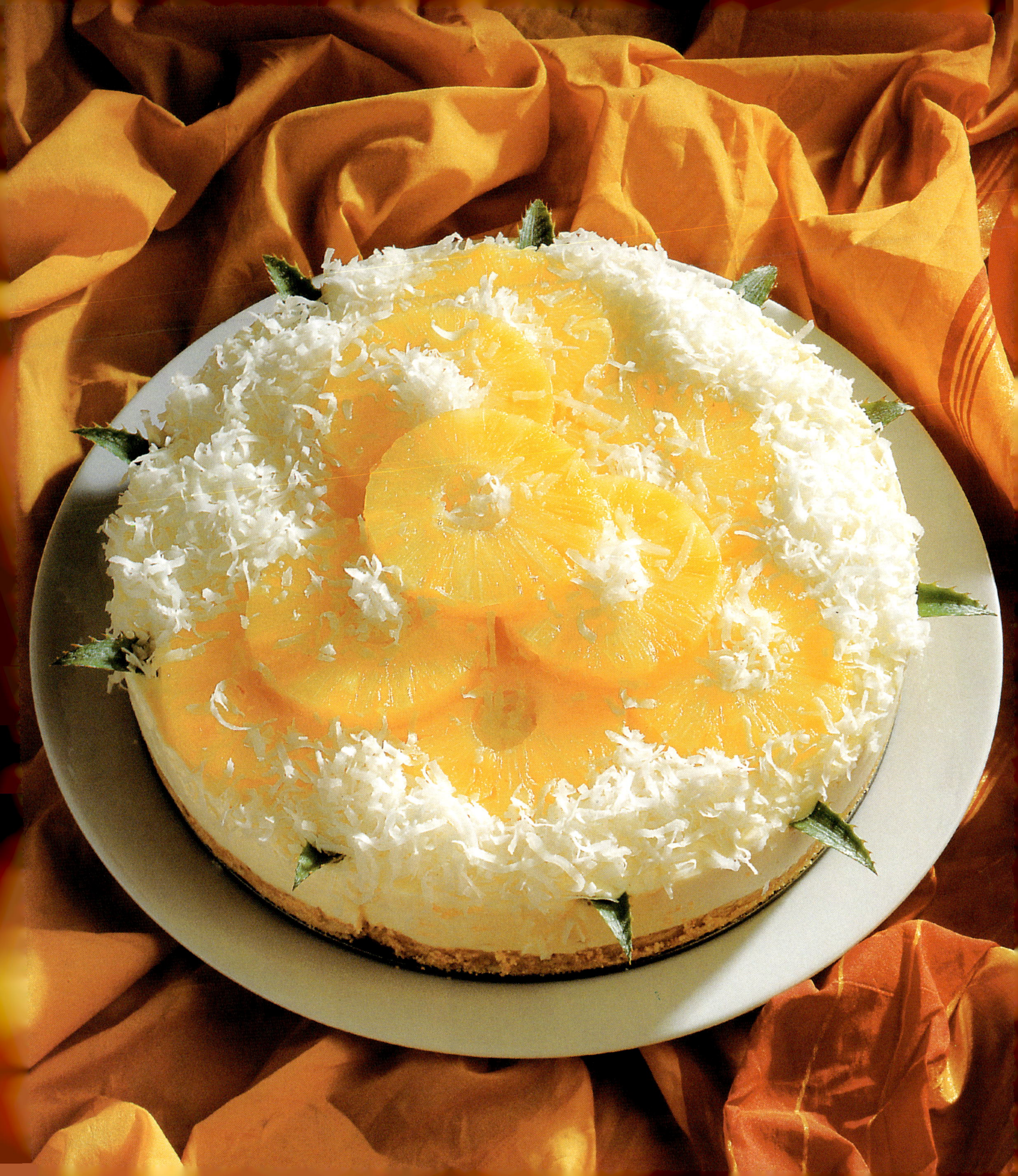

## Sunshine Cheesecake

*Base*

- 1½ cups fine graham cracker crumbs or ginger snap crumbs
- grated zest of 1 orange
- 2 tablespoons castor sugar
- 125 grams unsalted butter, melted and cooled

*Method*

Mix together all the ingredients and press onto the base and two-thirds up the sides of a 22-cm springform pan. Bake for eight minutes at 190°C/375°F and cool.

*Filling*

- 1¼ cups cream cheese, softened at room temperature
- ¾ cup castor sugar
- 3 eggs
- 1 cup sour cream
- 3 tablespoons custard powder
- ¾ cup orange juice, mixed with 1 tablespoon Grand Marnier or Cointreau
- 1 tablespoon grated orange zest
- 1 teaspoon orange essence

orange slices, orange zest and toasted almond slices, to decorate

*Method*

1. Beat cream cheese and sugar until smooth. Add eggs, one at a time. Add sour cream, custard powder, orange juice, orange zest and essence. Mix until smooth.
2. Pour into the pan. Bake at 190°C/375°F for 15 minutes and reduce to 170°C/340°F for an additional 50 to 55 minutes until the centre sets.
3. Cool overnight. Decorate with orange slices, orange zest and almond slices.

## Apricot Walnut Cheesecake

*Base*

- 1½ cups Marie biscuit crumbs
- ¼ cup ground walnuts
- ½ cup butter, melted

*Method*

Mix together all the ingredients and press onto the base of a 22-cm springform pan.

*Filling*

- 750 grams cream cheese
- ¾ cup brown sugar
- ¾ cup dried apricots, boiled, drained and finely chopped
- ¾ cup ground walnuts
- 2 eggs, lightly beaten
- 2 tablespoons all-purpose flour
- ¼ cup whipping cream

apricots and walnuts to decorate

*Method*

1. Beat cream cheese until smooth. Add sugar, apricots, walnuts, eggs, flour and whipping cream.
2. Pour into the prepared crust and bake at 170°C/340°F for an hour. Leave to cool in the oven before decorating with apricots and walnuts as desired.

## Orange Ginger Cheesecake

*Base*

- 2 cups shortbread cookie crumbs
- ¼ cup butter, melted
- ½ cup sliced almonds, toasted and finely crushed

*Method*

Combine all the ingredients and mix well. Press onto the base of a 22-cm springform pan. Chill.

*Filling*

- 500 grams cream cheese
- 1½ tablespoons powdered gelatine, dissolved in ½ cup hot water and cooled
- ½ cup castor sugar
- 150 ml evaporated milk, chilled
- 50 grams candied ginger, finely chopped
- 1 teaspoon fresh ginger juice
- ½ cup sweetened orange juice
- grated zest of 1 orange

orange segments to decorate

*Method*

Beat cream cheese until soft. Stir in the remaining ingredients. Pour into the prepared crust and chill overnight until firm. Decorate with orange segments.

Chef's Note: To slice a cheesecake cleanly, warm a knife over the stove and cut, wiping the knife clean and warming it again before making subsequent slices.

*Opposite: Sunshine Cheesecake.*

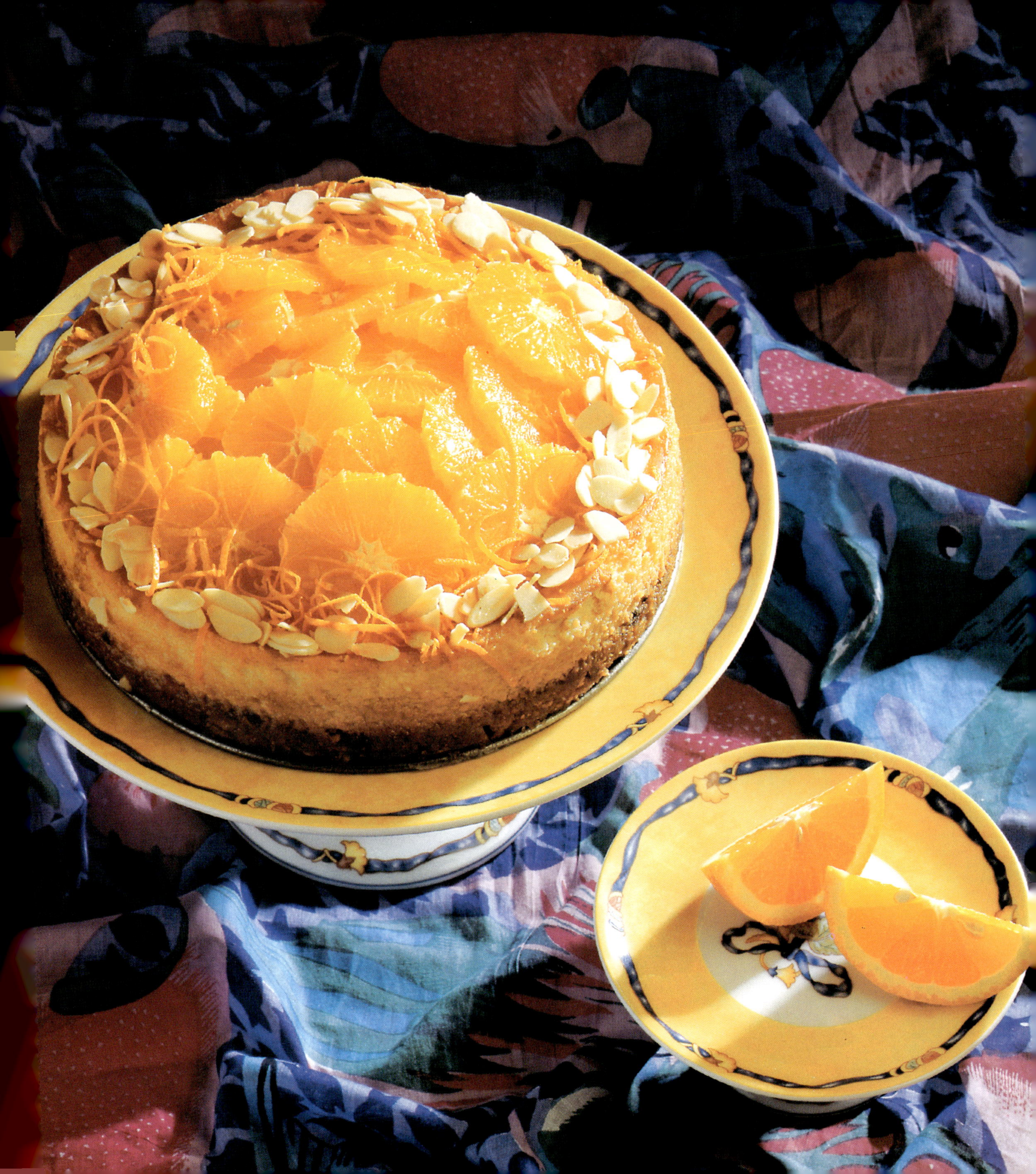

# Caramelised Apple Cheesecake

### Base

- 3 cups graham cracker crumbs, finely ground
- 1/2 cup toasted almonds, sliced
- 100 grams butter, melted

### Method

Mix together all the ingredients and press onto the base of a 22-cm springform pan.

### Filling

- 4 tablespoons butter
- 4 green apples, peeled, seeded and thinly sliced
- 1/2 cup brown sugar
- 1/2 teaspoon ground cinnamon
- 680 grams cream cheese, at room temperature
- 3/4 cup castor sugar
- 4 eggs
- 2 tablespoons Calvados, or other apple brandy, optional
- 100 grams white chocolate, melted

### Method

1. Melt butter and fry apples with brown sugar over medium heat until the apples start to caramelise. Stir in the cinnamon powder.
2. Arrange the apples in the base of the prepared crust.
3. In a separate bowl beat the cream cheese and sugar until smooth. Add the eggs one at a time. Add Calvados and melted chocolate.
4. Pour the batter into the prepared crust. Wrap a collar of foil around the outside of the springform pan and place the pan in a large baking dish half-filled with boiling water. Bake at 170°C/340°F for about an hour.
5. When the cheesecake is done, allow it to cool in the oven for 3 hours with the heat turned off and the oven door slightly ajar.

# Pumpkin Cheesecake with Pecan Topping

### Base

- 3/4 cup graham cracker crumbs
- 1/2 cup pecans, finely chopped
- 1/4 cup brown sugar, firmly packed
- 1/4 cup castor sugar
- 100 grams butter, melted and cooled

### Method

Grease a 22-cm springform pan. Combine crumbs, pecans, sugar and butter and press onto the base and two-thirds up the sides of the pan. Chill for an hour.

### Filling

- 1 1/2 cups solid-packed canned pumpkin, mashed
- 3 large eggs
- 1 teaspoon ground cinnamon
- 1/2 teaspoon ground nutmeg
- 1/2 teaspoon ground ginger
- 1/2 teaspoon salt
- 1/2 cup brown sugar
- 750 grams cream cheese, cut into pieces and softened at room temperature
- 1/2 cup castor sugar
- 2 tablespoons heavy cream
- 1 tablespoon custard powder
- 1 teaspoon vanilla essence

### Method

1. Whisk pumpkin, eggs, cinnamon, nutmeg, ginger, salt and brown sugar.
2. With an electric mixer blend together cream cheese, sugar, cream, custard powder, vanilla essence and the pumpkin mixture. Beat until smooth.
3. Pour the filling into the prepared crust, bake at 175°C/350°F for 50 to 55 minutes or until the centre just sets. Remove and cool on a wire rack for 5 minutes.

### Topping

- 2 cups sour cream
- 2 tablespoons castor sugar
- 1 tablespoon bourbon, optional
- 16 pecan halves, toasted, to decorate

### Method

Combine all ingredients and mix well. Spread the topping over the cheesecake and bake for an additional five minutes. Cool and chill before unmoulding. Decorate with pecans.

*Opposite: Pumpkin Cheesecake with Pecan Topping.*

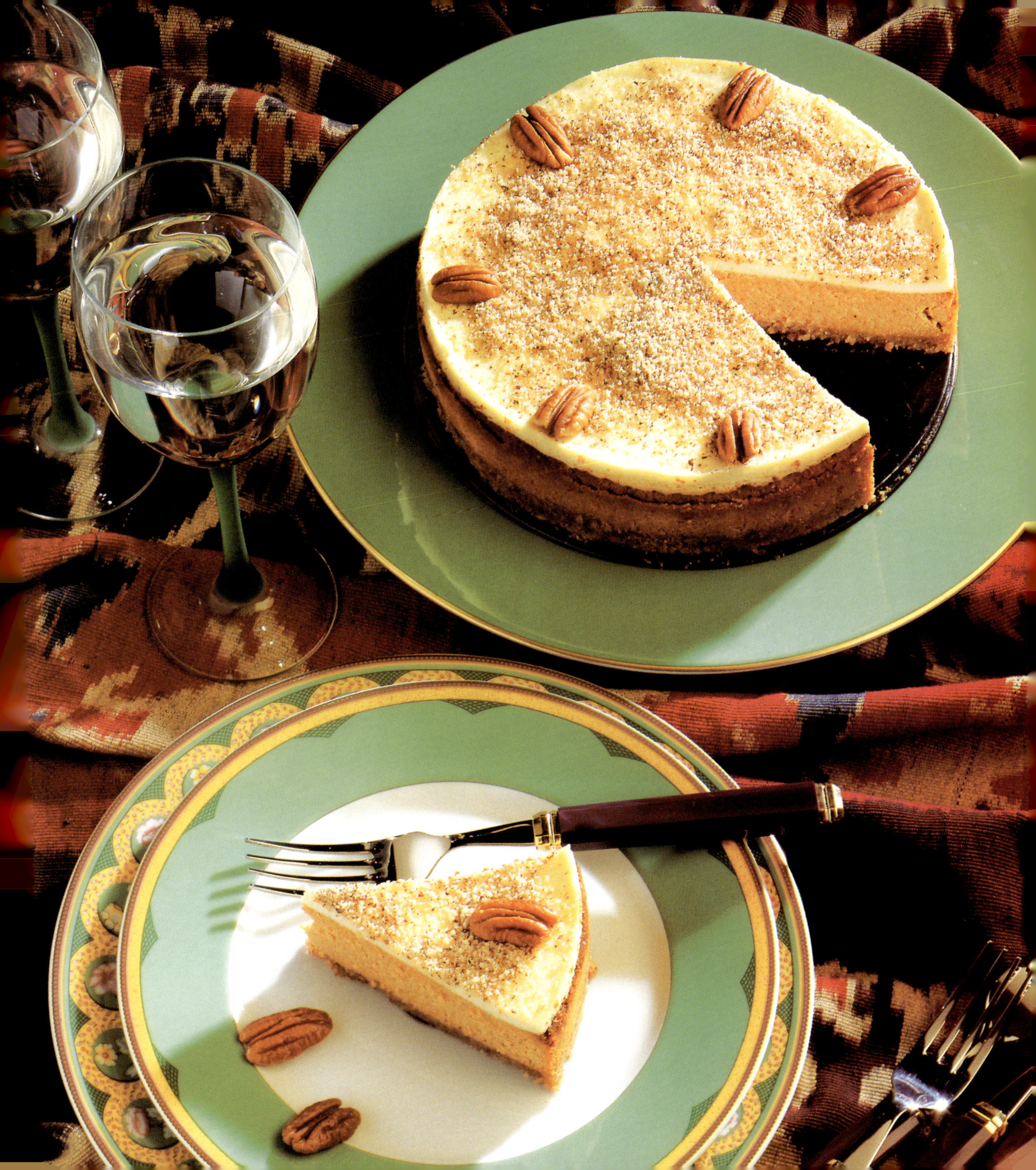

# Fresh Strawberries and Cream Cheesecake

*Ingredients*

1 raspberry or strawberry jam jelly roll, 15 cm long and cut into 2-cm slices (this can be bought ready-made)
500 grams cream cheese, softened at room temperature
½ cup castor sugar
2 tablespoons powdered gelatine, dissolved in ⅓ cup warm water
½ cup yoghurt
2 cups fresh strawberry puree
½ cup heavy cream, lightly whipped

whole strawberries to decorate
powdered sugar for dusting

*Method*

1. Arrange jelly roll slices on the base and up the sides of a 20-cm springform pan.
2. Beat cream cheese and sugar until smooth. Add gelatine, yoghurt and strawberry puree.
3. Gently fold in whipped cream and pour the batter over the jelly roll slices. Chill until firm. Decorate with strawberries and dust with powdered sugar.

# Brownie Cheesecake

*Base*

½ recipe for sweet pastry crust*

*Method*

Roll out the pastry to a thickness of about 6 mm. Line a 22 cm by 33 cm by 5 cm baking pan with the pastry. Make holes in the base with a fork. Bake blind, covered with foil and filled with beans, for 15 minutes at 180°C/360°F until golden. Discard the foil and beans and set aside.

*Filling*

230 grams cream cheese, at room temperature
250 grams butter
1½ cups castor sugar
4 eggs
1 teaspoon vanilla essence
a pinch of salt
150 grams semisweet chocolate, melted
1 cup all-purpose flour
1 cup walnuts, chopped

1 tablespoon unsweetened cocoa powder

*Method*

1. Beat cream cheese, butter and sugar until smooth. Add eggs one at a time, vanilla essence and salt.
2. Pour in the melted chocolate and gradually add the flour before folding in the nuts.
3. Pour the batter into the prepared pastry and bake for 45 minutes at 180°C/360°F. Cool and cut into 5 cm by 5 cm squares to serve. Dust with cocoa powder.

\* Refer to recipe for Fruit Tartlets on page 32.

# Coffee Cheesecake

*Base*

1 large, good-quality chocolate swiss roll, cut into 2-cm slices (this can be bought ready-made)

*Filling*

1 tablespoon powdered gelatine
1 tablespoon instant coffee powder
½ cup cold water
500 grams cream cheese
¾ cup castor sugar
300 grams semisweet chocolate, melted
150 grams evaporated milk, chilled

grated chocolate to decorate
whipped cream to serve

*Method*

1. Arrange slices of swiss roll on the base of a 22-cm springform pan.
2. Heat together gelatine, coffee powder and water until dissolved. Cool.
3. Cream together the cream cheese and sugar until smooth. Add melted chocolate and evaporated milk followed by cooled gelatine-and-coffee mixture. Pour into the prepared cake base and chill overnight.
4. Decorate with grated chocolate and serve with whipped cream.

*Opposite: Fresh Strawberries and Cream Cheesecake.*

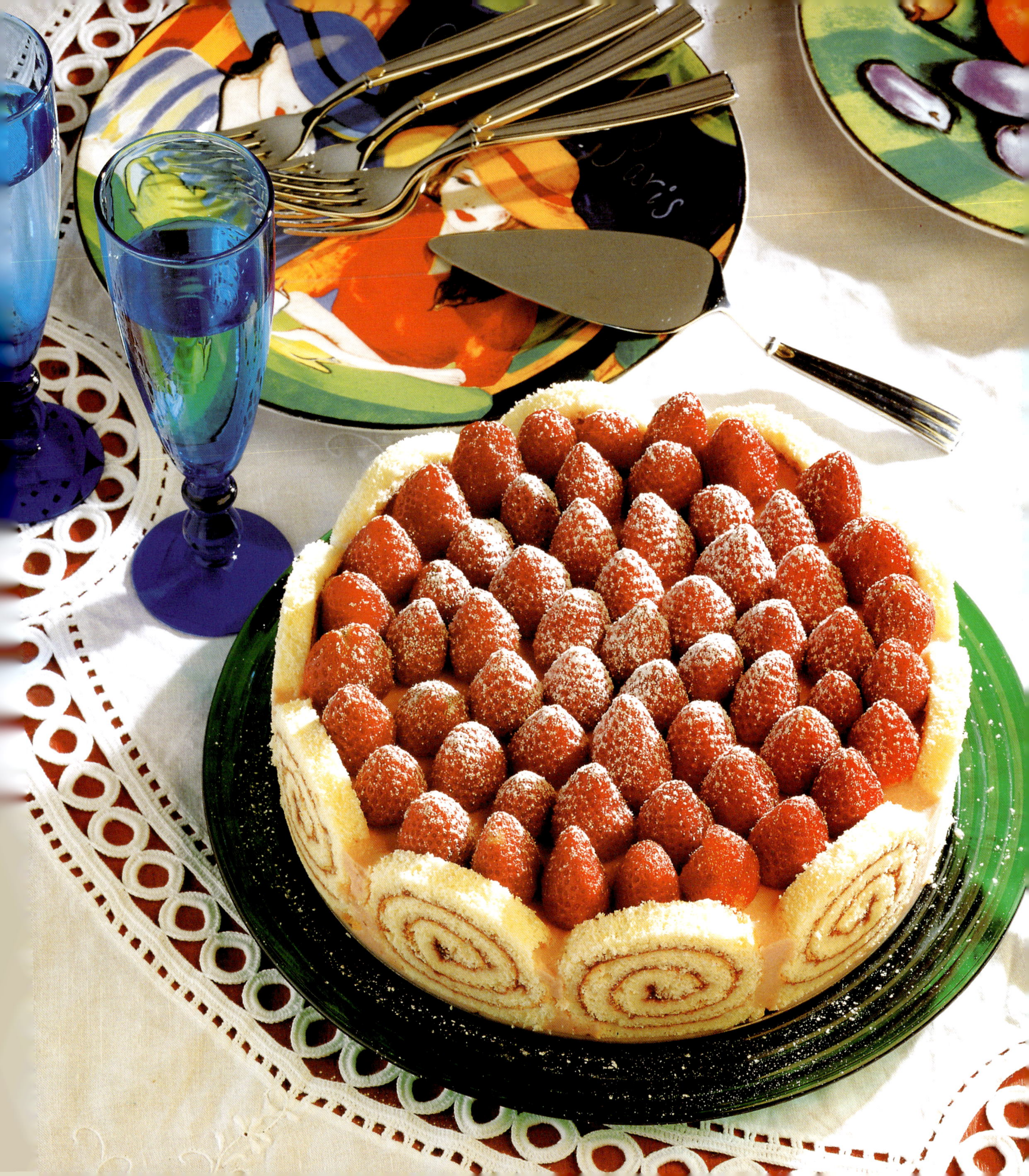

## Fresh Strawberries and White Chocolate Cheesecake

*Base*

- 2 cups Marie biscuits, crushed
- 1 cup almond slices, toasted
- 1/4 cup butter, melted

*Method*

Mix all the ingredients and press onto the base of a 25-cm springform pan.

*Filling*

- 980 grams cream cheese
- 1/2 cup castor sugar
- 4 whole eggs
- 2 egg yolks
- 2 tablespoons custard powder
- 1 teaspoon vanilla essence
- 250 grams white chocolate, melted
- 2 cups strawberries, chopped

- grated white chocolate
- 3 strawberries, halved, to decorate

*Method*

1. Beat together cream cheese and castor sugar. Add eggs, egg yolks, custard powder, vanilla essence and white chocolate.
2. Spread chopped strawberries on the base of the crust and pour in the filling.
3. Bake at 170°C/340°F for an hour. Leave to cool in the oven for a few hours before chilling.
4. Top the cake with grated white chocolate and arrange strawberry halves as desired.

## Marble Cheesecake

*Base*

- 3 cups chocolate chip cookie crumbs, finely ground
- 100 grams butter, melted
- 1/2 cup walnuts, coarsely chopped

*Method*

Combine all the ingredients and press onto the base of a 22-cm springform pan.

*Filling*

- 900 grams cream cheese
- 1 1/2 cups castor sugar
- 4 eggs
- 150 grams bittersweet chocolate, chopped and melted
- 2 teaspoons vanilla essence

*Method*

1. Beat cream cheese and sugar until smooth. Add eggs one at a time and mix well. Stir in vanilla essence.
2. Pour one-third of the batter into a separate bowl and whisk in the melted chocolate.
3. Alternately drop a spoonful of the plain batter and a spoonful of the chocolate batter into the prepared crust until all the batter is used. Lightly swirl with a knife. Bake at 170°C/340°F for an hour. Leave to cool for about 3 hours in the oven, with the oven door ajar, to prevent the cheesecake from cracking.

## Plain Chocolate Cheesecake

*Base*

- 35 pieces chocolate wafer, finely crushed
- 120 grams unsalted butter, melted
- 1/2 cup hazelnuts, toasted

*Method*

Mix all the ingredients and press onto the base of a well-buttered, 25-cm springform pan. Chill.

*Filling*

- 680 grams cream cheese, at room temperature
- 1 cup sugar
- 3 eggs
- 200 grams semisweet chocolate, melted and cooled
- 2 teaspoon cocoa powder
- 1 teaspoon vanilla essence
- 2 cups sour cream

*Method*

1. In a large bowl beat cream cheese and sugar until fluffy and smooth. Add eggs one at a time. Stir in chocolate, cocoa and vanilla essence, beating well after each addition.
2. Add sour cream and continue beating until smooth and well blended. Pour the custard into the prepared crust and bake at 170°C/340°F for an hour. Cake may appear too liquid but it will become firm when chilled. Cool to room temperature and chill overnight before serving.

*Opposite: Fresh Strawberries and White Chocolate Cheesecake.*

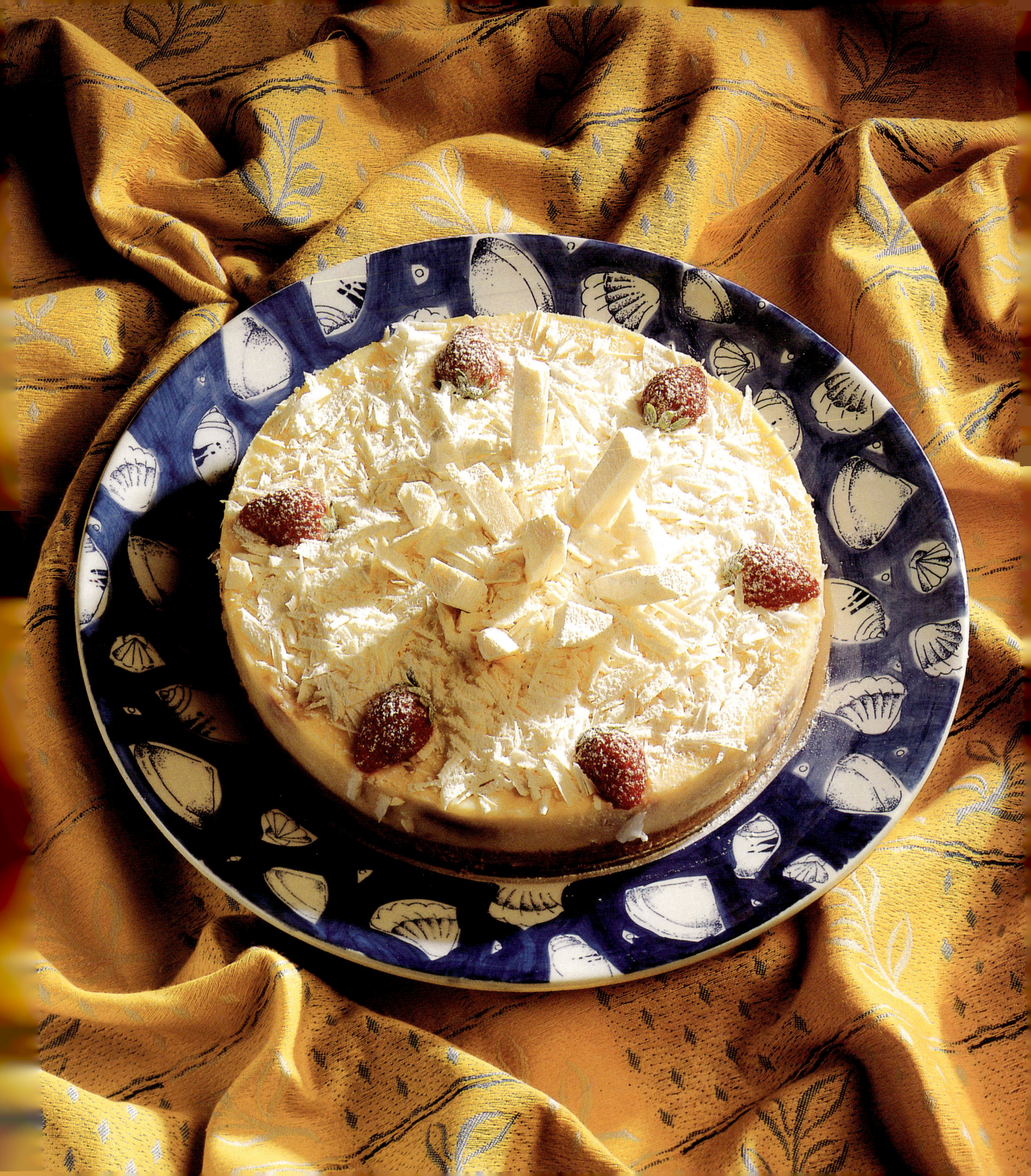

# Cookies

The Art of Baking Cookies, p90　1 Almond Accidents, p92　2 Chef Wan's Chocolate Chip Cookies, p92　3 Rugelash, p92　4 Chocolate Biscotti, p92　5 Almond Crunch Cookies, p94　6 Almond Drops, p94　7 Almond Rings, p94　8 Scottish Banbury Biscuits, p94　9 Coffee Whirls, p94　10 Cream Cheese Gems, p96　11 Savoury Cheese Fingers, p96　12 French Orange Biscuits, p96　13 Chocolate Oatmeal Cookies, p96　14 Caramel Apricot Swirl Cookies, p98　15 Cheesy Coin Cookies, p98　16 Orange Shortbread Biscuits, p98　17 Apricot Coconut Macaroons, p100　18 Cornflake Coffee Kisses, p100　19 Swiss Chocolate Rosettes, p100　20 Date and Pecan Pumpkin Squares, p100　21 Cornflake Crunchies, p102　22 Walnut Apricot Cookies, p102　23 Gingerbread Cookies, p102　24 Husarenkrapfert, p102　25 Oatmeal Biscuits, p102　26 Fruitcake Cookies, p104　27 Dried Shrimp Cornflake Cookies, p104　28 Ginger and Molasses Snaps, p104　29 Orange Shortbread Cookies, p104　30 Pecan Cookies, p106　31 Mom's Ginger Snaps, p106　32 Butter Cookies, p106　33 Lemon Custard Cookies, p106　34 Orange Marmalade Biscuits, p106　35 Hazelnut Shortbread, p108　36 Peanut Butter Cookies, p108　37 Pistachio Cantuccini Biscotti, p108　38 Dutch Kletskoppan, p108　39 Lemon Raspberry Cookies, p110　40 Mexican Wedding Cookies, p110　41 Sweet Dream Cookies, p110　42 Vienna Walnut Crescent, p110　43 Noel Nut Balls, p112　44 Orange Walnut Shortbread, p112　45 Sablé Cookies, p112　46 Raisin Oatmeal Cookies, p112　47 German Sand Biscuits, p114　48 Vanilla Kipferin, p114　49 Almond Biscuits, p114　50 Pistachio Lace Cookies, p114

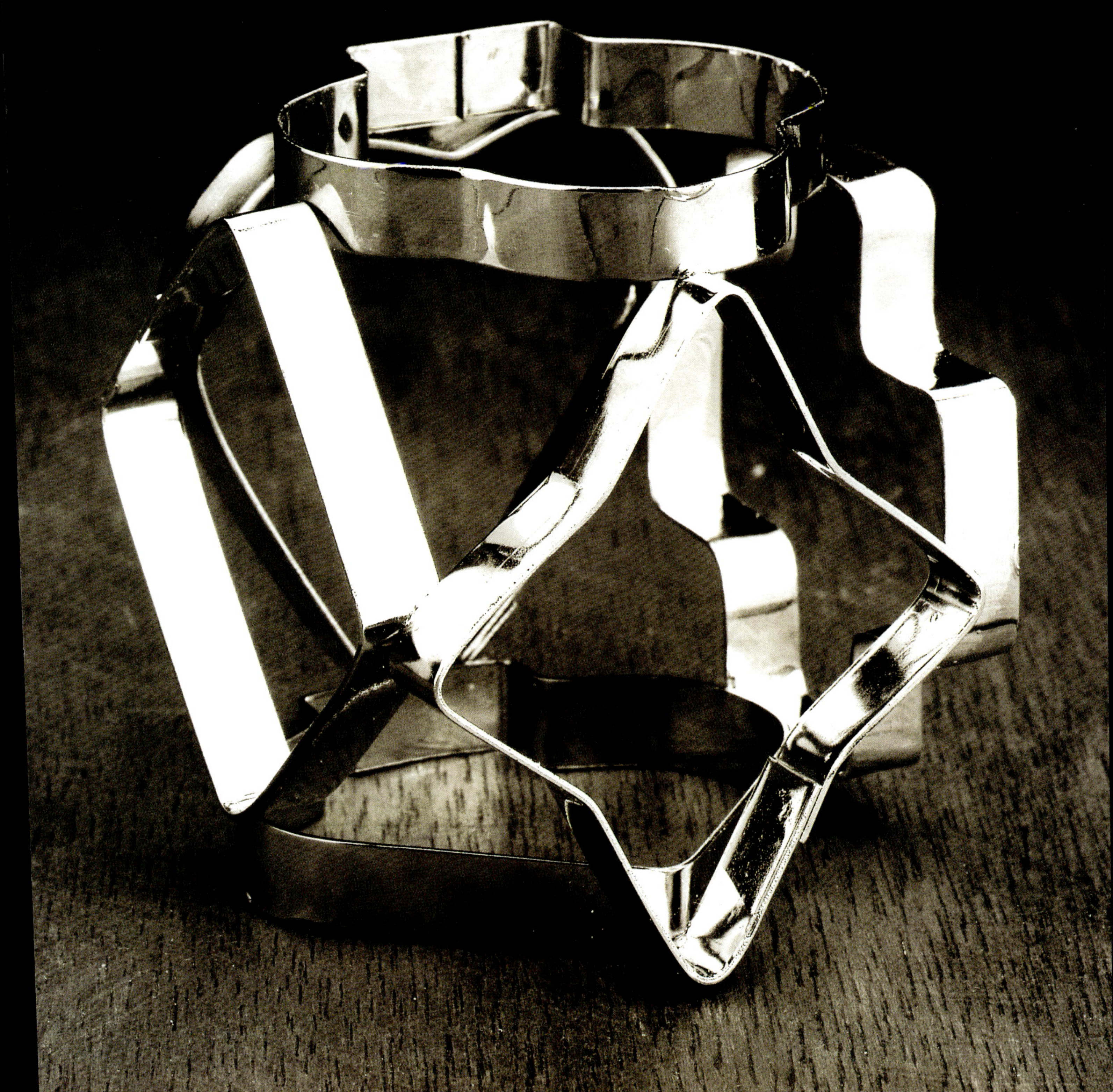

# The Art of Baking Cookies

I was introduced to baking when I was about seven. There were seven children in my family, and during the Hari Raya season we would all chip in to help my mother bake thousands of cookies for sale. We turned our small back kitchen into a cookie factory. I think we made up to 24 kinds of cookies during one of the festive seasons! To this day cookies are what I bake most often.

Cookies should look as good as they taste. You want to create petite, bite-sized morsels that your guests simply cannot resist, even if they are not hungry. Besides being small, cookies should be uniform in size and thickness.

The most common cookies are:

### Drop Cookies
These are so named because the dough is "dropped" by the spoonful onto baking trays. They include such simple, old-fashioned tidbits as oatmeal raisin cookies and chocolate chip cookies.

The story goes that the cookie began as a small spoonful of cake batter, baked prior to the baking of the cake so that the cook could judge the correctness of the oven temperature and the flavour and texture of the batter. Today drop cookies are often simple mounds studded with nuts, raisins or chocolate.

### Bar Cookies
Sometimes chewy, sometimes cake-like, and sometimes crisp and crunchy, bar cookies are quick to prepare as the batter is spread in a pan and the cookies baked and sliced all at once rather than being individually shaped. Bar cookies are good for picnics as they are easily wrapped and carried right in their baking pan. Popular bar cookies include fudge brownies, cheesecake squares and Scottish shortbread.

### Rolled Cookies
Children are big fans of rolled cookies, which are cookies cut from rolled-out dough. Some adults collect antique cookie cutters as a hobby. A knife can also be used for cutting the dough into shapes.

It is important that the dough be rolled to an even thickness, usually $\frac{1}{4}$ cm thick, so that the cookies will cook at the same rate.

### Icebox Cookies
Sometimes called refrigerator cookies, or slice-and-bake cookies, icebox cookies are sliced from logs of dough that have been chilled firm. The appeal of this method lies in the fact that the dough can be prepared days or even weeks in advance. Slicing and baking are done quickly and at your convenience.

This technique generally yields uniform, wafer-like cookies with a crisp texture. The logs may be square-sided or triangular. Fancy treats can be turned out by wrapping the dough around a filling, rolling the logs in nuts, or stacking different kinds of dough together.

### Moulded Cookies
Although hand-moulded cookies are time-consuming to shape as each morsel is individually crafted, most bakers consider them a labour of love. The dough can be rolled in sugar or nuts as in gingerbread, filled with jam as in pineapple tarts, or flattened with a fork for an interesting crisscross pattern.

A similar cookie is the pressed cookie,

shaped by forcing soft dough through a cookie press or pastry bag. Perhaps more than any other technique this yields professional-looking results, although you may need to practise a little before you can turn out perfectly shaped cookies with ease.

## INGREDIENTS

### All-Purpose Flour

All-purpose flour is suitable for all types of baking because it is a blend of hard and soft wheat. Hard wheat is higher in protein while soft wheat adds tenderness to cookies and pastries. Flour may absorb moisture in humid conditions; high humidity may call for slightly more flour while low humidity will require the opposite. Store flour in an airtight container in a cool, dry place. Flour may be frozen, but allow it to return to room temperature before use.

### Butter, Margarine and Shortening

Two types of butter are used in cooking and baking: salted and sweet. I prefer sweet butter for my pastries but salted butter can be used if the salt in the recipe is reduced by about 6 grams for every 455 grams of butter. If the recipe has little salt, or if the main ingredient in the recipe is butter, do not use salted butter.

The flavour of cookies made with margarine is pleasant but not as rich as the taste of cookies made with butter.

Shortening has little or no flavour and may replace other fats for frying and baking. Pie crust made with shortening rather than margarine produces a flakier pastry.

### Leavening

Baking powder is used in cookies as leavening. When baking powder comes into contact with liquid and heat, it releases carbon dioxide which causes the dough to rise. Cream of tartar, on the other hand, is most often used to stiffen egg whites for meringues.

### Molasses

Molasses is produced in the first stages of refining raw sugar. Used in bread and cakes, it adds a unique flavour and colour, and improves shelf life. Molasses may be labelled as sulphured or unsulphured depending on whether or not sulphur was used in the sugar-refining process.

## COOKIE-BAKING TIPS

1. Before baking read the entire recipe and assemble the ingredients and utensils.
2. Before sifting whisk the dry ingredients thoroughly for aeration. Dry ingredients should be measured by the dip and level method: dip the cup or measuring spoon in the ingredient and level with the back of a knife.
3. Use a glass measuring cup for liquid measurements. Check the level of the liquid at eye level.
4. Scrape down the sides of the bowl several times while mixing the batter to ensure that the ingredients are well mixed.
5. Space cookies out on the baking tray to ensure even baking.
6. Grease a baking tray with shortening, not butter or margarine which may burn. Place a spoonful of flour in the greased tray and shake, allowing the flour to coat all surfaces. Tap out the excess flour.
7. Bake one tray of cookies at a time so that hot air can circulate freely. Place the baking tray in the centre of the oven for even heat distribution. Some ovens have "hot spots". If your cookies tend to brown more quickly in one spot, rotate the baking tray midway through baking.
8. Preheat the oven before baking. It should take about 15 minutes, but this varies with different ovens.
9. An approximate baking time is suggested in each recipe. But oven temperature, humidity, altitude and other factors affect baking time. I always use a timer set at the minimum baking time, then test for doneness by touching a cookie lightly to see if there is a spring to it.
10. Before storing let freshly-baked cookies cool completely on a wire rack. Condensation on a baking tray softens cookies whereas the air that circulates underneath a wire rack speeds up the cooling process.
11. Store each type of cookie separately so that flavours do not mingle. For maximum freshness store cookies in airtight tins.
12. Most cookies freeze well for up to one month. Wrap them in foil or cling wrap, label and date them before freezing.

## Almond Accidents

*Ingredients*

- 226 grams butter, softened at room temperature
- 1 1/3 cups powdered sugar
- 1 teaspoon almond essence
- 2 1/4 cups cake flour
- 1/3 cup ground almonds

*Method*

1. Blend together the butter and sugar. Mix in almond essence, flour and almonds.

2. Roll each teaspoonful into a ball, place on a baking tray and bake at 175°C/350°F for approximately 15 minutes until light brown on the bottom and golden around the edges. Remove to a wire rack to cool.

## Chef Wan's Chocolate Chip Cookies

*Ingredients*

- 1 cup unsalted butter
- 1 teaspoon vanilla essence
- 1 cup castor sugar
- 1/2 cup dark brown sugar, firmly packed
- 1 egg
- 1/3 cup unsweetened cocoa powder
- 2 tablespoons fresh milk
- 1 3/4 cups all-purpose flour
- 1/4 teaspoon baking soda
- 1 cup chopped pecans or walnuts
- 70 grams dates, chopped
- 1 cup semisweet chocolate chips

*Method*

1. With an electric mixer cream the butter at high speed. Add vanilla essence and both types of sugar and beat until fluffy. Add egg. Decrease the mixer speed to low and beat in cocoa, followed by milk.

2. In a separate bowl stir together flour and baking soda with a wooden spoon. Mix in nuts, dates and chocolate chips, stirring to combine. Add to the batter.

3. Drop the batter by the rounded teaspoonful onto a foil-lined baking tray. Bake at 175°C/350°F for 12 to 13 minutes. Cool for two minutes before removing from the baking tray.

## Rugelash

*Dough*

- 250 grams cream cheese
- 1/2 cup unsalted butter
- 1/4 teaspoon salt
- 1 tablespoon castor sugar
- 1 teaspoon vanilla essence
- 1 cup all-purpose flour

*Filling*

- 1/2 cup raisins, chopped
- 1 cup walnuts, chopped
- 1/2 cup castor sugar
- 1 teaspoon ground cinnamon
- 1 egg, beaten
- powdered sugar for dusting

*Method*

1. Beat cream cheese, butter, salt, sugar and vanilla essence until light and smooth.

2. Fold in the flour until a dough forms. Chill in the refrigerator for a few hours.

3. Roll out the dough and cut with a round biscuit cutter.

4. Combine all the ingredients for the filling and mix well. Place a little filling on each circle of dough and fold the circle into two. Brush the edges with beaten egg to seal.

5. Bake at 185°C/365°F for 20 minutes until golden brown. Cool before dusting with powdered sugar.

## Chocolate Biscotti

*Ingredients*

- 2 cups all-purpose flour
- 1 cup castor sugar
- 1/2 teaspoon baking soda
- 1/2 teaspoon double-acting baking powder
- 1/2 teaspoon salt
- 1/2 teaspoon ground cinnamon
- 1/2 teaspoon ground cloves
- 1/4 cup espresso, cooled
- 2 tablespoons fresh milk
- 1 egg yolk
- 1 teaspoon vanilla essence
- 3/4 cup hazelnuts, toasted
- 1/2 cup semisweet chocolate chips

*Method*

1. Mix together flour, sugar, baking soda, baking powder, salt, cinnamon and cloves and stir well.

2. In a small bowl whisk espresso, milk, egg yolk and vanilla essence. Add to the flour mixture and beat until a dough forms. Stir in hazelnuts and chocolate chips.

3. Roll the dough into several logs 30 cm long and 5 cm wide. Arrange on a well-greased baking tray about 8 cm apart. Bake for 35 minutes at 175°C/350°F. Remove from the oven and cool for 10 minutes. Reduce the temperature to 170°C/340°F. On a cutting board cut the logs crosswise into slices. Arrange on the tray again with cut sides down. Bake for another 5 minutes until golden.

*Opposite: Chef Wan's Chocolate Chip Cookies (left) and Rugelash (right).*

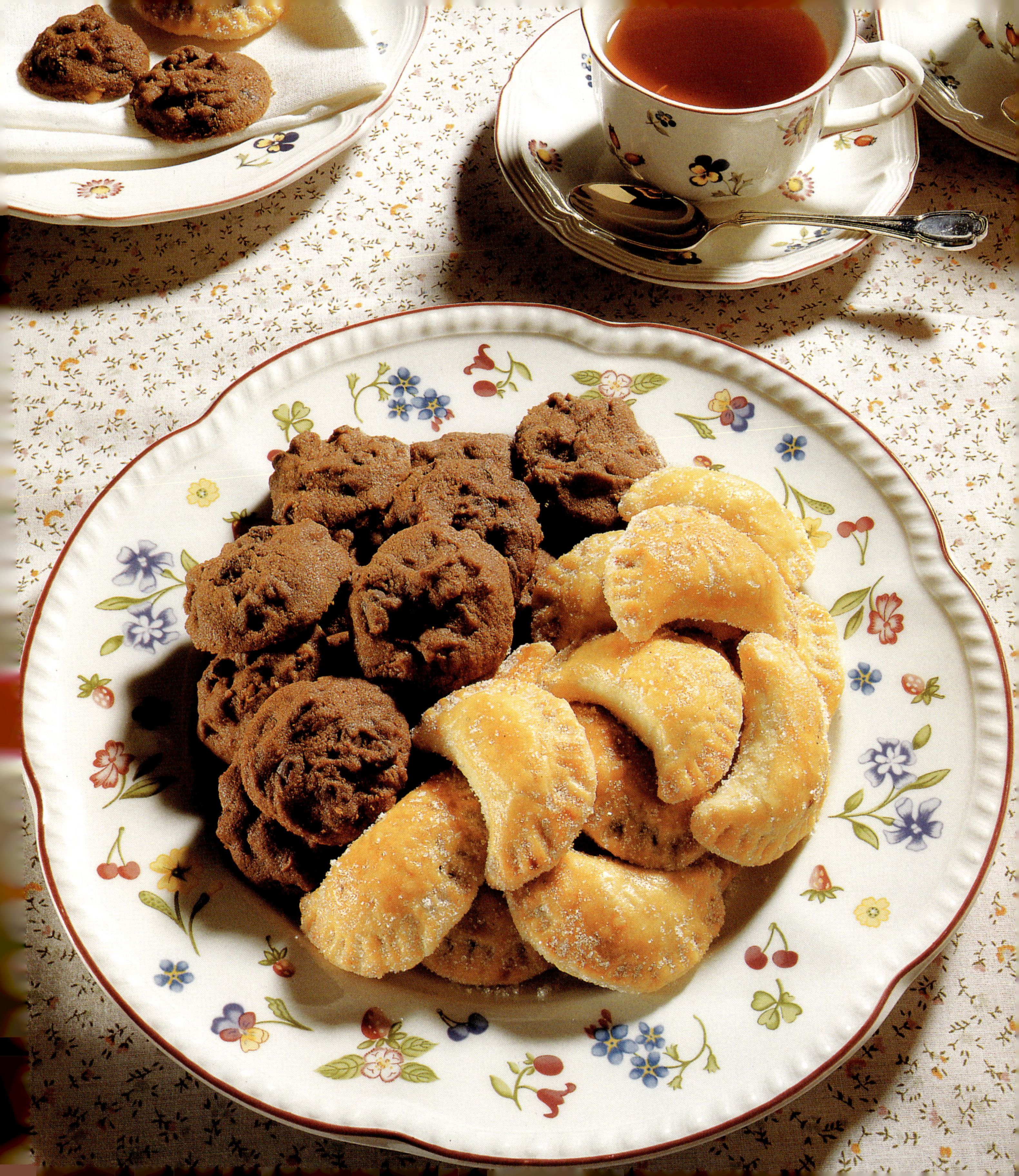

# Almond Crunch Cookies

*Ingredients*

    170 grams unsalted butter
    200 grams powdered sugar
    4 egg yolks
    1 teaspoon vanilla essence
    1 teaspoon almond essence
    285 grams all-purpose flour
    170 grams cornflour
    140 grams ground almonds

    1/2 cup slivered almonds to decorate
    a little egg yolk, beaten, to glaze

*Method*

1. Beat butter and sugar until creamy. Add egg yolks, vanilla essence and almond essence.
2. Add both types of flour and ground almonds. Mix the dough well and chill for an hour before rolling out.
3. Cut into desired shapes with a cookie cutter. Top with slivered almonds and glaze with egg yolk. Bake for 12 to 15 minutes at 175°C/350°F until golden.

# Almond Drops

*Ingredients*

    250 grams egg whites
    45 grams cornflour
    150 grams castor sugar
    150 ground almonds
    1 tablespoon vanilla essence

    slivered almonds to decorate

*Method*

1. Whip egg whites into stiff peaks. Fold in cornflour, sugar, ground almonds and vanilla essence.
2. Fill a piping bag with the pastry and pipe cookies onto a baking tray lined with greased parchment paper. Decorate each cookie with a slivered almond.
3. Bake at 180°C/360°F for 10 minutes until golden.

# Almond Rings

*Ingredients*

    3/4 cup butter, at room temperature
    1 egg yolk
    1/4 cup powdered sugar
    1/2 teaspoon pure almond essence
    2 cups all-purpose flour
    1/2 cup ground almonds
    1/4 teaspoon salt

    1 egg white, slightly beaten, for dipping
    crushed almonds to decorate

*Method*

1. Place butter, egg yolk, sugar and almond essence in a large bowl and mix well with a wooden spoon. Add flour, ground almonds and salt. Mix thoroughly until well blended.
2. Chill the dough for 1 hour. Break off pieces of dough the size of a walnut and roll into thick lengths. Form into rings and dip in egg white.
3. Sprinkle with crushed almonds and place on an ungreased baking tray. Bake for 10 minutes at 175°C/350°F until golden.

# Scottish Banbury Biscuits

*Ingredients*

    250 grams butter
    250 grams castor sugar
    1/2 teaspoon ground cinnamon
    60 grams eggs
    500 grams all-purpose flour
    180 grams currants

    castor sugar for dusting

*Method*

1. Mix together butter, sugar, cinnamon and eggs. Add flour and currants and mix into an elastic dough.
2. Roll out to a 4-mm thickness and cut out with a 4-cm fluted cutter. Dust with sugar and bake at 170°C/340°F for 15 minutes.

# Coffee Whirls

*Dough*

    225 grams butter
    50 grams powdered sugar
    1 tablespoon coffee essence
    175 grams all-purpose flour
    50 grams custard powder

*Method*

1. Cream butter until softened. Add powdered sugar and blend well. Add coffee essence.
2. Sift together the flour and custard powder. Fold into the butter mixture. Spoon into a piping bag fitted with a 1-cm star nozzle and pipe cookies on a greased baking tray. Bake at 190°C/375°F for 10 to 15 minutes. Cool.

*Filling*

    75 grams butter
    175 grams powdered sugar
    1 tablespoon milk
    1 teaspoon coffee essence

*Method*

Cream together butter, sugar, milk and coffee essence. Place filling between double pieces of baked cookies until all the cookies have been filled this way.

*Opposite: Almond Rings (above), Almond Drops (below left) and Almond Crunch Cookies (below right).*

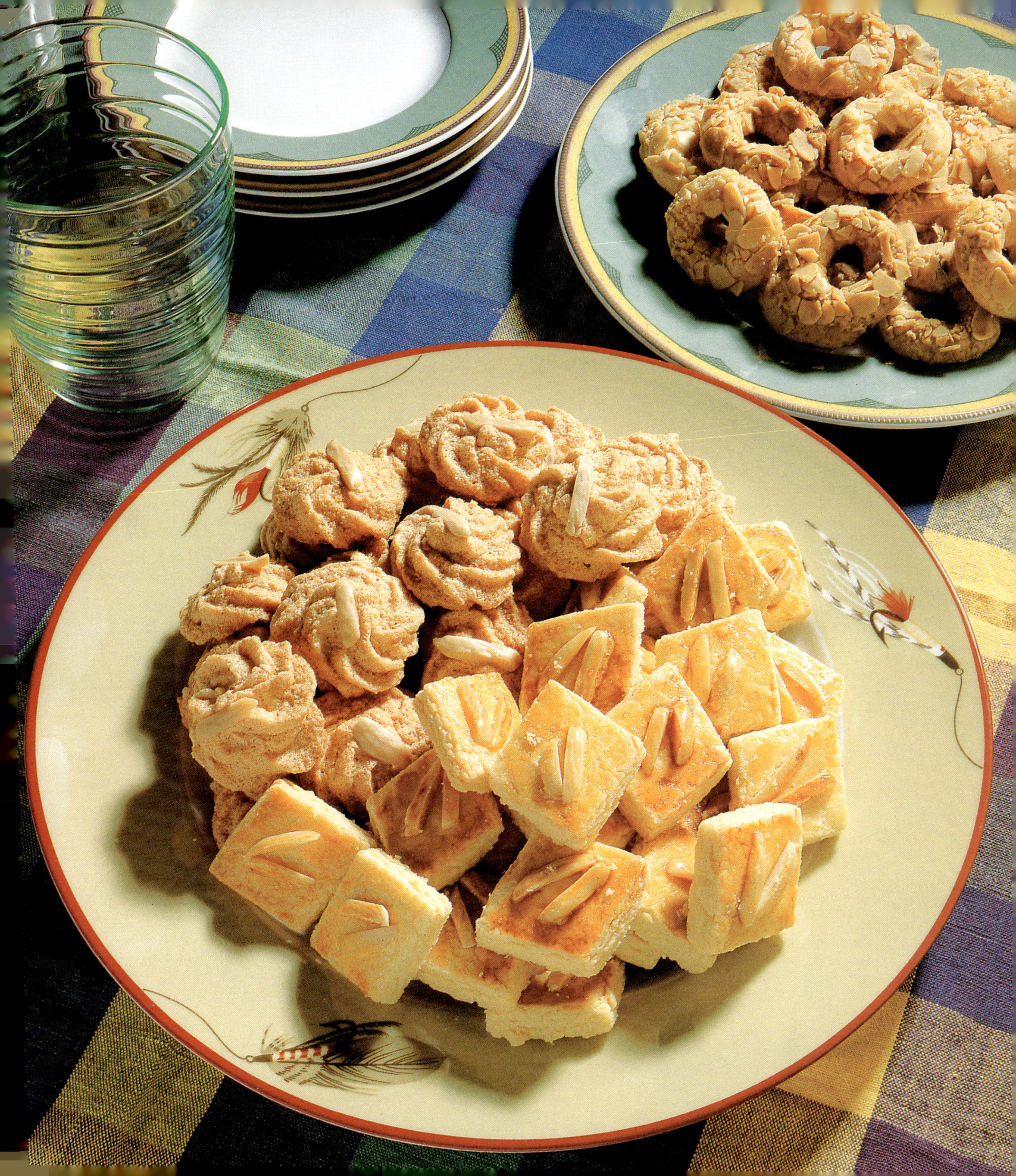

# Cream Cheese Gems

*Ingredients*

　1/2 cup butter
　113 grams cream cheese, at room temperature
　1 cup castor sugar
　1/2 teaspoon vanilla essence
　1 teaspoon grated lemon zest
　1 cup all-purpose flour
　30 whole almonds, blanched and skinned, to decorate

*Method*

1. With an electric mixer beat butter, cream cheese and sugar until smooth. Beat in vanilla essence and lemon zest. Gradually add flour, mixing thoroughly.

2. Drop the dough by the rounded teaspoonful onto an ungreased baking tray, spacing the cookies about 5 cm apart. Top with an almond. Bake at 175°C/350°F for about 12 minutes or until the edges are golden. Transfer to a wire rack and cool. Store in an airtight container.

# Savoury Cheese Fingers

*Ingredients*

　300 grams flour
　40 grams cornflour
　1/2 teaspoon pepper
　1/2 teaspoon mustard
　1/2 teaspoon chilli powder
　a pinch of salt
　200 grams butter
　30 grams vegetable shortening
　200 grams grated cheddar cheese
　2 egg yolks, mixed with 2 to 3 tablespoons milk

　almond slices to decorate
　1 egg, beaten, to glaze

*Method*

1. Place flour, cornflour, pepper, mustard, chilli and salt in a bowl. Cut in butter and shortening until the mixture resembles breadcrumbs.

2. Add cheese and egg yolk mixture. Mix well until a soft dough forms.

3. Roll out the dough to a thickness of 3 mm. Cut into rectangles 1.5 cm by 5 cm each.

4. Top each rectangle with almond slices and arrange on a greased baking tray.

5. Glaze with egg and bake for 8 to 12 minutes at 180°C/360°F.

# French Orange Biscuits

*Ingredients*

　375 grams butter
　500 grams castor sugar
　500 grams ground almonds
　500 grams orange and lemon peel, finely chopped
　125 grams all-purpose flour, sifted
　125 grams fresh milk

*Method*

1. Cream butter and sugar. Add almonds, citrus peel, flour and milk.

2. Drop in little heaps, the size of walnuts, on a lightly greased baking tray. Flatten slightly with a wet fork. Bake at 170°C/340°F for 15 minutes.

Chef's Note: As these cookies are very fragile, they should not be removed from the baking tray until they are almost cold.

# Chocolate Oatmeal Cookies

*Ingredients*

　1 1/4 cups all-purpose flour
　1/2 teaspoon baking powder
　1/2 teaspoon baking soda
　1/2 teaspoon ground cinnamon
　1/4 teaspoon salt
　3/4 cup unsalted butter, at room temperature
　3/4 cup packed brown sugar
　1 1/2 teaspoons vanilla essence
　1 egg
　2 tablespoons fresh milk
　1 cup rolled oats
　1/2 cup chocolate chips
　1/2 cup raisins

*Method*

1. Sift together flour, baking powder, baking soda, cinnamon and salt.

2. In another bowl beat butter, sugar and vanilla essence until creamy. Add egg and milk.

3. Gradually beat in sifted ingredients. Stir in oats, chocolate chips and raisins.

4. Drop by the rounded tablespoonful onto ungreased baking trays. Bake at 180°C/360°F for about 12 minutes until the edges are crisp but the centres are still soft. Cool on a wire rack.

*Opposite: Cream Cheese Gems (left) and Savoury Cheese Fingers (right).*

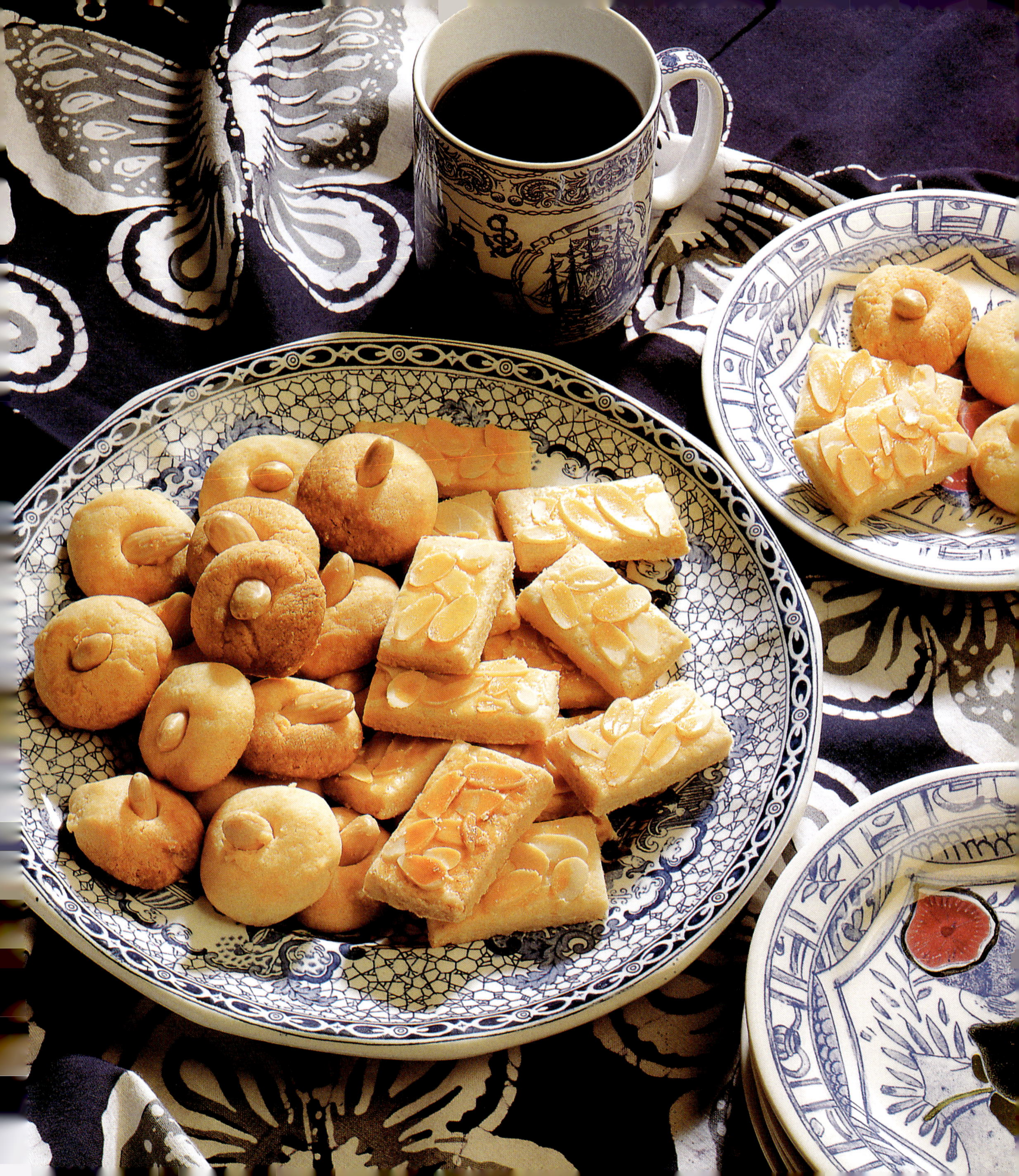

# Caramel Apricot Swirl Cookies

*Dough*

- ½ cup butter, softened
- ¼ cup vegetable shortening
- 1 cup brown sugar, firmly packed
- ½ teaspoon vanilla essence
- 1 egg yolk
- 1⅓ cup all-purpose flour
- ½ teaspoon baking powder
- ¼ teaspoon salt

*Method*

1. Beat butter and shortening together in an electric mixer. Add brown sugar and beat until fluffy. Add vanilla essence followed by egg yolk.
2. In a separate bowl sift together flour, baking powder and salt. Gradually add the sifted ingredients to the butter mixture, beating until just blended. Wrap the dough in cling wrap and refrigerate for about two hours until firm.

*Ginger Apricot Filling*

- 1 cup dried apricot, coarsely chopped
- ½ cup water
- ⅓ cup castor sugar
- 1 tablespoon lemon juice
- ½ teaspoon ground ginger

*Method*

1. Combine all ingredients in a saucepan. Simmer for about 15 minutes. Process in a food processor until coarsely pureed. Cool to room temperature.
2. Place the dough between two sheets of cling wrap and roll into a 30 cm by 15 cm rectangle. Evenly spread the filling over the dough to within 1 cm of the edges.
3. Starting with the shorter edge, roll the pastry up like a jelly roll. Remove the cling wrap as you roll. Cut the roll in half to make two long rolls. Stretch the rolls until they are about 20 cm long each. Wrap the rolls individually in cling wrap and refrigerate for at least 3 hours or overnight.
4. Preheat the oven to 175°C/350°F. Remove one roll of cookie dough at a time and cut into 6-mm thick slices. Arrange the slices about 2.5 cm apart on a greased baking tray. Bake for 8 to 10 minutes until golden brown and firm to the touch. Leave to cool on the baking tray for two minutes before transferring to a wire rack.

# Cheesy Coin Cookies

*Ingredients*

- 1 cup all-purpose flour
- ¼ teaspoon paprika
- ¼ teaspoon dry mustard
- ¼ teaspoon salt
- ½ cup butter or margarine
- 1 egg yolk
- 1 cup grated cheddar cheese
- a few tablespoons milk for moistening

*Method*

1. Sift together flour, paprika, mustard and salt. Cut in butter or margarine until the mixture resembles coarse crumbs.
2. Add egg yolk and cheese. Mix quickly to form a dough. If the dough is too dry, add a few tablespoons of milk. Wrap the dough in cling wrap and refrigerate for a few hours until firm.
3. Preheat the oven to 170°C/340°F. On a lightly floured board or pastry cloth, roll out the dough to a thickness of about 3 mm. Using a round cookie cutter, cut out coin-sized cookies. Space them out slightly on an ungreased baking tray. Pierce several times with a fork.
4. Bake for about 10 to 12 minutes until golden brown. Transfer to a wire rack and cool slightly. Serve warm or at room temperature.

# Orange Shortbread Biscuits

*Ingredients*

- 2 cups unsalted butter, softened
- 1½ cups brown sugar, firmly packed
- 4 cups all-purpose flour
- a pinch of salt
- grated zest of 2 oranges
- 2 large eggs, beaten with 2 tablespoons water, to glaze

*Method*

1. Cream butter and brown sugar. Gradually add flour and salt to make a fairly stiff dough. Stir in orange zest. Wrap in cling wrap and refrigerate for at least 2 hours.
2. Turn the dough out onto a lightly floured board and roll to a thickness of 1 cm. Cut out with assorted 2.5-cm to 4-cm cookie cutters and place on a greased baking tray.
3. Beat together eggs and water and glaze cookies. Bake at 180°C/360°F for 15 to 20 minutes until golden brown.

Chef's Note: Shortbread can be formed into different shapes such as wedges and even seashells. To make wedges, shortbread dough is spread thickly in pie pans and scored into wedges before baking.

*Opposite: Caramel Apricot Swirl Cookies (above) and Cheesy Coin Cookies (below).*

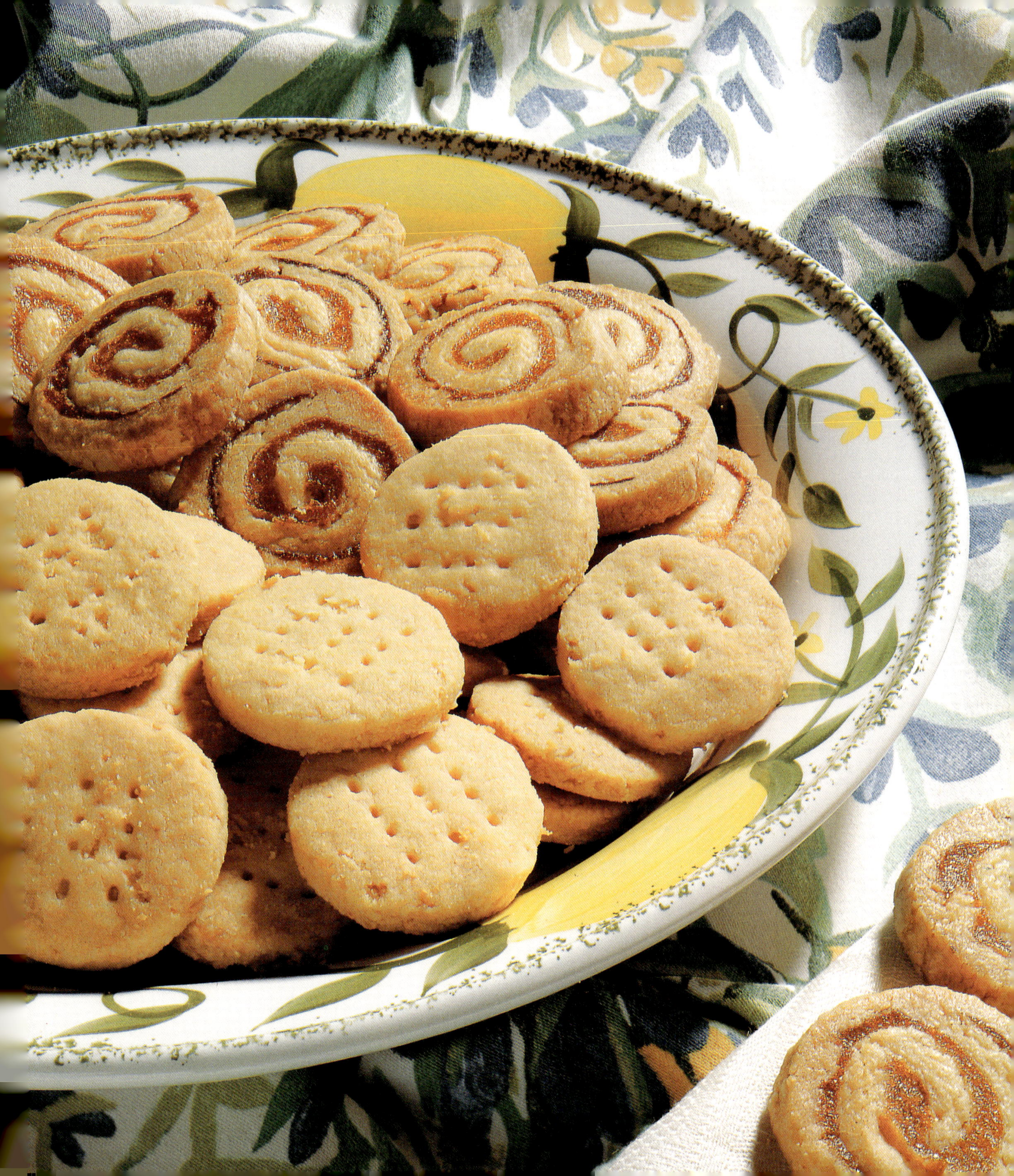

## Apricot Coconut Macaroons

### Ingredients

- 1/2 cup packed dried apricots, quartered
- 1/2 cup water + 1 tablespoon castor sugar
- 3/4 cup castor sugar
- 1/2 cup + 2 cups unsweetened flaked coconut
- 3 egg whites
- 1 tablespoon custard powder
- 2 tablespoons butter, melted
- 1 teaspoon vanilla essence

### Method

1. In a saucepan combine apricots, water and 1 tablespoon sugar, and poach on low heat until the liquid is reduced to 1 tablespoon. Cool and place in a food processor.

2. Add 3/4 cup sugar, 1/2 cup coconut, egg whites, custard powder, butter and vanilla essence to the liquid in the food processor and puree. Transfer to a cake mixer and add the remaining coconut. Beat at medium speed until well mixed.

3. Form the dough into balls and bake at 175°C/350°F for 12 to 20 minutes.

Chef's Note: If you are using canned apricots, marinate them in a little Grand Marnier or apricot brandy before use.

## Cornflake Coffee Kisses

### Ingredients

- 125 grams butter
- 20 grams vegetable shortening
- 70 grams powdered sugar
- 1 egg yolk
- 1 tablespoon peanut butter
- 1/2 teaspoon coffee essence
- 180 grams all-purpose flour
- 50 grams cornflour
- 30 grams cashew nuts, ground
- 1/2 teaspoon baking powder
- 1 egg white, beaten, to glaze
- almond flakes and cornflakes, coarsely crushed, to decorate

### Method

1. Beat butter, shortening, powdered sugar and egg yolk for 4 minutes. Add peanut butter and coffee essence and beat for another two minutes.

2. Mix together both types of flour, cashews and baking powder. Fold into the butter mixture. Mix well. Leave the dough to chill in the refrigerator for 10 minutes.

3. Roll out the dough and cut lengthwise into rectangles with a serrated knife. Glaze with egg white and sprinkle with crushed almonds and cornflakes.

4. Bake for 13 minutes at 180°C/360°F.

## Swiss Chocolate Rosettes

### Ingredients

- 200 grams powdered sugar
- 500 grams butter
- 150 grams eggs
- 1 teaspoon orange essence
- 700 grams all-purpose flour
- 45 grams cocoa powder

powdered sugar for dusting

### Method

1. Beat together sugar, butter, eggs and orange essence until smooth.

2. Sift together flour and cocoa. Fold into the batter.

3. Using a No.7 star tube, pipe out rosettes onto a lightly greased baking tray. Bake at 205°C/400°F for 15 minutes. Dust with powdered sugar.

## Date and Pecan Pumpkin Squares

### Ingredients

- 2 1/2 cups all-purpose flour
- 1 1/2 teaspoons double-acting baking powder
- 3/4 teaspoon ground cinnamon
- 1/2 teaspoon ground nutmeg
- 1/2 teaspoon ground cloves
- 1/2 teaspoon salt
- 1 cup unsalted butter, softened
- 2 cups brown sugar, packed
- 2 large eggs
- 1 cup cooked pumpkin
- 1 teaspoon vanilla essence
- 1/4 cup water
- 2 cups pitted dates cut into thirds and tossed with 1/4 cup flour until well coated
- 1 1/2 cups pecans, chopped

caramel sauce or vanilla ice-cream to serve

### Method

1. Sift together flour, baking powder, cinnamon, nutmeg, cloves and salt.

2. In another bowl cream butter and sugar and add eggs one at a time, beating well with each addition.

3. Add pumpkin, vanilla essence and water. Gradually add the sifted ingredients to the pumpkin mixture, beating slowly. Stir in dates and pecans.

4. Pour the batter into a greased, 33 cm by 22 cm baking pan and bake at 175°C/350°F for 1 hour until a skewer inserted in the centre of the pastry comes away cleanly. Cool and cut into squares. Serve with caramel sauce or vanilla ice-cream.

Chef's Note: If you prefer you can use walnuts or hazelnuts in place of pecans.

*Opposite: Swiss Chocolate Rosettes (above) and Cornflake Coffee Kisses (below).*

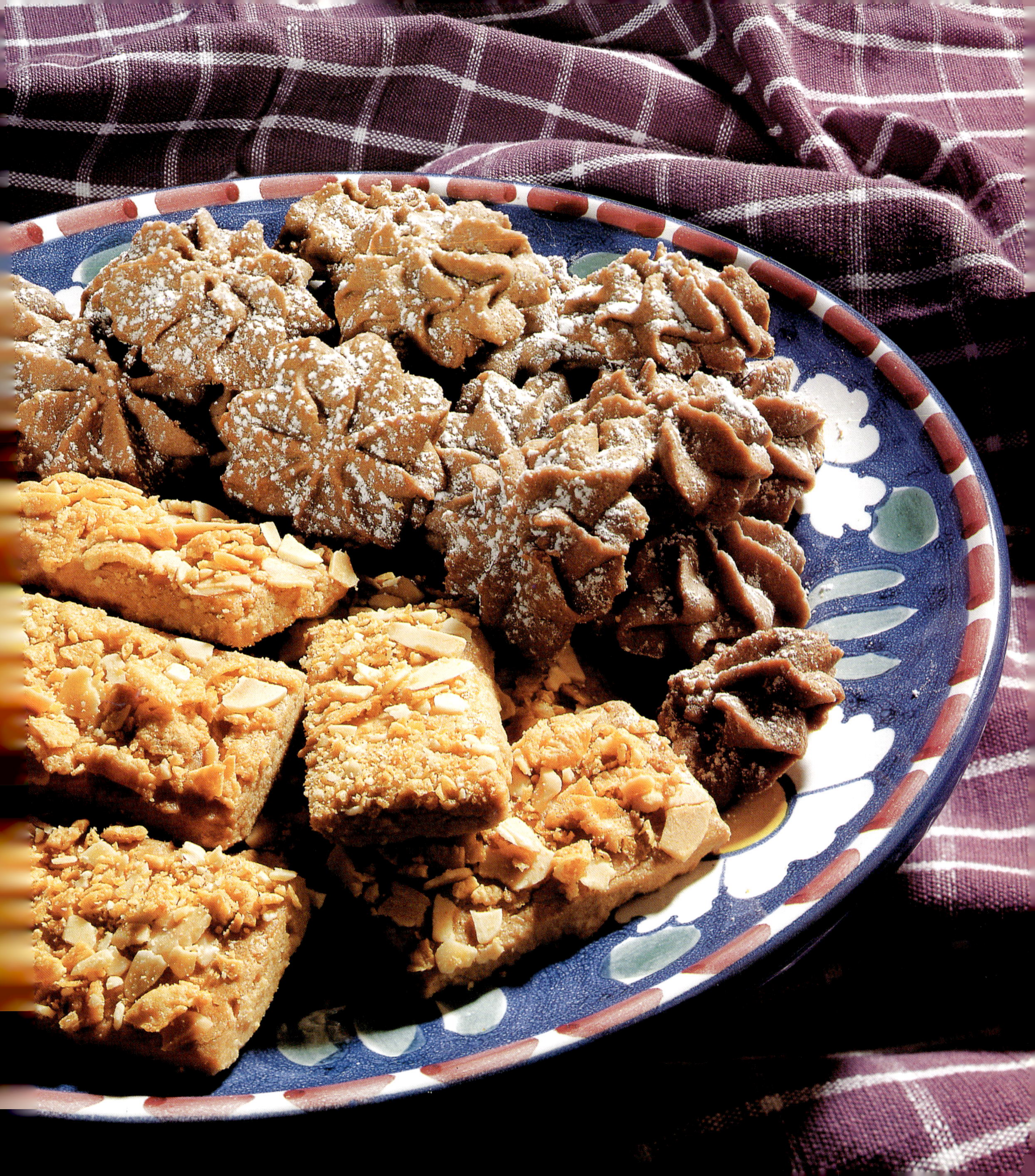

## Cornflake Crunchies

*Ingredients*

- 105 grams butter or margarine
- 1/2 cup castor sugar
- 1 egg yolk
- 3/4 cup self-raising flour, sifted
- 100 grams cornflakes, lightly crushed
- 1/4 cup red glace cherries, chopped
- 1/4 cup toasted almonds, skinned and chopped

*Method*

1. Cream butter and sugar until light and creamy. Add egg yolk and mix well. Fold in flour, cornflakes, cherries and almonds, and mix well.

2. Shape the dough into small balls and lightly flatten the tops with a wet fork. Place on a lightly greased baking tray. Bake in a preheated 170°C/340°F oven until lightly browned.

## Walnut Apricot Cookies

*Ingredients*

- 225 grams unsalted butter
- 3/4 cup powdered sugar
- 1 1/2 cups self-raising flour
- 1 1/4 cups cornflakes, finely crushed
- 1/2 cup dried apricots, finely chopped
- grated zest of 1/2 orange
- 1 egg, beaten, to glaze
- 3/4 cup walnuts, chopped
- walnuts, halved, to decorate

*Method*

1. Beat butter and sugar until well mixed. In a separate bowl mix together flour, cornflakes, apricots and orange zest. Fold into the butter mixture.

2. Shape the dough into a 2.5 cm-wide log. Wrap in parchment paper and chill in the refrigerator overnight. Slice into circles, brush with egg and sprinkle with chopped walnuts. Top each cookie with a walnut half.

3. Bake in a preheated 175°C/350°F oven for 10 to 15 minutes or until golden.

## Gingerbread Cookies

*Ingredients*

- 1 cup dark molasses
- 1/2 cup light brown sugar
- 1/2 cup castor sugar
- 4 teaspoons ground ginger
- 4 teaspoons ground cinnamon
- 3/4 tablespoon baking soda
- 1 cup unsalted butter
- 2 large eggs
- 6 cups all-purpose flour

*Method*

1. Heat molasses, both types of sugar, ginger and cinnamon in a double boiler at medium heat. When the sugar melts, add baking soda and stir. Remove from heat when bubbling.

2. Place butter in a large bowl and add the hot molasses. Stir well. Cool slightly before adding eggs. Transfer to an electric mixer and gradually add flour one cup at a time.

3. Roll out the dough to a thickness of 6 mm on a well-floured board and cut into desired shapes. Place the cookies on a baking tray and bake at 180°C/360°F for 15 to 20 minutes until firm. Cool on a wire rack. Store in an airtight container.

## Husarenkrapfert

*Ingredients*

- 210 grams all-purpose flour
- 150 grams butter
- 70 grams castor sugar
- 1 teaspoon vanilla essence
- a pinch of salt
- juice of 1/4 lemon
- grated zest of 1 lemon
- 2 egg yolks
- 50 grams almonds or hazelnuts, ground
- 1 egg yolk, mixed with 1 tablespoon honey, to glaze
- red currant jam

*Method*

1. Mix flour and butter by hand. Add sugar, vanilla essence, salt, lemon juice, lemon zest, egg yolks and almonds and quickly knead into a dough. Chill in the refrigerator for one hour. Form into balls and place on a parchment-lined baking tray. Use a thimble or the tip of a chopstick to make a depression in each cookie and glaze with egg yolk and honey.

2. Bake at 170°C/340°F for 15 to 20 minutes. Fill the cooled cookies with red currant jam.

## Oatmeal Biscuits

*Ingredients*

- 250 grams all-purpose flour
- 125 grams butter
- 265 grams oatmeal
- 5 grams bicarbonate of soda
- 62 grams fresh milk
- 62 grams castor sugar
- 200 grams golden syrup

*Method*

1. Sift flour and cut in butter until the mixture resembles coarse breadcrumbs. Mix in oatmeal.

2. Dissolve bicarbonate of soda in the milk. Add oatmeal mixture. Add sugar and syrup to form a smooth dough. Shape into balls, flatten the tops and arrange on a lightly greased tray. Bake at 170°C/340°F for 15 minutes.

*Opposite: Walnut Apricot Cookies (above) and Cornflake Crunchies (below).*

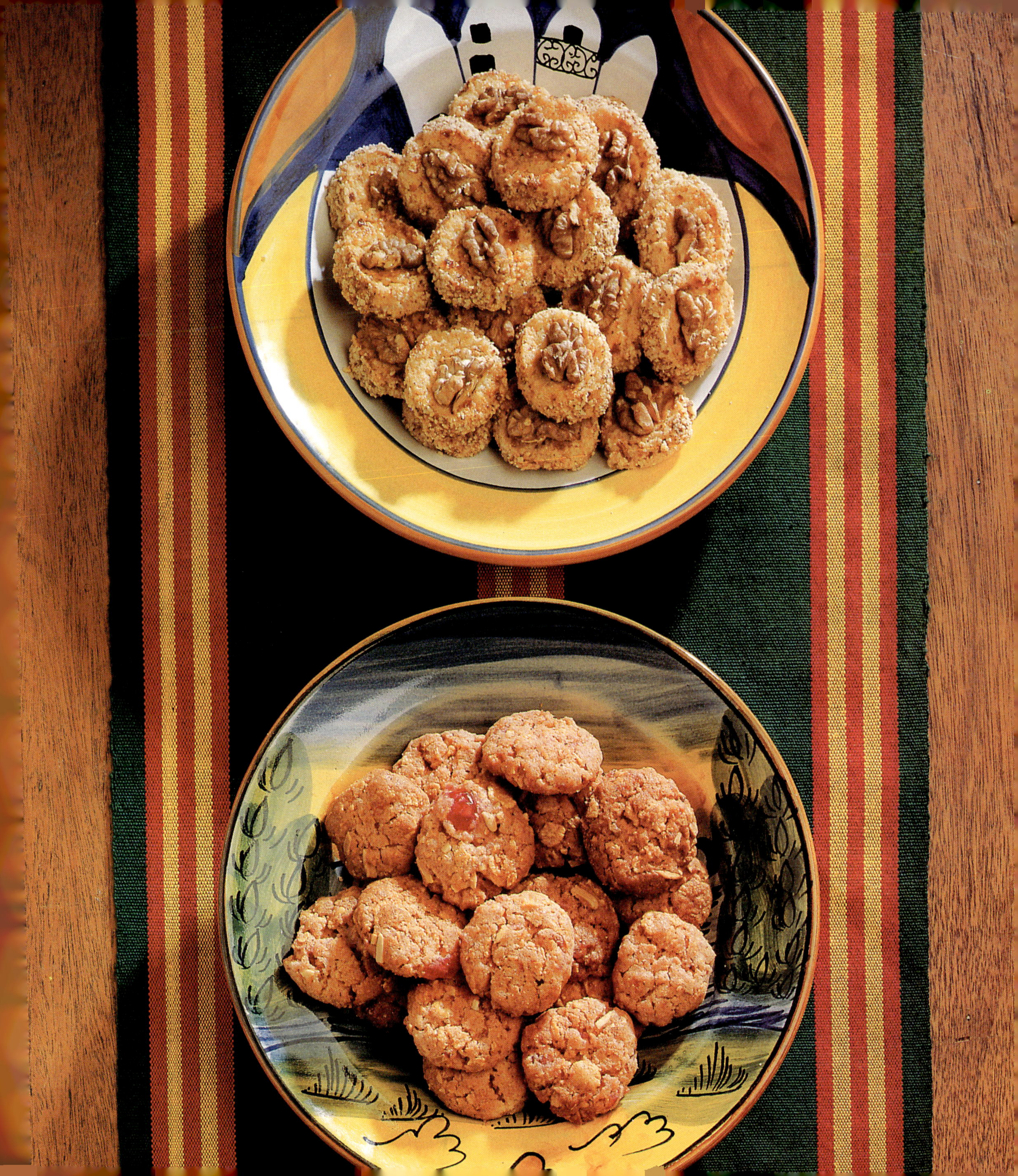

## Fruitcake Cookies

*Ingredients*

- 115 grams + 4 tablespoons unsalted butter, softened
- 1/3 cup dark brown sugar, packed
- 1/2 teaspoon ground cinnamon
- 1/2 teaspoon ground ginger
- 1/4 teaspoon nutmeg
- a pinch of salt
- 1 cup + 2 tablespoons all-purpose flour
- 1/2 cup toasted almonds, chopped
- 3/4 cup dates, chopped
- 1/4 cup raisins
- 1/2 cup toasted hazelnuts, chopped coarsely
- 2 tablespoons honey
- 1 egg, lightly beaten

*Method*

1. Cream 115 grams butter with brown sugar, cinnamon, ginger, nutmeg and salt until light and fluffy.
2. Reduce the speed to low and beat in 1 cup flour. Wrap the dough tightly in cling wrap and refrigerate for about 15 minutes until chilled.
3. Meanwhile mix together almonds, dates, raisins and hazelnuts. Set aside.
4. In a separate bowl cream the remaining 4 tablespoons butter with the honey until light and fluffy. Gradually beat in the egg. Reduce the speed to low and beat in the remaining 2 tablespoons flour until just combined. Fold in dried fruit and nuts until completely coated. Set aside.
5. Lightly grease a heavy baking tray. On a lightly floured surface roll out the chilled dough to a thickness of 6 mm. Using a 5-cm fluted cookie cutter, cut out cookies as close together as possible. Place on a baking tray. Heap one tablespoon fruit mixture on each cookie. Bake for 10 minutes at 175°C/350°F until the tops begin to brown.

Chef's Note: These cookies are best eaten a few days after they are baked. They keep for up to a month in an airtight container.

## Dried Shrimp Cornflake Cookies

*Ingredients*

- 250 grams all-purpose flour, sifted
- 1 cup cornflakes, finely ground
- 50 grams dried shrimp, finely ground
- 1/2 teaspoon baking powder
- 200 grams butter or margarine
- 80 grams powdered sugar, sifted
- 1 egg, beaten, to glaze
- dried shrimp to decorate

*Method*

1. Mix together flour, cornflakes, ground shrimp and baking powder.
2. With an electric mixer beat butter and sugar until soft. Add flour mixture to form a dough. Roll out to a thickness of 1 cm and cut with a cookie cutter into desired shapes.
3. Place the cookies on a greased baking tray. Glaze with egg and decorate with dried shrimp. Bake in a preheated 170°C/340°F oven until golden.

## Ginger and Molasses Snaps

*Ingredients*

- 3/4 cup vegetable shortening
- 1 cup castor sugar
- 1 egg
- 1/4 cup molasses
- 2 cups all-purpose flour
- 2 teaspoon baking soda
- 1/2 teaspoon salt
- 1 tablespoon ground ginger
- 1 teaspoon ground cinnamon

castor sugar to decorate

*Method*

1. With an electric mixer beat together vegetable shortening and sugar. Add egg and beat until fluffy. Add molasses.
2. Sift together flour, baking soda, salt, ginger and cinnamon. Fold into the shortening until a dough forms.
3. Shape the dough into balls and roll in castor sugar. Place the cookies on a greased baking tray 5 cm apart and bake at 175°C/350°F for 10 to 12 minutes until the tops crack.

## Orange Shortbread Cookies

*Ingredients*

- 300 grams unsalted butter
- 160 grams castor sugar, divided into two equal parts
- 300 grams all-purpose flour
- 100 grams cornflour
- 1 teaspoon grated orange zest
- 1 teaspoon orange essence

powdered sugar to decorate

*Method*

1. Cream butter and half of the sugar.
2. Sift together flour and cornflour. Add to the butter with the remaining sugar, orange zest and orange essence. Chill in the refrigerator for an hour until the dough is firm enough to roll out.
3. Roll out on a floured surface to a thickness of 5 cm and cut into rectangles. Bake for 15 minutes at 175°C/350°F until golden. Cool before rolling in powdered sugar.

*Opposite: Fruitcake Cookies (left) and Dried Shrimp Cornflake Cookies (right).*

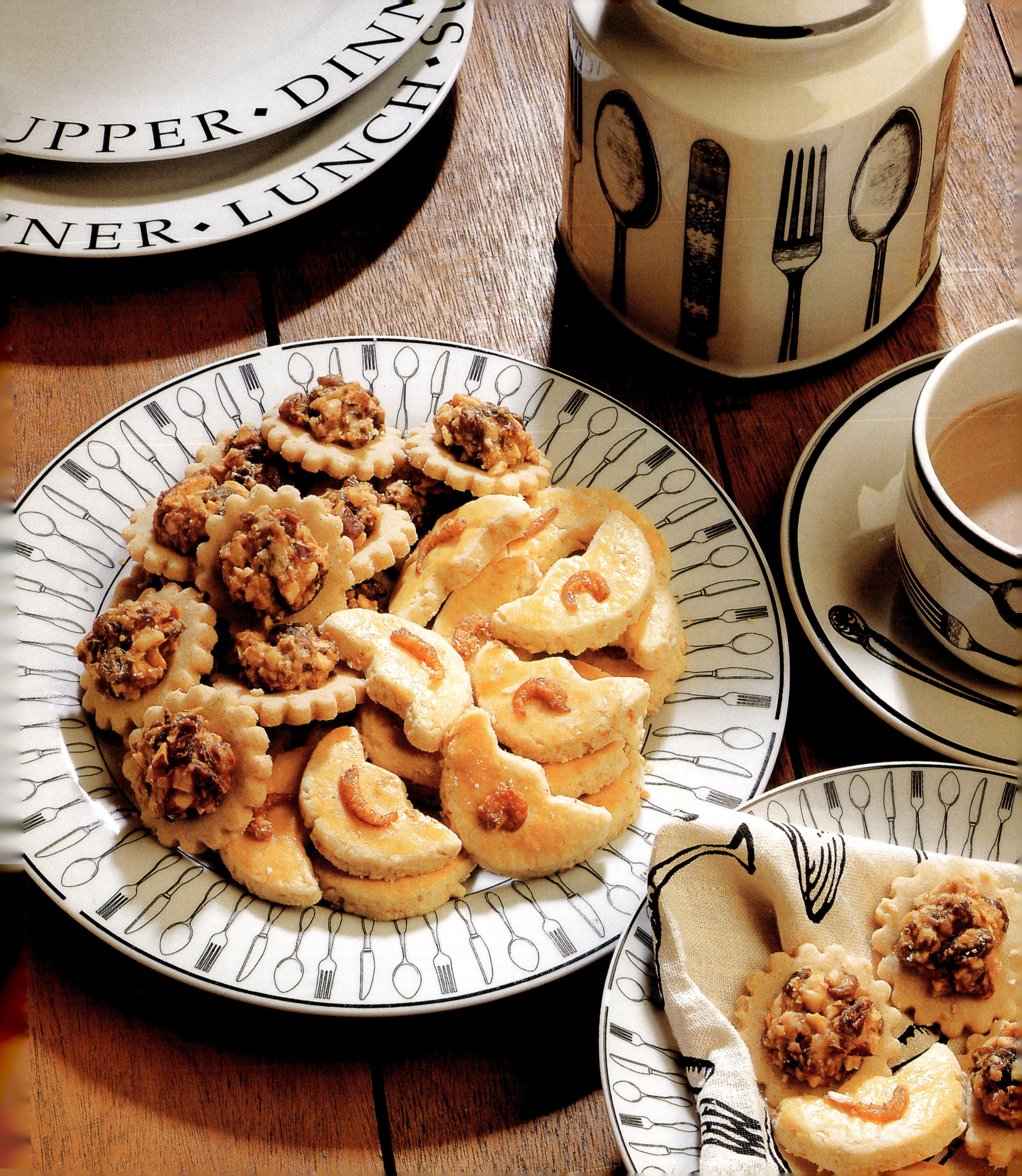
UPPER • DINN
NER • LUNCH • SU

## Pecan Cookies

*Ingredients*

60 grams unsalted butter
1/4 cup powdered sugar
1 teaspoon vanilla essence
125 grams toasted pecans, coarsely ground
1/2 cup all-purpose flour

whole pecans to decorate
powdered sugar for dusting

*Method*

1. Beat butter with sugar until light and creamy. Add vanilla essence, pecans and flour. Mix into a dough.
2. Roll each cookie into a marble and place on a greased baking tray. Top with a pecan and flatten slightly. Bake for 8 to 10 minutes at 175°C/350°F. When cool, dust with powdered sugar.

## Mom's Ginger Snaps

*Ingredients*

2 teaspoons baking soda
2 cups all-purpose flour
1 teaspoon ground ginger
1 teaspoon ground cloves
1 teaspoon ground cinnamon
3/4 cup vegetable shortening
1 cup castor sugar
4 tablespoons molasses
1 egg

castor sugar to decorate

*Method*

1. Sift all dry ingredients together.
2. Beat shortening and sugar. Add molasses, egg and the sifted ingredients. Mix until dough forms.
3. Roll the dough into 4-cm balls without flattening them. Roll the balls in castor sugar and bake at 175°C/350°F for 8 to 10 minutes.

## Butter Cookies

*Ingredients*

455 grams butter
340 grams powdered sugar, sifted
6 eggs
570 grams cake flour, sifted
a dash of vanilla essence
grated zest of 1 lemon

*Method*

1. Cream together butter and sugar. Add eggs one at a time until well-blended.
2. Fold flour, vanilla essence and lemon zest into the butter mixture.
3. Fit a no.7 star nozzle on a piping bag, fill the bag with pastry and pipe small shells onto a greased baking tray. Chill for 5 minutes to prevent the cookies from expanding too much during baking. Bake at 175°C/350°F until golden. Cool.

Chef's Note: As an option fill the cooled cookies with apricot jam to make sandwiches. Decorate by dipping the tip of each cookie in melted chocolate.

## Lemon Custard Cookies

*Ingredients*

200 grams soft margarine
100 grams powdered sugar
1/2 teaspoon vanilla essence
4 tablespoons lemon juice
grated zest of 1 lemon
2 egg yolks
300 grams all-purpose flour
50 grams custard powder
1/2 teaspoon baking powder

glace cherries or whole almonds to decorate

*Method*

1. Cream margarine with powdered sugar until smooth. Add vanilla essence, lemon juice, lemon zest and egg yolks and beat well.
2. Sift together flour, custard powder and baking powder and add to the batter to form a soft pastry.
3. Fill a piping bag, fitted with a 1-cm star nozzle, with pastry. Pipe about 20 cookies onto a greased baking tray. Decorate each cookie with a cherry. Bake at 180°C/360°F for 12 to 15 minutes until golden.

## Orange Marmalade Biscuits

*Ingredients*

2 eggs
1 1/2 cups castor sugar
1 teaspoon salt
1/3 cup vegetable shortening, melted and cooled
3/4 cup orange marmalade
grated zest of 1 lemon
3 tablespoons lemon juice
3 cups all-purpose flour
2 teaspoons baking powder
1 cup walnuts, chopped

*Method*

1. Whisk eggs and sugar until fluffy. Add salt, shortening, orange marmalade, lemon zest and lemon juice, whisking again until well mixed.
2. Sift together flour and baking powder. Fold into the batter. Add walnuts.
3. Drop the cookies by the tablespoonful on a greased baking tray about 2.5 cm apart. Bake for 12 minutes at 170°C/340°F until the edges are golden.

*Opposite: Pecan Cookies (above left), Mom's Ginger Snaps (above right) and Butter Cookies (below).*

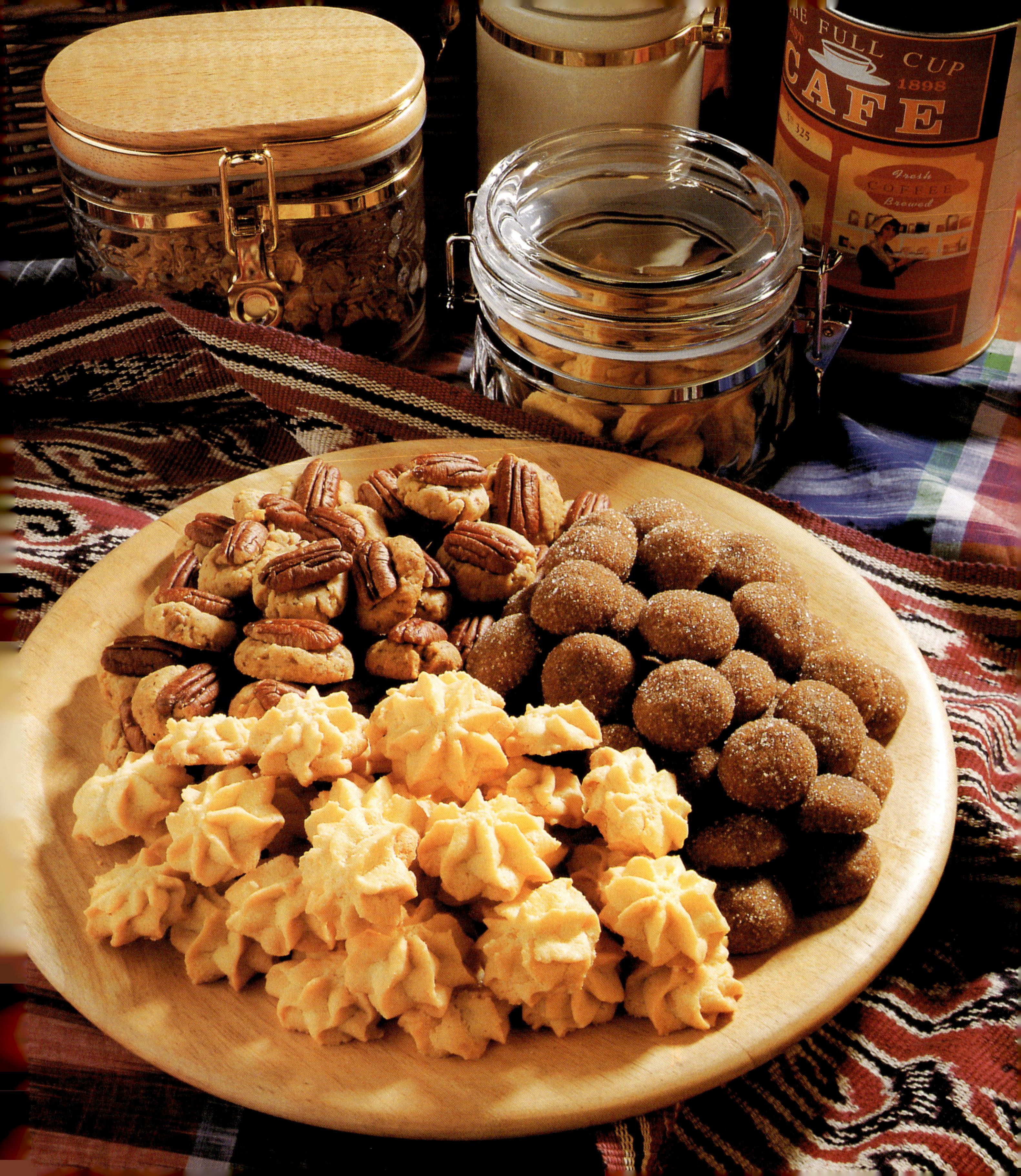
FULL CUP
CAFE
1898
Fresh
COFFEE
Brewed

## Hazelnut Shortbread

*Ingredients*

    225 grams unsalted butter
    1 cup powdered sugar
    1 teaspoon vanilla essence
    a pinch of salt
    1/4 cup custard powder
    2 cups all-purpose flour
    1 cup hazelnuts, finely ground
    2 tablespoons fresh milk

    1 cup castor sugar to decorate

*Method*

1. Cream butter and sugar until fluffy. Add vanilla essence.
2. Sift together salt, custard powder and flour. Stir in ground hazelnuts. Alternately add flour mixture and milk to the butter mixture. Form into a dough and shape into three logs. Wrap individually in parchment paper. Chill for a few hours.
3. When the dough is firm, cut each roll into 1 cm-thick slices. Arrange on a greased baking tray and bake for 15 minutes at 180°C/360°F until golden. Cool before rolling in castor sugar.

## Peanut Butter Cookies

*Ingredients*

    1/2 cup butter, softened
    1/2 cup vegetable shortening
    1/2 cup peanut butter
    1 cup castor sugar
    1 cup brown sugar
    1/4 teaspoon salt
    2 eggs
    1 teaspoon baking soda
    1/4 cup warm water
    3 cups all-purpose flour, sifted

    1 cup whole peanuts, toasted, to decorate
    a little egg, beaten, to glaze

*Method*

1. Cream butter, shortening and peanut butter until smooth. Add castor sugar, brown sugar and salt. Beat in eggs one at a time.
2. In a small bowl dissolve baking soda in warm water and add to the butter mixture. Stir in flour and mix until smooth.
3. Wrap in cling wrap and refrigerate until firm. Roll by hand into 2.5-cm balls. Arrange on an ungreased cookie tray and gently press each ball flat. Top with a peanut and glaze with beaten egg. Bake the cookies for 15 minutes at 180°C/360°F until golden brown.

## Pistachio Cantuccini Biscotti

*Ingredients*

    1 3/4 cups all-purpose flour
    1 cup + 1 teaspoon castor sugar
    1/2 teaspoon baking powder
    1/4 teaspoon salt
    4 tablespoons cold unsalted butter, cut into small pieces
    1 teaspoon vanilla essence
    1/2 cup glace cherries, diced
    1 1/2 cups shelled pistachios, preferably unroasted
    2 eggs, lightly beaten

*Method*

1. Preheat the oven to 175°C/350°F. Lightly butter a large, heavy baking tray.
2. In a food processor combine the flour with 1 cup of the sugar, baking powder and salt. Process for a few seconds to blend.
3. Add butter, vanilla essence and cherries. Pulse until the mixture resembles coarse breadcrumbs. Add pistachios and eggs, pulsing 10 times to blend. Scrape down the dough and pulse another five times until the dough is evenly moistened.
4. On a lightly floured work surface divide the dough into four equal parts. Roll each into a 20-cm log. Flatten each log to a width of about 5 cm. Sprinkle with the remaining 1 teaspoon sugar. Bake for 25 minutes or until golden brown. Use a metal spatula to transfer the logs to a wire rack and let the dough rest for 15 to 20 minutes.
5. Transfer to a work surface. Use a sharp knife to quickly slice each log diagonally into 1 cm thick fingers. Place the cantuccini back on the baking tray, cut sides down, and bake for about seven minutes until golden brown. Transfer to a wire rack. Cool before storing.

## Dutch Kletskoppan

*Ingredients*

    180 grams butter or margarine
    200 grams castor sugar
    30 grams water
    100 grams all-purpose flour
    a little ground cinnamon

    almond halves, toasted, to decorate

*Method*

1. Mix all the ingredients, except almonds, to make a soft paste. Fill a piping bag with the paste and pipe small circles onto a greased baking tray, setting them slightly apart.
2. Decorate with almond halves. Bake at 170°C/340°F for 15 minutes. Loosen the cookies from the baking tray before they are cold.

*Opposite: Hazelnut Shortbread (left) and Peanut Butter Cookies (right).*

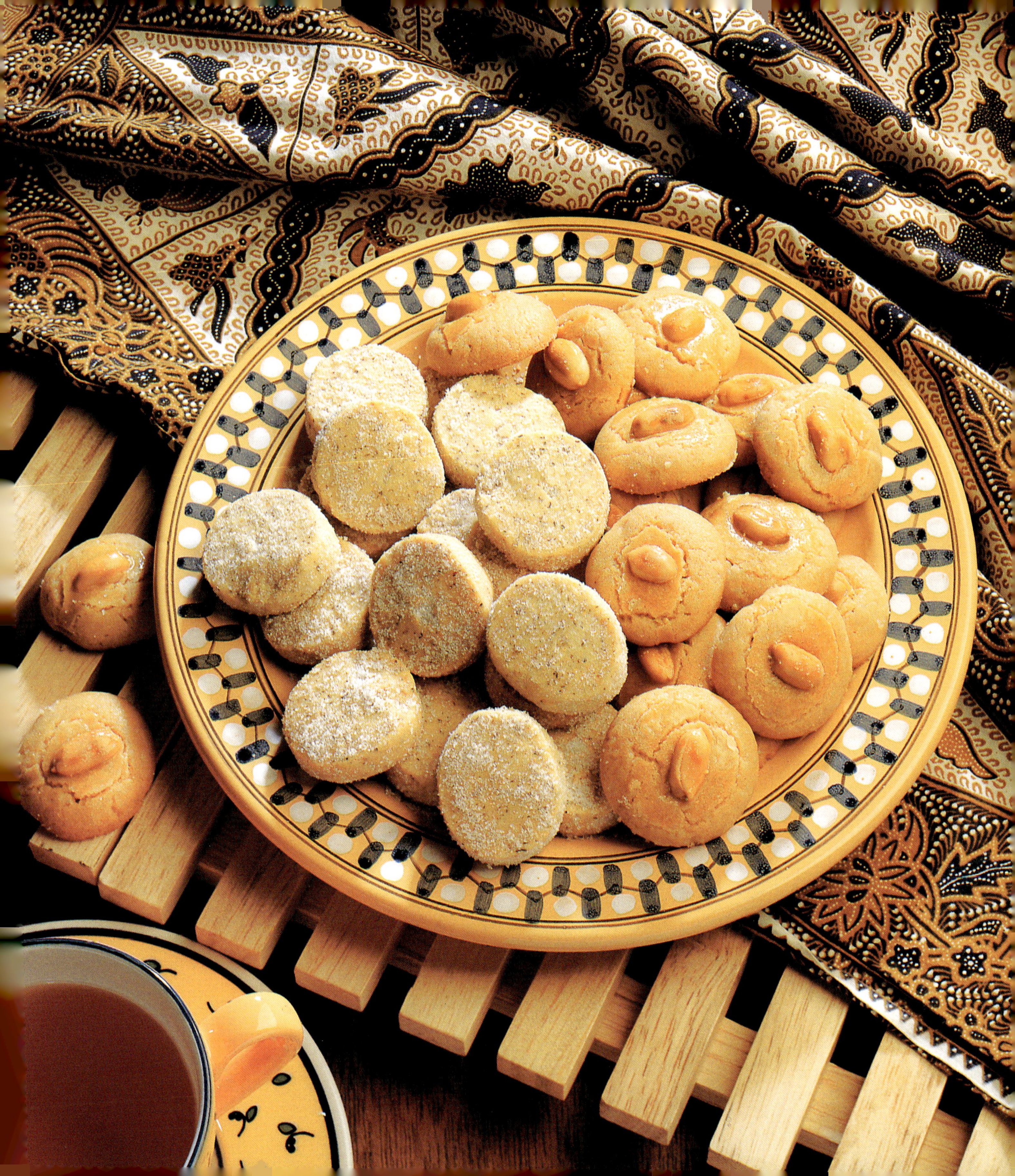

## Lemon Raspberry Cookies

*Ingredients*

210 grams all-purpose flour
150 grams unsalted butter
70 grams castor sugar
a pinch of salt
grated zest of 1½ lemons
2 tablespoons lemon juice
2 egg yolks
50 grams almonds, ground

1 teaspoon honey, mixed with ½ cup raspberry jam
a little egg yolk, beaten, to glaze

*Method*

1. In a food processor combine flour, butter, sugar, salt, lemon zest, lemon juice, egg yolks and almond to form a dough. Chill for a few hours.
2. Roll out the dough into small marbles. Flatten each ball slightly with a wet fork and make a small depression in the centre.
3. Mix together the honey and raspberry jam. Fill the cookies with jam. Brush the sides with beaten egg yolk and bake for 8 to 10 minutes at 170°C/340°F until golden.

## Mexican Wedding Cookies

*Ingredients*

2½ cups all-purpose flour
¼ teaspoon salt
1 cup chopped pecans
1 cup butter
½ cup powdered sugar
2 teaspoons vanilla essence

½ cup powdered sugar
½ teaspoon ground cinnamon

*Method*

1. Mix together flour, salt and pecans.
2. In another bowl cream butter and sugar until fluffy. Add vanilla essence.
3. Slowly add the flour mixture to the butter mixture until a dough forms. Shape the dough into marbles. Place on a greased baking tray and bake at 175°C/350°F for 15 minutes until golden. Remove and place on a wire rack. Dust with powdered sugar, followed by ground cinnamon. Place in paper cups to serve.

Chef's Note: You may use any other nuts in place of pecans.

## Sweet Dream Cookies

*Ingredients*

8 tablespoons salted butter, melted
1 cup castor sugar
1 whole egg
2 egg yolks
2 cups all-purpose flour
½ teaspoon baking soda
a pinch of salt

castor sugar to decorate

*Method*

1. Beat butter and sugar until creamy. Add egg and egg yolks, beating well.
2. In a separate bowl mix together flour, baking soda and salt. Gradually add enough to the butter mixture to make a dough that holds together and can be rolled. Form the dough into two balls, wrap in foil and refrigerate for several hours.
3. When chilled, roll out thinly on a floured board. Cut into shapes with cookie cutters and sprinkle with castor sugar. Place on a greased baking tray and bake for 10 minutes at 180°C/360°F until the cookies are golden.

Chef's Note: For an attractive presentation, colour the sugar with food colouring before topping the cookies.

## Vienna Walnut Crescent

*Pastry Crust*

½ cup unsalted butter
85 grams cream cheese
1 cup all-purpose flour, sifted

*Method*

Cream butter and cheese until fluffy. Add flour and knead until smooth. Wrap and refrigerate the dough for at least 3 hours.

*Filling*

¼ cup apricot jam
1 egg, beaten with 2 tablespoons fresh milk, to glaze

¼ cup walnuts, finely chopped, to decorate
powdered sugar for dusting

*Method*

1. Roll out the dough thinly and cut into 5 cm squares. Place ¼ teaspoon jam in one corner of each square. Fold the corner diagonally to completely cover the jam, press down to seal and roll to form crescents. Place on a cookie sheet.
2. Beat together the egg and milk to make a glaze. Brush the crescents with glaze and sprinkle with chopped nuts. Bake at 180°C/360°F for 12 to 15 minutes until golden. Cool and dust with powdered sugar.

*Opposite: Mexican Wedding Cookies (left) and Lemon Raspberry Cookies (right).*

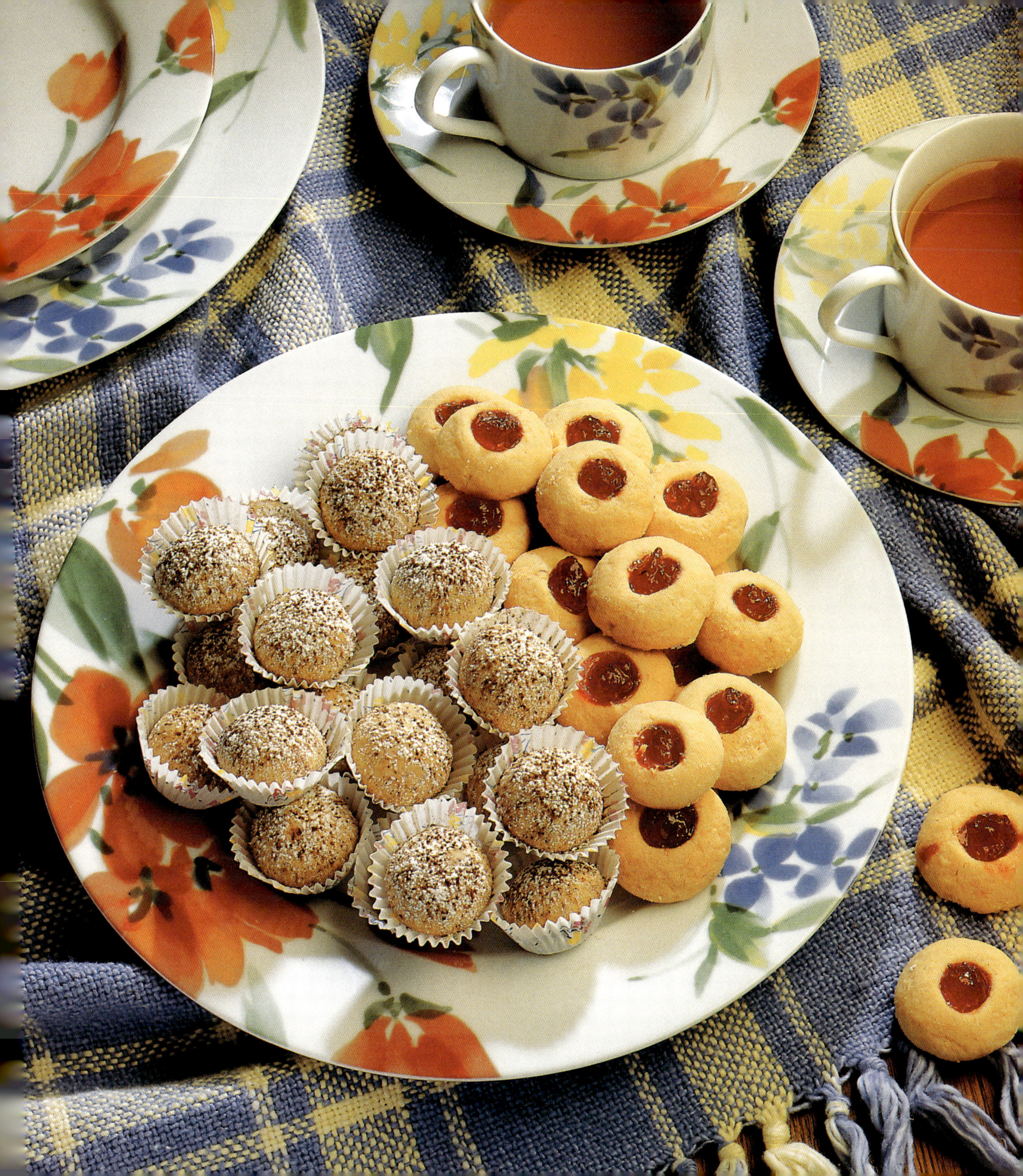

# Noel Nut Balls

*Ingredients*

- 1 cup unsalted butter
- 2 tablespoons honey
- 1/2 cup powdered sugar
- 2 1/4 cups all-purpose flour, sifted
- 1/4 teaspoon salt
- 1 teaspoon orange juice
- 3/4 cup pecans, finely chopped

powdered sugar to decorate

*Method*

1. Cream butter and honey until fluffy. Stir in sugar, flour, salt, orange juice and pecans. Wrap the dough in cling wrap and refrigerate for several hours.

2. Roll 1 teaspoon of dough at a time into balls. Place on a greased baking tray and bake at 180°C/360°F for 12 to 13 minutes. Cool on a wire rack, then roll in powdered sugar.

# Orange Walnut Shortbread

*Ingredients*

- 250 grams unsalted butter
- 3/4 cup brown sugar
- 1 teaspoon orange essence
- grated zest of 1 orange
- 2 cups all-purpose flour
- a pinch of salt
- 1/2 cup toasted walnuts, finely ground

- 1 egg, beaten, to glaze
- powdered sugar for dusting

*Method*

1. Cream butter and sugar. Add orange essence, orange zest, flour, salt and walnuts. Mix well. Chill for a few hours.

2. Roll out, a little at a time, on a well floured board to a thickness of 1 cm. Cut into rectangles and place on a greased baking tray. Brush lightly with beaten egg and make several holes in each cookie with a fork. Bake at 175°C/350°F for about 20 minutes until golden. Cool the shortbread on a wire rack. Roll in powdered sugar before storing in an airtight container.

# Sablé Cookies

*White Dough*

- 454 grams cake flour, sifted
- 354 grams butter
- 150 grams powdered sugar, sifted

powdered sugar to decorate

*Method*

1. Make a well in the centre of the sifted flour and cut in the butter. Add sugar. Mix well and knead by hand.

2. Form three logs, each measuring about 38 cm long. Roll in powdered sugar and refrigerate until firm.

*Chocolate Dough*

- 370 grams cake flour
- 150 grams powdered sugar
- 85 grams cocoa powder
- 354 grams butter

powdered sugar to decorate

*Method*

1. Sift together cake flour, sugar and cocoa. Make a well in the centre. Cut in butter and mix until a dough forms.

2. Form three logs each measuring about 38 cm long. Roll in powdered sugar and refrigerate until firm.

*To Assemble Sablé Cookies:*
Cut each white log into quarters. Do the same with the chocolate logs. Stack the logs together, alternating the white and chocolate quarters. Use a little moisture to stick them together. Refrigerate until firm. Slice into 1-cm circles and bake at 175°C/350°F for 20 minutes until golden.

# Raisin Oatmeal Cookies

*Ingredients*

- 540 grams butter, softened
- 350 grams castor sugar
- 240 grams dark raisins
- 225 grams oat flakes
- 1/2 teaspoon vanilla essence
- 595 grams bread flour
- 1/2 teaspoon baking soda

*Method*

1. Lightly mix butter and sugar. Add raisins, oat flakes and vanilla essence. Stir in flour and baking soda.

2. Refrigerate the dough for an hour. When firm divide the dough into 285 grams each and roll between two sheets of parchment or wax paper. At this point the dough may be frozen if the cookies are not being baked immediately.

3. To bake, cut the chilled dough into 5 cm-long slices. If the dough had been frozen, allow the cookies to thaw for 5 minutes. Bake at 175°C/350°F for about 15 to 20 minutes until golden.

*Opposite: Noel Nut Balls (above), Sablé Cookies (centre) and Orange Walnut Shortbread (below).*

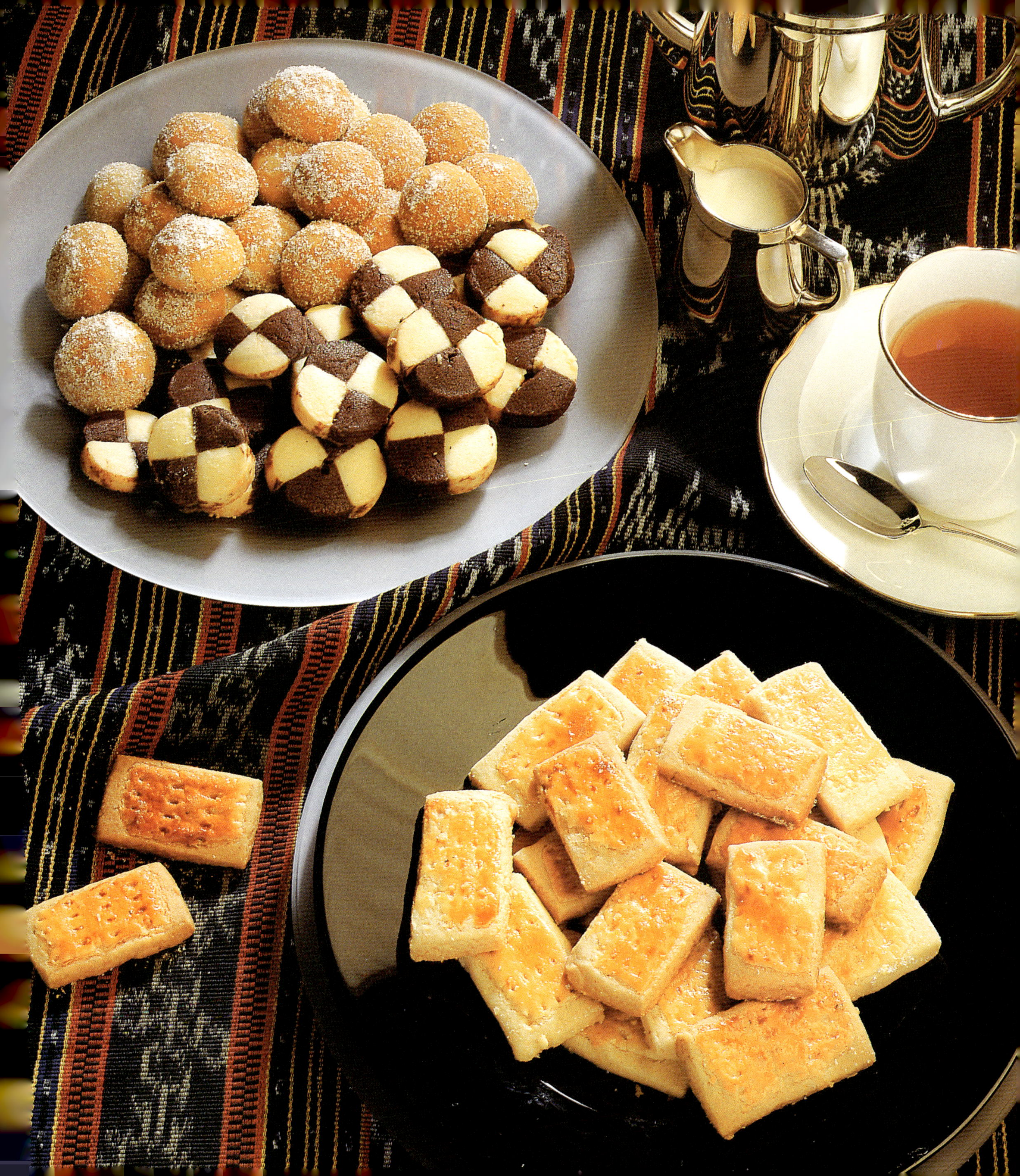

## German Sand Biscuits

### Ingredients

- 375 grams butter
- 250 grams powdered sugar
- 140 grams fresh milk
- grated zest of 1 lemon
- 1 teaspoon vanilla essence
- 750 grams all-purpose flour

apricot jam

### Method

1. Cream butter and sugar until light. Add milk a little at a time, followed by lemon zest and vanilla essence. Stir in flour.
2. Use a piping bag fitted with a plain nozzle to pipe the dough onto a lightly greased baking tray. Make a small depression in the centre of each cookie and pipe in apricot jam. Bake at 205°C/400°F for 20 minutes.

## Vanilla Kipferin

### Ingredients

- 210 grams all-purpose flour
- 70 grams ground almonds
- 50 grams castor sugar
- 180 grams cold, unsalted butter, cut into small pieces
- 2 egg yolks

powdered sugar for dusting

### Method

1. Combine flour, almonds and sugar in a bowl. Cut in cold butter until the mixture resembles breadcrumbs. Add egg yolks and form the dough into a ball. Chill for an hour.
2. Roll the dough into marbles by hand, then form into crescents. Bake at 180°C/360°F for about 8 minutes until golden. Dust with powdered sugar.

*Chef's Note: This is a popular Christmas cookie in Austria and Switzerland. Because of their shape they are sometimes known as Moon Crescents.*

## Almond Biscuits

### Ingredients

- 375 grams unsalted butter
- 500 grams castor sugar
- grated zest of 2 limes
- 500 grams almonds, finely ground
- 125 grams all-purpose flour
- 125 grams fresh milk

### Method

1. Beat butter and sugar until fluffy. Add lime zest, almonds, flour and milk. Press the dough into a 33 cm by 9.5 cm baking pan.
2. Bake for 15 minutes at 170°C/340°F until golden brown. Remove to a wire rack to cool. Cut into bars to serve.

## Pistachio Lace Cookies

### Ingredients

- 1 cup unsalted pistachios, shelled and coarsely chopped
- 115 grams + 1 tablespoon unsalted butter
- 2/3 cup packed brown sugar
- 1/3 cup light corn syrup
- 2 tablespoons Grand Marnier
- 2 teaspoons grated orange zest
- 1 cup all-purpose flour

### Method

1. Preheat oven to 190°C/375°F. Heat one tablespoon butter in a small skillet. Saute the pistachios, stirring constantly until lightly browned. Drain on paper towels.
2. In a saucepan combine the remaining butter, brown sugar, corn syrup, Grand Marnier and zest. Bring to a boil, stirring constantly. Gradually beat in flour. Stir in the pistachios.
3. Drop the dough by the teaspoonful on a lightly buttered cookie tray, making sure they are evenly spaced.
4. Bake for 3 to 5 minutes or until the cookies spread to 8 or 10 cm wide and are golden brown. Cool on the cookie tray for 3 to 5 minutes. Transfer to a wire rack using a spatula.

*Chef's Note: You can shape the warm cookies by wrapping each one around the handle of a wooden spoon before it cools and hardens.*

*Opposite: Vanilla Kipferin (above left), German Sand Biscuits (above right) and Almond Biscuits (below).*

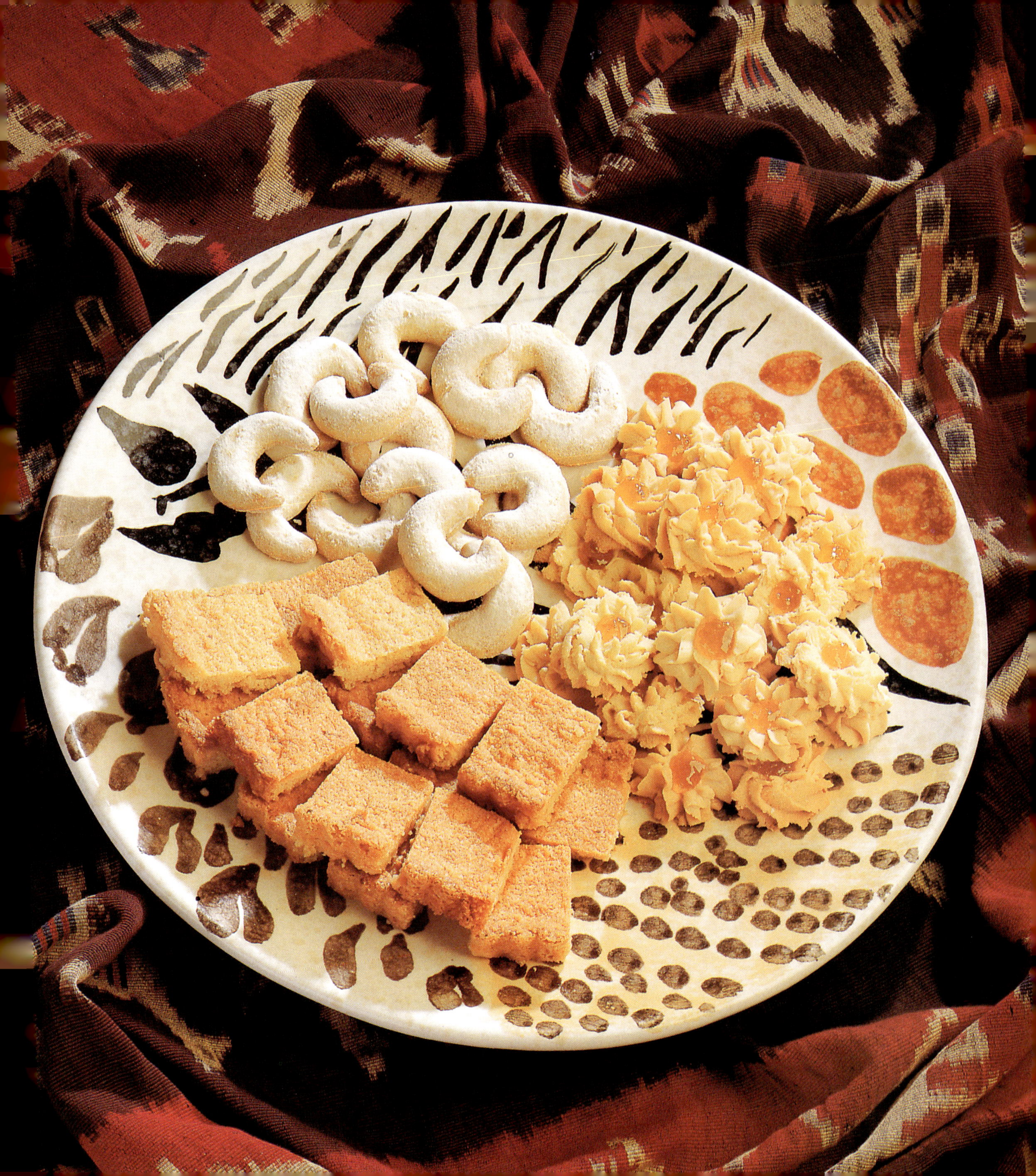

# Bread

The Art of Making Bread, p118  **1** Almond Bread, p120  **2** Brioche, p120  **3** Spicy Corn Bread, p120  **4** German Potato Bread, p120  **5** Banana Walnut Loaf, p122  **6** Sweet Corn Bread, p122  **7** Dried Fruit and Orange Loaf, p122  **8** Dried Fruit and Apricot Loaf, p122  **9** Dutch Apple Bread, p124  **10** Pumpkin Walnut Loaf, p124  **11** Turkish Calzone, p124  **12** Christmas Stollen, p126  **13** Danish Fruit Ring, p126  **14** Lebanese Flat Bread, p126  **15** Corn and Cheddar Cheese Loaf, p128  **16** Raisin Pumpkin Roll, p128  **17** Onion Walnut Bread, p128  **18** Farmer's Country Loaf, p130  **19** French Peasant Bread, p130  **20** Norwegian Christmas Bread, p130  **21** Foccaccia à la Provence, p132  **22** Foccaccia with Red Onions and Rosemary, p132  **23** Tropical Fruit Loaf, p132  **24** Prune and Pecan Sticky Bun, p134  **25** Swiss Braided Bread, p134  **26** Carrot Cheese Bread, p134

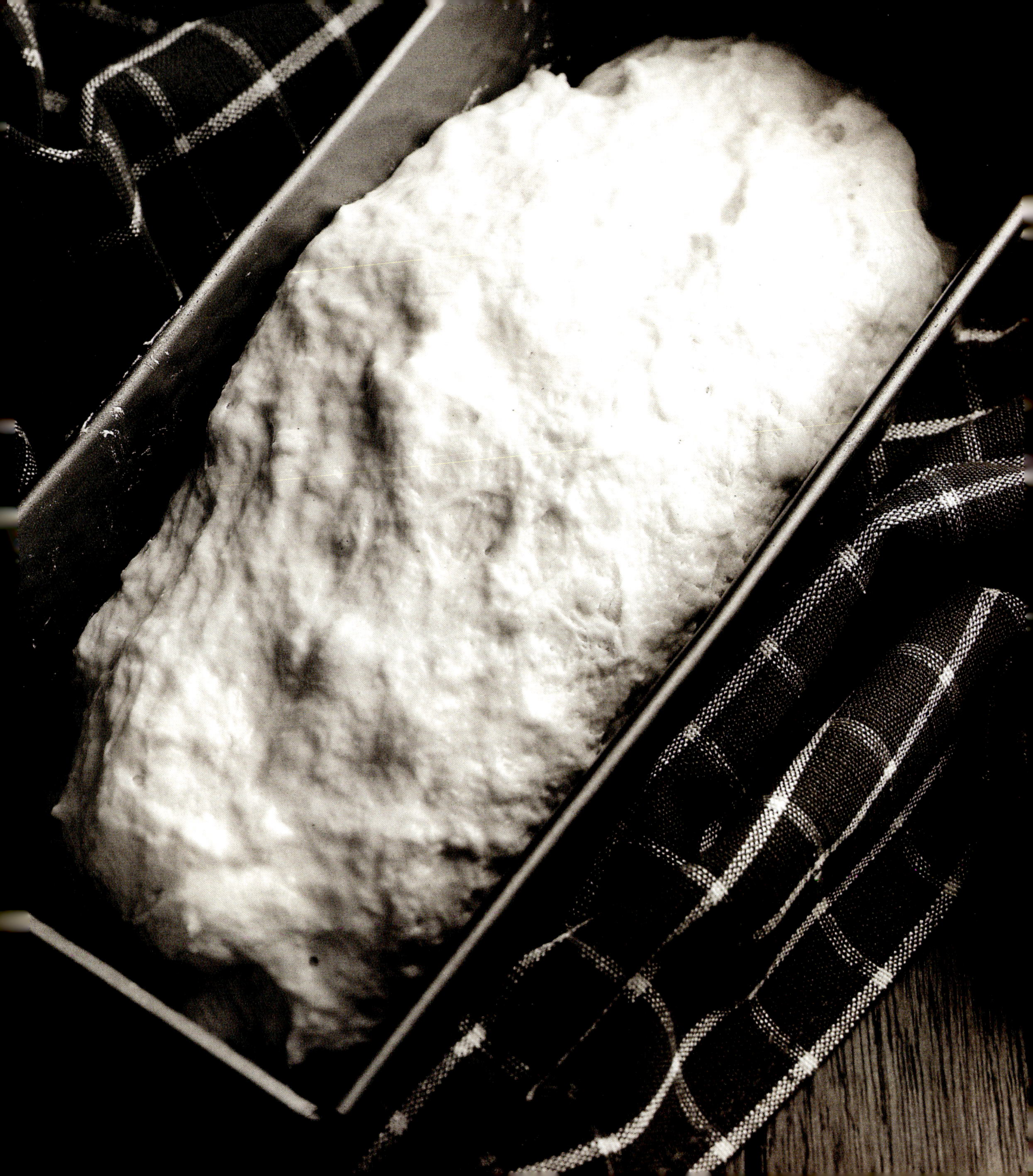

# The Art of Making Bread

There is really nothing quite like fresh bread, warm and fragrant, spread with butter and slowly savoured. Good bread is even more delicious when you have made it yourself.

I am always surprised to hear people say that bread-making requires great skill. This is not true. Working with yeast is simple and straightforward. As long as you do not destroy the yeast by using liquid that is too hot, there is very little that can go wrong in bread-making, unlike in pastry-making and cake-making where a lighter touch is required. It is only the dough-kneading stage that requires time and effort. But even a child can successfully knead dough and shape a loaf.

Once you begin making bread, you may find yourself becoming absorbed in the art and the endless variety. Bread comes in a multitude of shapes, sizes, textures and tastes. It is also a good source of fibre, proteins and minerals. Interestingly enough, simple loaves can be regarded as peasant food in one part of the world and sophisticated gourmet fare in another.

I started seriously making bread while attending the Ritz Hotel cooking school in Paris six years ago. We used to bake so much bread that after each class I would distribute loaves to people at the metro subway.

Bread making dates back to the Stone Age, when people first learnt to grind grain, probably barley and millet, in stone mills. Early bread, heavy and unleavened, was cooked on a heated stone. Over time the process of milling grain was refined.

Early Egyptians used wind-powered fans and sieves to separate the chaff from the bran. Romans and Greeks further developed grain cultivation and milling methods and produced flour refined to different degrees.

Bread making has always had an important place in the European home. Different regions in the same country can produce breads that differ in flavour and shape. Although most bread-making is done commercially nowadays, many people around the world still make bread as a hobby.

## RISING

One lesson I've learnt over years of working with international chefs is that haste makes waste, not taste. There are bakers who only make their bread dough with very warm liquid and leave their dough to rise slowly in a warm place. Unlike dough that has risen quickly, dough that has been allowed to rise slowly has a deeper flavour and is not filled with air bubbles. The slow-rising bread also stays fresh longer.

Any large bowl is suitable for placing your dough while it rises, but I prefer ceramic or glass bowls. Metal bowls are conductors of heat and can "cook" the dough, especially if the bowl is placed in a warm place such as the top of a warm oven. Allow your dough to rise at room temperature in a greased bowl. Cover the bowl with a kitchen towel or with cling wrap to allow the dough to retain moisture and to prevent a skin from forming on it. Turn the dough once, while it is rising, to grease it.

Generally dough takes one to two hours to rise until it is double the original bulk. But different ingredients and conditions affect rising time. Drafts will cause dough to rise slowly and unevenly. Wholegrain doughs take longer to rise than doughs made with white flour. Doughs high in fat and fruit take longer to rise as well. Test the dough by poking it with two fingers: if the indentations remain, the dough is adequately risen. Otherwise leave the dough to rise for a further 15 to 30 minutes before testing it again. I like to leave my dough to rise overnight. Sometimes, to slow down the rising process, I even allow my dough to rise in the refrigerator for eight hours or more. Bread that is forced to rise too quickly in an overly warm place will yield a sour-tasting loaf.

## TYPES OF BREAD

There are three basic breads: the loaf, which may be long, oval, round, or elaborately shaped; the breakfast bread such as the croissant and danish; and cake-bread such as muffins and doughnuts.

## YEAST

Baking with yeast demands precise measurements. Yeast needs sugar in order to be activated, however too much sugar can slow the leavening process to a point where it stops altogether.

Yeast dough often contains sugar, which colours and flavours the bread. Salt is used for the same purpose as well as for the additional purpose of retarding the yeast just a little so that the texture will not be too coarse and filled with holes.

Bread that is pale in colour rather than a healthy brown has either been baked at too low a temperature or has had the salt omitted.

Yeast is damaged at temperatures above 46°C/115°F and it is killed at 63°C/145°F. On the other hand, yeast fermentation is nonexistent at 4°C/40°F or below. In certain types of dough such as danish pastry dough, braided white bread dough, or croissant dough, it is essential that the yeast be kept cold to prevent fermentation while the dough is being shaped. White bread made with cold milk, for example, slows yeast fermentation long enough to allow time to braid the dough or form it into different shapes.

The easiest bread to make is plain white bread baked with white flour and only enough sugar to help the yeast along. With a sweet flour such as rye, or wholewheat flours that have little or no gluten structure, it is very important to keep the dough from getting too cold.

## KNEADING

It is both satisfying and important for a beginner to mix the bread dough by hand. A baker should learn how bread dough responds to the touch. Once you are experienced, you can choose to mix the dough with an electric mixer, food processor, or by hand.

Working on a lightly floured surface, knead the dough by gently bringing the far edge towards you and folding it over. Push the dough away with the heel of your hands. Give the dough a quarter turn and repeat the kneading process until the dough is smooth. This can take anywhere from two to 10 minutes. If your dough is too stiff you are adding too much flour. This is the most common mistake. Don't worry if not all of the flour called for in the recipe is used.

When making bread, aim for a loaf that, when cooked, has a firm crust and a moist, interestingly irregular texture.

# Almond Bread

## Bread

- 1½ teaspoons active dry yeast, dissolved in ¼ cup lukewarm water and set aside for 10 minutes
- ¾ cup butter, softened
- ¾ cup castor sugar
- ⅓ cup fresh milk
- ½ teaspoon salt
- 4 eggs
- 1 egg yolk
- 1 teaspoon almond essence
- 1 cup golden raisins
- 4¾–5 cups all-purpose flour

## Method

1. Combine dissolved yeast, butter, sugar, milk, salt, eggs, egg yolk, almond essence and raisins. Mix well.
2. Gradually fold in flour and knead until a dough forms. Place in a bowl and cover tightly, leaving the dough to rise for about an hour or until double in bulk.
3. Punch down the dough and divide it into two parts. Form into balls and flatten into 20 cm-wide circles. Set aside for 45 minutes to allow the dough to rise further.

## Topping

- ⅓ cup castor sugar
- 1 teaspoon vanilla essence
- 1 egg
- ½ cup ground almonds
- 4 tablespoons butter, melted
- 1½ tablespoons cornflour
- 1 egg white, beaten with a little water, to glaze
- ½ cup almond slices to decorate
- powdered sugar for dusting

## Method

1. Beat together sugar, vanilla essence and egg. Add ground almonds, cornflour and melted butter.
2. Glaze the risen dough with egg white and spread with topping. Sprinkle with almond slices and bake at 175°C/350°F for 35 minutes until golden brown. Dust with powdered sugar when cooled. Score into wedges before serving.

# Brioche

## Ingredients

- 1 tablespoon dry yeast
- ⅔ cup milk
- 1 teaspoon salt
- 4 tablespoons sugar
- 500 grams bread flour
- 4 eggs
- 230 grams butter, diced

## Method

1. Dissolve yeast in milk, salt and sugar. Add flour and eggs.
2. Stretch and knead for 5 minutes on a marble-topped surface. Add butter and knead again for 10 minutes. Leave to rise in the refrigerator for a few hours.
3. Punch down, shape into small rolls and place each ball into a ramekin dish.
4. Bake at 180°C/360°F for 20 minutes.

# Spicy Corn Bread

## Ingredients

- 255 grams cornmeal
- 170 grams cake flour
- 85 grams castor sugar
- 1 teaspoon salt
- ¾ teaspoon baking powder
- 3 egg yolks
- 1 cup cream
- 1¼ cups milk
- 200 grams butter, melted and cooled
- 1 225-gram can creamed corn
- 2 red chillies, sliced
- 1 onion, diced
- 1½ cups cheddar cheese, grated
- 3 egg whites

## Method

1. Combine cornmeal, flour, sugar, salt and baking powder.
2. In a separate bowl combine egg yolks, cream and milk. Set aside for 10 minutes. Add butter, corn, chillies, onion and cheese. Add the dry ingredients.
3. In a separate bowl beat egg whites until stiff peaks form. Add to the batter and fold to mix.
4. Bake in a loaf pan at 175°C/350°F for about 40 minutes.

# German Potato Bread

## Ingredients

- 4 teaspoons active dry yeast, dissolved in ¼ cup lukewarm milk for 15 minutes
- 4 medium potatoes, boiled and mashed, retaining 250 ml of the potato cooking liquid
- 2 tablespoons corn oil
- 4 teaspoons salt
- 850–900 grams all-purpose flour

## Method

1. Combine dissolved yeast, mashed potatoes, oil and salt and mix well. Stir in the retained cooking liquid and flour, a little at a time, until a stiff dough forms.
2. Transfer to a floured surface and knead dough until smooth and elastic. Return the dough to the bowl, cover and leave in warm place for 1 to 1½ hours until double in bulk. Punch down and leave to rise for another 40 minutes.
3. Grease two 23 cm by 13 cm loaf tins. Roll the dough into small balls. Place two rows of balls in each tin. Allow the dough to rise above the rim of the tins.
4. Bake at 200°C/390°F for 10 minutes, then lower the heat to 180°C/360°F and continue baking for another 40 minutes until the bottom of the loaf tin sounds hollow when tapped. Cool.

*Opposite: Almond Bread (above left), German Potato Bread (above right), Brioche Loaf (below) and individual Brioche (left).*

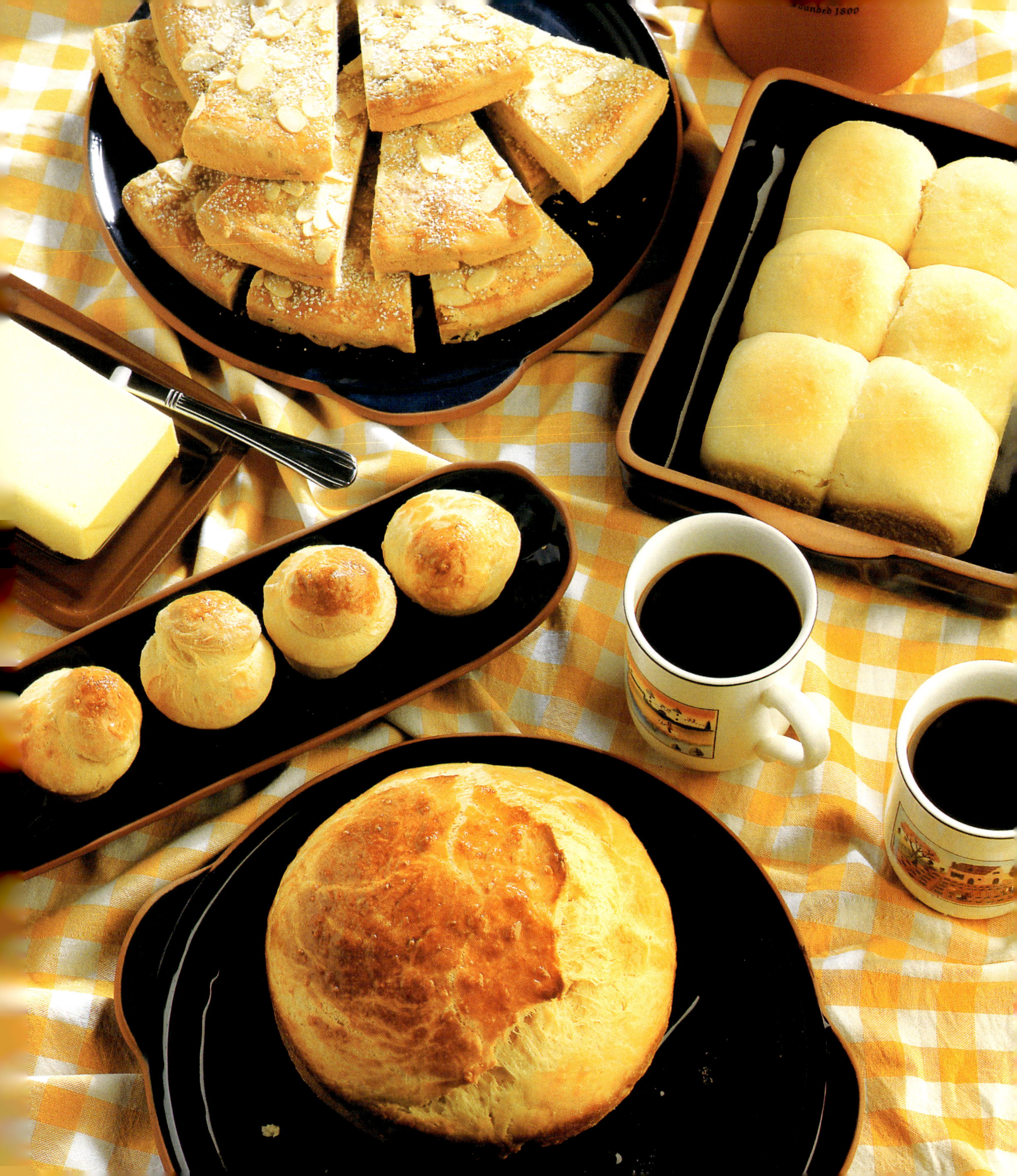

## Banana Walnut Loaf

*Ingredients*

    2 eggs
    12 ripe bananas, mashed
    145 grams castor sugar
    280 grams all-purpose flour
    1 teaspoon salt
    1 teaspoon baking soda
    1/2 cup walnuts, chopped

*Method*

1. Beat eggs and add mashed bananas. Add sugar.
2. Sift together flour, salt and baking soda and fold into the banana mixture.
3. Add walnuts. Pour the batter into a greased loaf tin. Bake at 175°C/350°F for an hour.

## Sweet Corn Bread

*Ingredients*

    3/4 cup all-purpose flour
    3/4 cup rye flour
    1/2 cup cornmeal
    3 teaspoons baking powder
    a pinch of salt
    2 eggs
    1/2 cup castor sugar
    1/2 cup butter, melted
    1 cup evaporated milk
    1/2 cup creamed corn

*Method*

1. Combine the first five ingredients in a bowl.
2. In a separate bowl beat eggs and sugar and add butter.
3. Fold dry ingredients into the batter alternately with milk until well mixed. Add creamed corn.
4. Pour into a 22-cm square baking dish. Bake at 205°C/400°F for 20 minutes.

## Dried Fruit and Orange Loaf

*Ingredients*

    1 cup golden raisins
    1/2 cup currants
    grated zest of 1 orange
    1/4 cup orange juice
    1/3 cup castor sugar
    2 1/2 cups all-purpose flour
    1/2 teaspoon salt
    1 teaspoon baking soda
    1 tablespoon baking powder
    2 eggs
    1/2 cup corn oil
    1 cup brown sugar
    1/4 teaspoon ground nutmeg
    1 cup fresh milk

*Method*

1. Mix together raisins, currants, orange juice, orange zest and sugar and leave to soak for an hour.
2. Sift together flour, salt, baking soda and baking powder. Set aside.
3. Whisk eggs, corn oil, brown sugar and nutmeg until well mixed. Fold in sifted ingredients alternately with milk. Add soaked fruit.
4. Pour the batter into a greased and floured loaf pan. Bake at 170°C/340°F for an hour until a skewer inserted in the centre comes away cleanly.

## Dried Fruit and Apricot Loaf

*Ingredients*

    1 1/2 cups water
    1 cup figs
    1 cup dried apricots
    1 cup golden raisins
    1 cup dates
    2 cups all-purpose flour
    2 teaspoons baking powder
    1 teaspoon baking soda
    1 teaspoon salt
    1/4 cup vegetable shortening
    3/4 cup castor sugar
    1 egg
    grated zest of 1 lemon

*Method*

1. Mix together water, figs, apricots, raisins and dates and cook for five minutes. Drain for 2/3 cup liquid. Set aside.
2. Sift together flour, baking powder, baking soda and salt. Set aside.
3. In a separate bowl beat vegetable shortening, sugar, egg and lemon zest until fluffy. Alternately fold in sifted ingredients, fruit and fruit liquid.
4. Grease two 21 cm by 11 cm by 8 cm loaf pans and line with wax paper. Pour in the batter. Leave to rest for five minutes before baking at 175°C/350°F for 45 minutes.

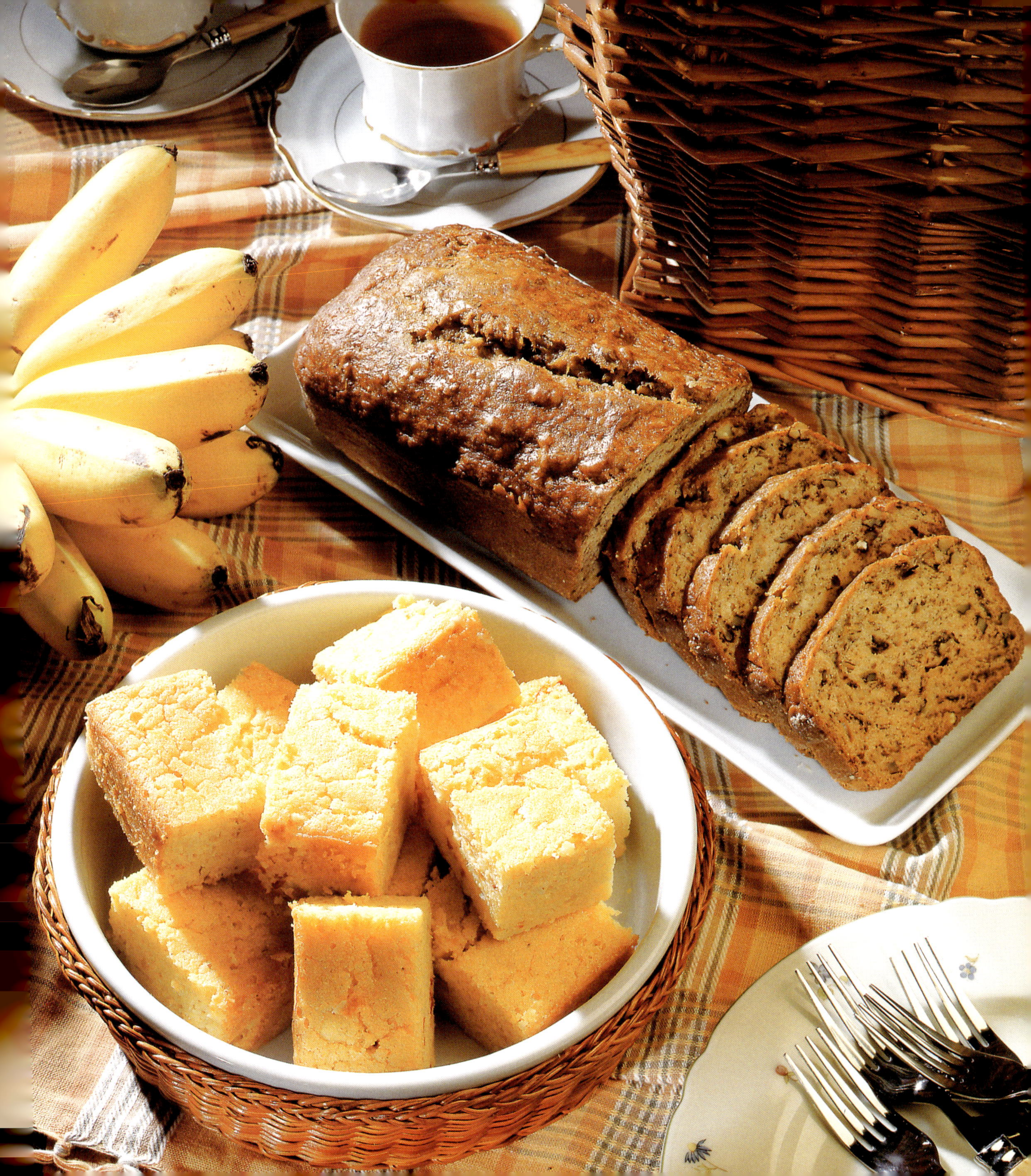

# Dutch Apple Bread

*Bread*

- ¼ cup butter
- ½ cup fresh milk
- ¼ cup castor sugar
- 7 grams active dry yeast
- ¼ cup lukewarm water
- 3½ cups all-purpose flour
- 2 eggs
- 1 apple, peeled and diced

*Method*

1. Heat butter, milk and sugar.
2. Dissolve yeast in lukewarm water. Add to the milk mixture. Add flour, eggs and apples. Knead slowly for 10 minutes.
3. Leave the dough to rise for about an hour until double in bulk.

*Topping*

- ⅓ cup all-purpose flour
- ¼ cup castor sugar
- 2 tablespoons butter
- ½ teaspoon ground cinnamon

*Method*

1. Mix well all the topping ingredients.
2. Punch down the dough, roll out to form a 22 cm by 35 cm rectangle and spread with three-quarters of the topping. Roll up jelly-roll style and place in a loaf pan. Leave to rise for an hour.
3. Sprinkle with the remaining topping and bake at 175°C/350°F for 40 minutes.

# Pumpkin Walnut Loaf

*Ingredients*

- 1⅔ cups all-purpose flour
- ¼ teaspoon baking powder
- 1 teaspoon baking soda
- ¾ teaspoon salt
- 1 teaspoon ground cinnamon
- 1 teaspoon ground cloves
- ½ teaspoon ground nutmeg
- 2 eggs, beaten
- 1½ cups castor sugar
- ½ cup vegetable oil
- ½ cup water
- 1 cup pumpkin, boiled or baked and then mashed
- ½ cup walnuts, chopped

*Method*

1. Sift together first seven ingredients.
2. In a separate bowl beat eggs and sugar. Add oil, water and mashed pumpkin. Gradually fold in sifted ingredients. Mix well and add walnuts.
3. Pour the batter into a greased and floured 18-cm loaf pan.
4. Bake at 170°C/340°F for an hour. Prick the loaf surface with a toothpick to test for doneness. If the toothpick comes away cleanly, the loaf is ready.

Chef's Note: It is better to bake than to boil the pumpkin as baking produces a better aroma.

# Turkish Calzone

*Bread*

- 7 grams active dry yeast
- ½ teaspoon castor sugar
- ½ cup lukewarm water
- ¾ cup fresh milk
- 2 tablespoons olive oil
- 3 cups all-purpose flour
- 1½ teaspoons salt
- 2 tablespoons ghee to glaze

*Method*

1. Dissolve yeast and sugar in warm water until frothy. Mix together with the remaining ingredients for the bread and knead for 10 minutes.
2. Cover and leave in a warm place until double in bulk.

*Filling*

- some cooking oil
- 1 onion, finely chopped
- 6-cm knob of ginger, finely chopped
- 1 green chilli, finely sliced
- 2 tablespoons meat curry powder
- 300 grams minced meat
- salt and sugar to taste
- 1 sprig coriander leaves, finely chopped

*Method*

1. Heat oil in a frying pan and fry the onion, ginger, green chilli and curry powder. Add meat and fry for another 5 minutes. Add salt, sugar and coriander leaves. Cool.
2. Divide the dough into two portions. Roll out one portion and place half of the filling in the centre. Fold into two horizontally. Brush the top with ghee. Repeat for the second loaf.
3. Bake at 180°C/360°F for 20 minutes until golden brown.

*Opposite: Dutch Apple Bread (above left), Pumpkin Walnut Loaf (above right) and Turkish Calzone (below).*

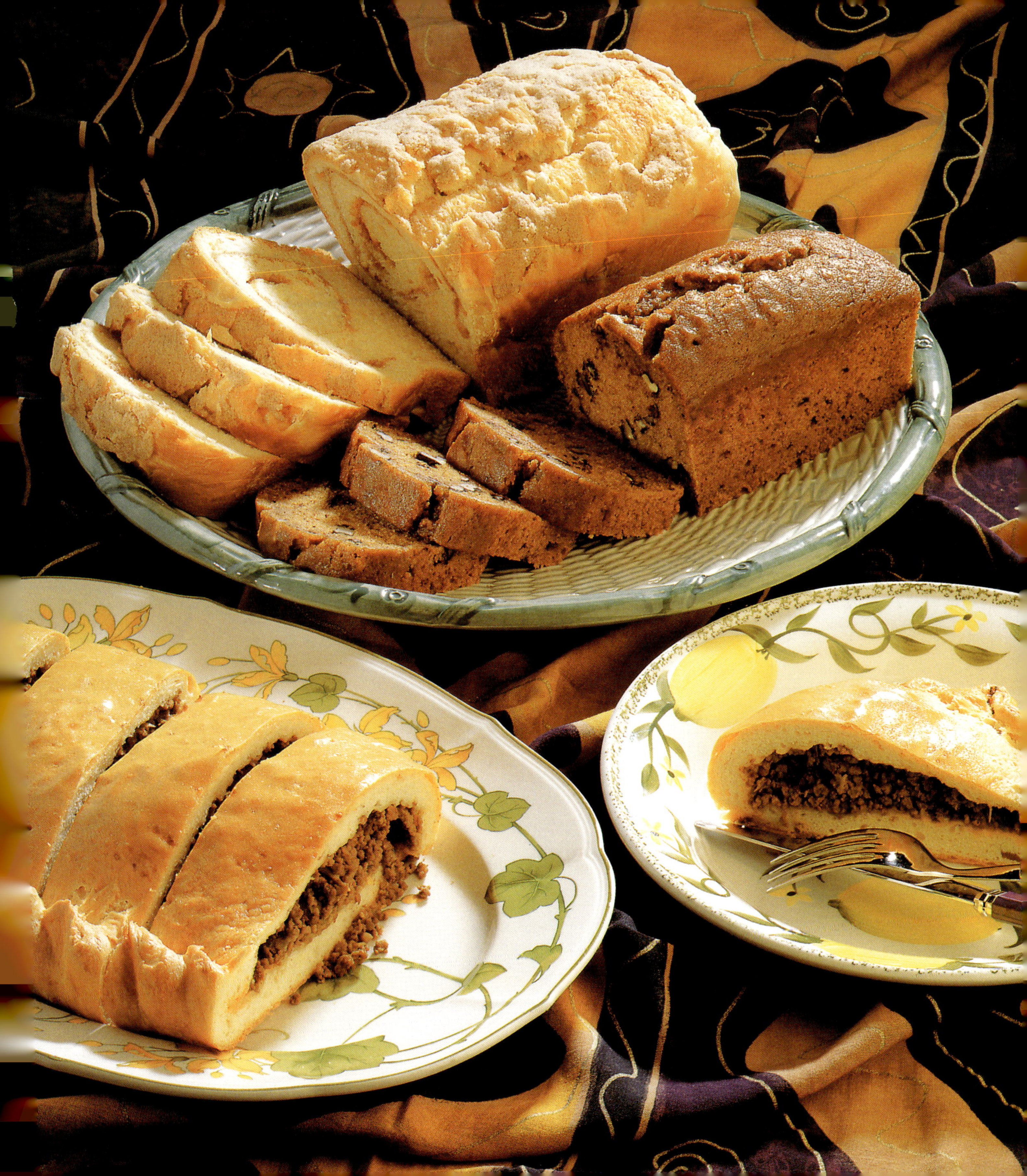

# Christmas Stollen

*Ingredients*

    150 grams currants
    150 grams golden raisins
    1/2 cup orange juice
    1/2 cup cognac
    5 1/2 cups all-purpose flour
    1/2 cup castor sugar
    1/2 teaspoon salt
    a pinch of ground mace
    1/4 teaspoon ground nutmeg
    1 cup warm milk
    2/3 cup butter, melted + a little extra for brushing
    28 grams cake yeast, dissolved in 1/4 cup lukewarm water
    3 large eggs, beaten
    285 grams almonds, chopped
    grated zest of 2 lemons
    powdered sugar for dusting

*Method*

1. Soak currants and raisins in orange juice and cognac. Set aside. Sift together flour, sugar, salt, mace and nutmeg. Stir in warm milk and melted butter. Add dissolved yeast and eggs. Knead until fairly smooth.

2. Add soaked fruit, almonds and lemon zest and continue kneading on a floured board for about 10 minutes. If the dough is too sticky, knead in more flour.

3. Place the dough in a buttered bowl. Cover with cling wrap and allow it to rise for 1 to 2 hours in a warm place until double in bulk.

4. Punch down and roll out into a 30 cm by 20 cm rectangle. Brush with melted butter.

5. Fold one long edge towards centre. Fold other long edge towards centre, overlapping first edge by 2.5 cm. Turn over, taper ends and place on a parchment-lined baking tray. Cover with cling wrap and allow the dough to rise again in a warm place for 1 to 1 1/2 hours.

6. Preheat the oven to 170°C/340°F. Bake for 35 to 40 minutes until golden brown. Cool on a wire rack and dust with powdered sugar.

# Danish Fruit Ring

*Bread*

    15 grams dried yeast
    3 tablespoons warm water
    2 teaspoons + 1/3 cup castor sugar
    3 1/2 cups all-purpose flour
    1 1/2 teaspoons salt
    1/2 teaspoon ground cinnamon
    170 grams butter, diced
    4 eggs, beaten
    1/3 cup fresh milk

*Filling*

    1 cup walnuts or any mixed nuts, finely chopped
    3/4 cup brown sugar
    1 teaspoon ground cinnamon
    a pinch of salt
    1 cup dark raisins
    1/2 cup golden raisins
    1/2 cup prunes
    1/2 cup dried apricots
    1 tablespoon all-purpose flour
    1 tablespoon corn syrup
    powdered sugar for dusting

*Method*

1. Crumble yeast into the warm water, add 2 teaspoons sugar and set aside until frothy. Add remaining sugar to the yeast mixture.

2. Sift together flour, salt and cinnamon. Add to the yeast mixture with the butter. Add eggs and milk. Knead until dough forms. Knead again for 10 minutes. Place the dough in a bowl, cover and set aside until double in bulk.

3. Punch down the dough, fold into three and leave to rise overnight in the refrigerator.

4. Combine all the ingredients for the filling until well mixed. Roll out half of the dough to form a square 6 mm thick. Trim the corners for decoration.

5. Spread the filling over the dough, roll up into a log and join the ends together to form a ring. Secure the edges with water. Arrange the ring on a baking tray. Cover with a tea towel and leave to rise until double in bulk.

6. Trim all around the roll and bake at 180°C/360°F for 45 minutes. Dust with powdered sugar.

# Lebanese Flat Bread

*Ingredients*

    1 1/2 teaspoons dry yeast
    2 cups lukewarm water
    1 teaspoon sugar
    6 cups all-purpose flour
    1 tablespoon olive oil
    1 1/2 teaspoons salt

*Method*

1. Dissolve the yeast in lukewarm water and sugar. Set aside for 15 minutes. Mix the yeast with 2 cups of flour. Cover and set aside for an hour until frothy.

2. Stir in the rest of the flour, oil and salt. Knead for 10 minutes. Allow the dough to rise for 2 hours until double in bulk.

3. Punch down the dough, knead for a further five minutes and shape into eight equal parts. On a lightly floured piece of cloth, roll each part into a ball and flatten into 25 cm circles. Cover with another piece of cloth and set aside for 20 minutes. Transfer to baking tray.

4. Heat the oven to 180°C/360°F and bake for 15 minutes until golden brown.

Chef's Note: This bread is delicious filled with grilled lamb and topped with sour cream, chopped onions and chilli sauce. The Lebanese call this Donna Kebab. Traditionally flat bread, or khoubiz, contains no fat but I find that a little olive oil in the dough improves the flavour and texture.

*Opposite: Christmas Stollen (above) and Danish Fruit Ring (below).*

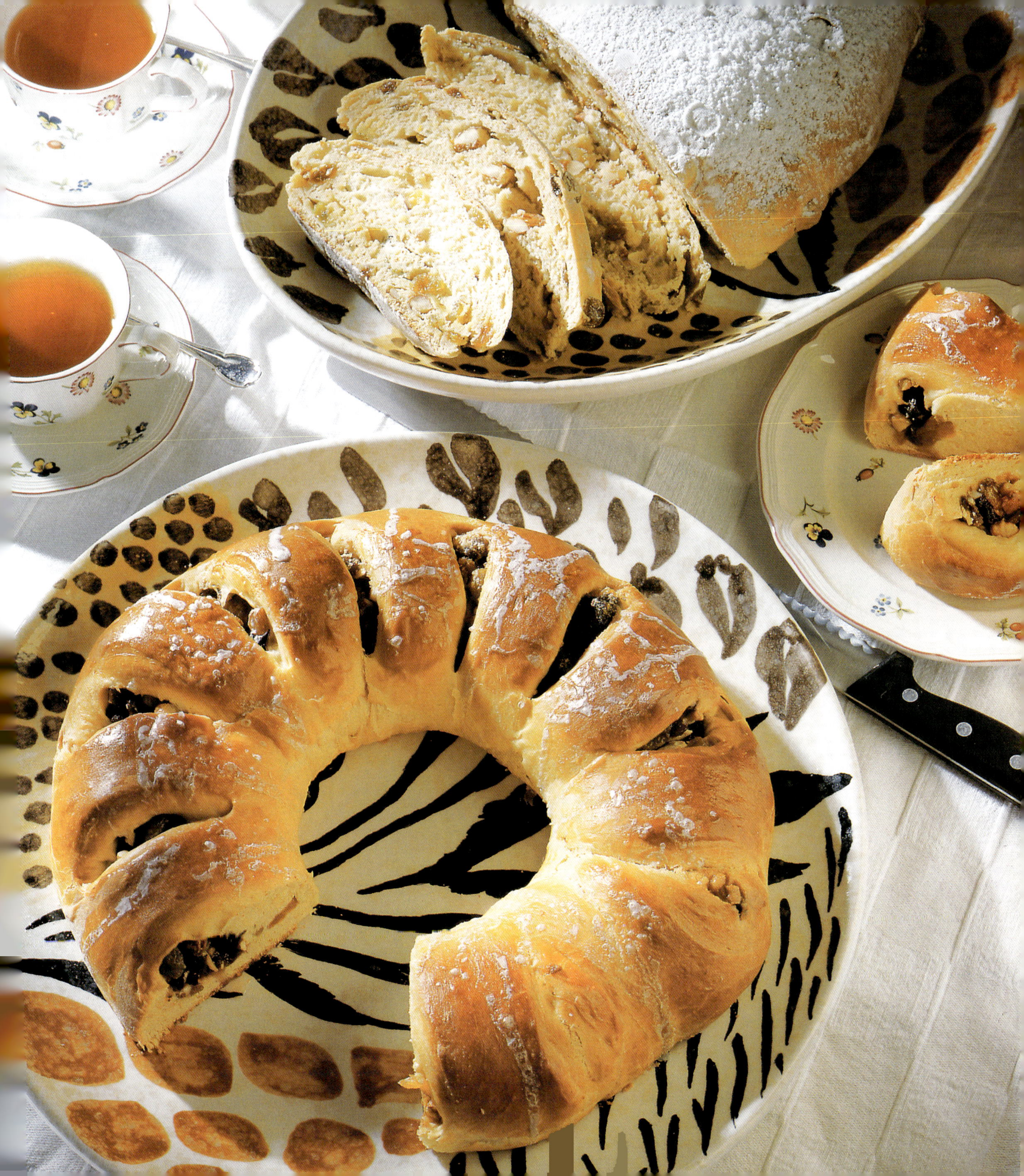

## Corn and Cheddar Cheese Loaf

### Ingredients

- 1 tablespoon active dry yeast, or 30 grams fresh yeast
- 1/2 cup warm water
- 1 cup cornmeal
- 2 teaspoons salt
- 1 tablespoon sugar
- 1/2 teaspoon baking soda
- 2 eggs
- 1 cup yoghurt
- 1/2 cup corn oil
- 1 cup creamed sweetcorn
- 5 cups + a little extra all-purpose flour
- 1 1/2 cups cheddar cheese, grated
- 2 green chillies, finely chopped
- 1 onion, diced and fried until golden brown

### Method

1. Crumble yeast into warm water and allow it to dissolve for 5 minutes until frothy. Mix together yeast, cornmeal, salt, sugar and baking soda.
2. Add eggs, yoghurt, oil, sweetcorn, flour, cheese, chillies, onion and a little more flour. Knead until dough forms. Allow the dough to rest for 10 minutes, then knead again. Place in a bowl and set aside until double in bulk.
3. Punch down the dough, divide into two parts and place each portion in a baking pan. Allow the dough to double in bulk. Bake at 170°C/340°F for an hour.

## Raisin Pumpkin Roll

### Ingredients

- 1 1/2 tablespoons active dry yeast
- 1/4 cup water, warmed to a temperature of 40°C/105°F to 46°C/115°F
- 1 cup pumpkin, cooked and mashed
- 1 cup milk, warmed to a temperature of 40°C/105°F to 46°C/115°F
- 3/4 cup castor sugar
- 2 1/2 tablespoons vegetable oil
- 2 1/4 teaspoons salt
- 1/2 cup raisins
- 4 1/2 cups all-purpose flour
- 4 tablespoons unsalted butter, melted, to glaze

### Method

1. Sprinkle yeast over warm water and stir to dissolve.
2. In a heavy-duty electric mixer, attached with a dough hook, mix pumpkin, milk, sugar, oil, salt and raisins. Blend in yeast mixture. Gradually beat in enough flour, one cup at a time, to form a stiff dough. Continue beating until the dough balls up.
3. Lightly oil a large bowl. Place the dough in the bowl, turning to coat in oil. Cover with cling wrap and allow the dough to rise for about 1 1/2 hours in a warm place until double in bulk.
4. Lightly grease two large cookie trays. Punch down the dough. Turn out onto a lightly floured surface. Divide into three parts. Divide each part into 12 pieces. Cover with a towel for 10 minutes.
5. Roll each piece into a ball. Place one ball in the centre of the cookie sheet. Arrange 17 balls around the central ball in concentric circles, with sides just touching. Cover the rolls with a towel and let them rise for 45 minutes in a warm, draft-free area until double in bulk.
6. Preheat the oven to 175°C/350°F. Brush the rolls lightly with 2 tablespoons butter. Bake for about 30 minutes until golden brown. Remove from oven and immediately glaze with the remaining melted butter. Serve warm.

## Onion Walnut Bread

### Ingredients

- 2 1/2 cups fresh milk
- 30 grams fresh yeast
- 1 teaspoon castor sugar
- 1 kg + 25 grams bread flour
- 3/4 teaspoon salt
- 1/2 cup corn oil
- 1 cup toasted walnuts, chopped
- 2 large onions, sauteed until golden
- 1 egg, beaten, to glaze
- wholewheat flour for dipping

### Method

1. Knead milk, yeast, sugar, flour, salt and oil in an electric mixer attached with a dough hook for 10 minutes. Add walnuts and onions and knead for another 2 minutes. Allow the dough to rest for 20 minutes, then punch down.
2. Divide the dough into two equal parts, shaping each into an oval. Glaze with egg and dip in wholewheat flour. Allow the dough to rise until 1 1/2 times its original size. Bake at 200°C/390°F for 40 to 50 minutes.

*Opposite: Corn and Cheddar Cheese Loaf (above left), Raisin Pumpkin Roll (right) and Onion Walnut Bread (below).*

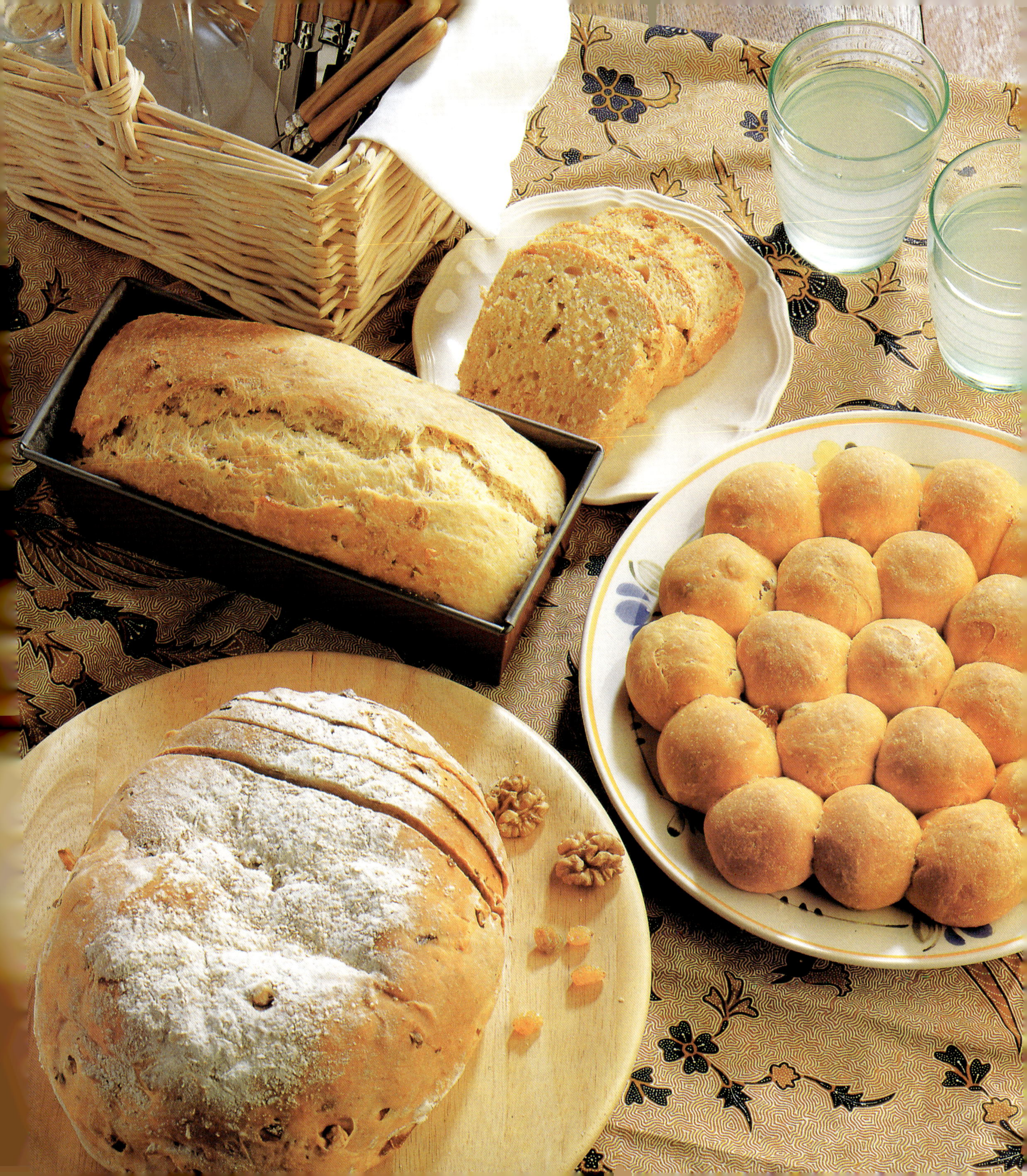

## Farmer's Country Loaf

*Ingredients*

    350 grams bread flour,
        divided into three parts
    350 grams wholewheat flour,
        divided into three parts
    15 grams salt
    15 grams fresh yeast
    430 ml lukewarm water

    corn oil to glaze
    flour for dusting

*Method*

1. Mix one part bread flour and one part wholewheat flour with half of the salt in a bowl. Make a well in the middle.
2. Dissolve yeast in 4 tablespoons lukewarm water. Pour into the flour. Add the remaining water.
3. Blend together the flour and yeast mixture with your fingertips until the mixture thickens. Sprinkle over some flour to prevent the batter from forming a skin. Set aside for 20 minutes until double in bulk.
4. Mix together the remaining flour and salt and add to the yeast mixture. Knead until a dough forms.
5. Transfer the dough to a floured surface and knead for 10 minutes, stretching the dough away from yourself.
6. Roll the dough into a tight ball and use your fingertips to give it a quarter turn. Repeat the process three times.
7. Roll the dough up into a ball and place it in a bowl. Cover with a wet towel. Leave to rise for 1½ to 2 hours.
8. To see if the dough is properly risen, poke the dough with your fingertips. If it does not spring back, it is ready. Punch down and shape into an oval. Turn the oval upside down and make a crease lengthwise for decoration. Place on a baking sheet right side up. With a sharp knife slash the dough diagonally 3 times. Cover and leave to rise until double in bulk.
9. Preheat the oven to 220°C/425°F.
10. Glaze the dough with corn oil and sprinkle with flour. Bake for 15 minutes until golden brown, then lower the temperature to 190°C/375°F and continue baking for 20 to 25 minutes. To test for doneness, tap the bottom of the loaf. If it sounds hollow the loaf is cooked, otherwise return the loaf to the oven for another 5 minutes or so.

## French Peasant Bread

*Ingredients*

    2 cups lukewarm water
    1 tablespoon active dry yeast
    1 tablespoon castor sugar
    2 teaspoons salt
    4 cups bread flour
    1 tablespoon cornmeal

    butter, melted, to glaze

*Method*

1. Mix together lukewarm water, yeast, sugar, salt and flour. Cover and leave to rise until double in bulk.
2. Grease a baking tray and sprinkle it with cornmeal.
3. Divide the dough into two portions. Without kneading, shape each portion into an oval. Place on a baking tray and allow the dough to rise for about an hour until double in bulk.
4. Brush with melted butter. Bake at 220°C/425°F for 10 minutes then lower the temperature to 190°C/375°F and bake for another 20 minutes until cooked.

## Norwegian Christmas Bread

*Ingredients*

    2 cups fresh milk
    1 cup castor sugar
    1 cup butter
    1 teaspoon salt
    3 tablespoons active dry yeast, dissolved
        in ½ cup lukewarm water
    3 cups + 6 cups all-purpose flour
    1 teaspoon ground cardamom or 2
        teaspoons vanilla essence
    3 eggs, beaten
    1 cup glace cherries and candied
        pineapples, coarsely chopped
    1½ cups golden raisins
    1 cup sifted powdered sugar, dissolved
        in 1½ tablespoons milk

*Method*

1. Heat milk, sugar, butter and salt and cool until lukewarm. Add dissolved yeast and 3 cups flour, cover the mixture and set aside for 1 hour.
2. Add cardamom, eggs, fruit and enough of the remaining flour to make an elastic dough. Knead for 10 minutes. Allow the dough to rise for one hour. Punch down.
3. Preheat the oven to 200°C/390°F. Generously butter a 22 cm by 12 cm loaf pan. Place in a loaf tin. Bake for 10 minutes. Reduce the heat to 170°C/340°F and bake for another 50 minutes until nicely browned. Drizzle dissolved sugar over the cooled bread.

*Opposite: Farmer's Country Loaf (above left), French Peasant Bread (above right) and Norwegian Christmas Bread (below).*

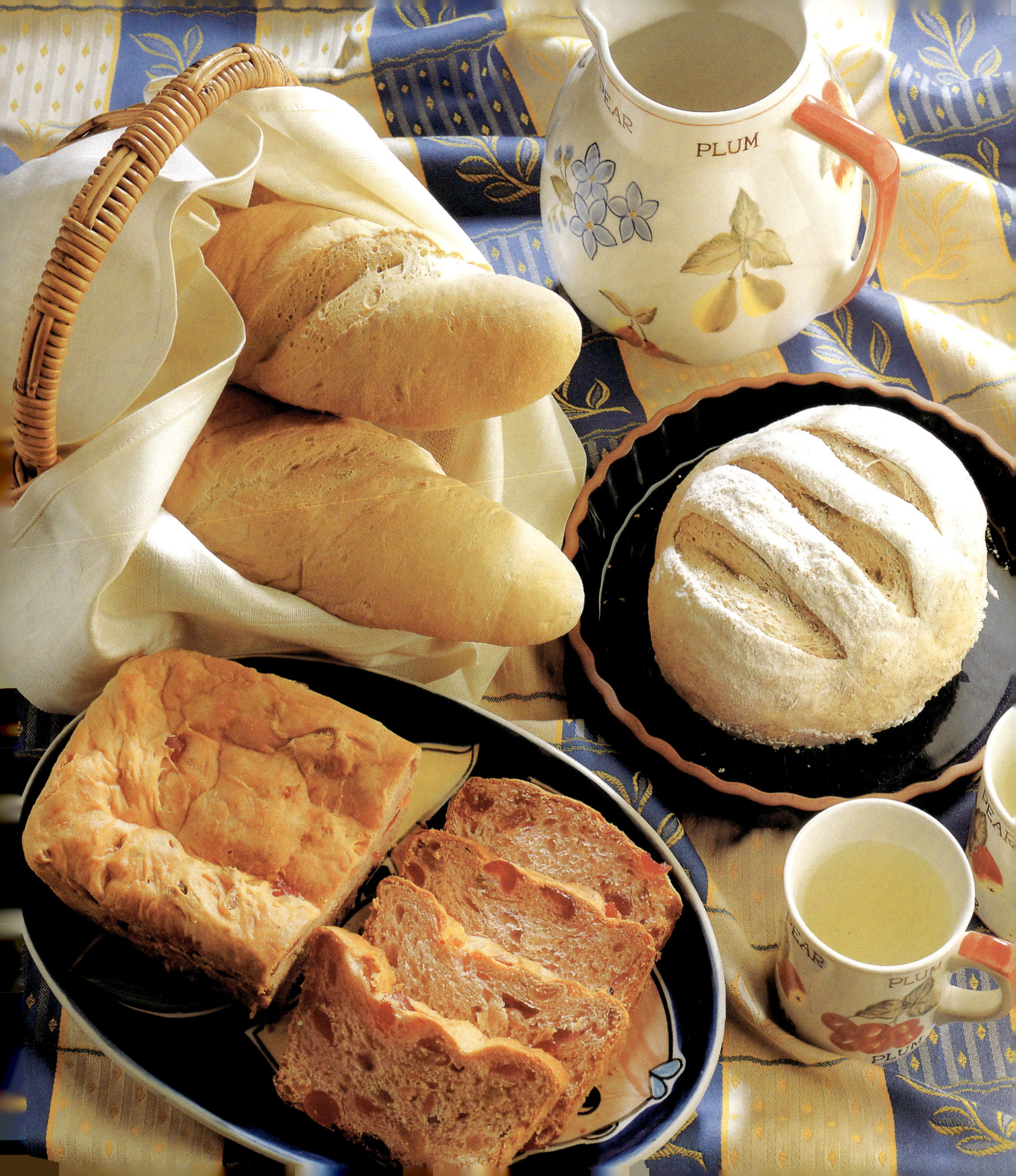
PEAR
PLUM
PEAR
PLUM
PLUM

## Foccaccia à la Provence

*Dough*

- 1 teaspoon active dry yeast
- 3/4 cup lukewarm water
- 3/4 cup all-purpose flour
- 1 teaspoon active dry yeast
- 1 cup lukewarm water
- 3 tablespoons olive oil
- 2 teaspoons salt
- 2 1/2 cups all-purpose flour, sifted with 3/4 cup wholewheat flour

*Method*

1. Combine yeast with lukewarm water and 3/4 cup flour. Set aside for 45 minutes.
2. Add remaining yeast, lukewarm water and olive oil. Add salt and stir with a wooden spoon.
3. Gradually fold in both types of the remaining flour until a dough forms. Place the dough in a bowl, cover and allow it to rise for two to three hours until double in bulk.
4. Punch down the dough and spread in a baking tray. Leave to rise again for half an hour.

*Topping*

- some olive oil for frying
- 2 cloves garlic, diced
- 1/2 onion, finely diced
- 1 teaspoon basil
- 1 brinjal, finely diced
- 1 red capsicum, diced
- 2 tomatoes
- 2 tablespoons tomato paste
- 1 tablespoon sugar
- salt and pepper to taste

*Method*

1. Heat olive oil in a pan and fry the garlic, onion and basil. Add vegetables, tomato paste, sugar, salt and pepper. Add a little water if the mixture is too dry and fry until the brinjal is soft. Cool.
2. Make depressions in the dough with your fingertips and spread with the topping. Bake at 200°C/390°F for 25 minutes.

## Foccaccia with Red Onions and Rosemary

*Dough*

- 2 1/2 teaspoons active dry yeast
- 1/2 cup UHT milk, warmed to 40°C/105°F and 46°C/115°F
- 1 1/2 tablespoons olive oil
- 1 cup water, at room temperature
- 500 grams all-purpose flour
- 2 teaspoons salt

*Method*

1. Dissolve yeast in milk until frothy. Add olive oil and water.
2. Combine flour and salt. Make a well in the flour and pour in the yeast mixture. Mix well and knead the dough for 10 minutes. Cover the dough and allow it to rise for 2 hours in a greased bowl until double in bulk.
3. Punch down and divide into two equal parts. Shape each part into a round loaf.

*Topping*

- 3/4 cup walnuts, toasted and chopped
- 2 red onions, sliced and fried in olive oil
- 10 black olives, chopped
- 1 teaspoon fresh rosemary, chopped

*Method*

Combine all ingredients and sprinkle over the loaves. Leave to rise for another hour before baking in a 200°C/390°F oven for half an hour.

## Tropical Fruit Loaf

*Ingredients*

- 25 dried apricots
- 10 prunes
- 5 slices dried pear
- 2 cups water
- 3 bananas
- 1/2 cup ground almonds
- 1 cup wholemeal flour
- 2 teaspoons baking powder
- 1/4 teaspoon ground cinnamon
- 1 teaspoon grated orange zest

*Method*

1. Boil apricots, prunes and pear in the water. Cover and set aside for 5 minutes. Strain the cooking liquid. Remove 10 boiled apricots from the fruit mixture and add to the cooking liquid. Blend well. Set aside.
2. Mix together the almonds, flour, baking powder, boiled fruit, cinnamon, orange zest and the pureed apricot
3. Grease and line a 20-cm loaf pan. Pour the batter in and bake at 180°C/360°F for 40 minutes.

*Opposite: Foccaccia with Red Onions and Rosemary (left) and Foccaccia à la Provence (right).*

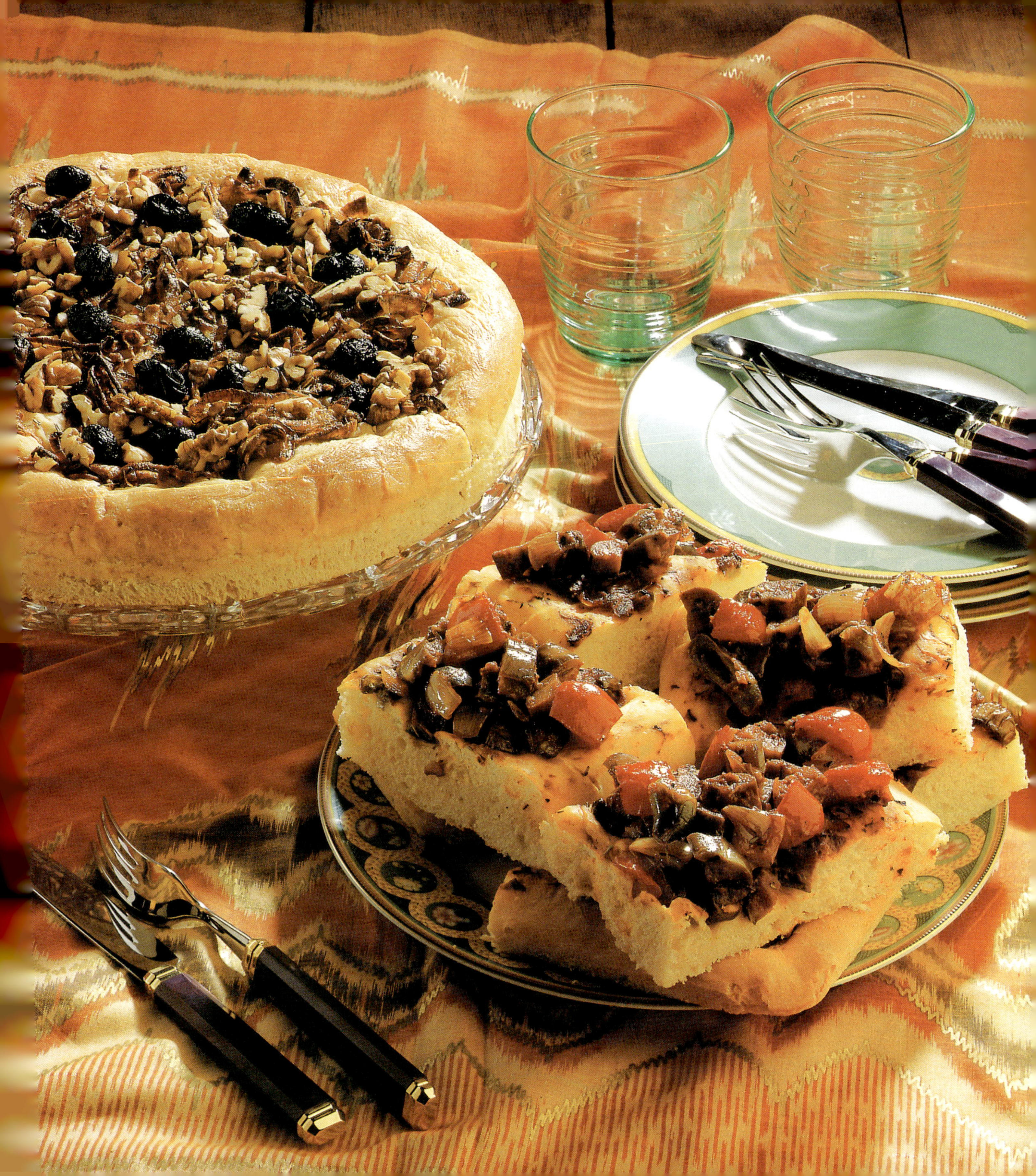

# Prune and Pecan Sticky Bun

### Caramel Topping

- 4 tablespoons butter
- 1 cup brown sugar
- 1 cup pecans, coarsely chopped
- lukewarm water

### Method

Melt butter and sugar in a small saucepan. Add pecan nuts and cook over slow heat for 3 minutes. Add water and stir well until dissolved.

### Dough

- 2 tablespoons dried yeast
- 1/2 cup lukewarm water
- 2/3 cup milk
- 3 tablespoons castor sugar
- 1 teaspoon salt
- 1/2 cup butter, diced
- 5–6 cups all-purpose flour
- 2 eggs, lightly beaten

- butter, melted, to glaze
- 1/2 cup castor sugar, mixed with 1 tablespoon cinnamon powder

### Method

1. Dissolve yeast in lukewarm water.
2. Heat milk, sugar, salt and butter. Add the yeast and mix well.
3. Place 3 cups flour in a bowl. Add eggs and warm milk mixture. Stir well.
4. Transfer the dough to a floured surface and knead for 10 minutes, adding more flour until the dough is elastic rather than sticky. Place the dough in a bowl. Brush with some melted butter and cover tightly for two to three hours until double in bulk.
5. Punch down the dough and knead for five minutes. Roll out into a 60 cm by 45 cm rectangle. Spread evenly with more melted butter and sprinkle with the cinnamon and sugar mixture.
6. Roll up like a jelly roll and secure the edges with water. Cut the roll into six slices and arrange them flat on a baking tray with caramel topping underneath. Cover with a tea towel and leave to rise for an hour until double in bulk. Brush the surface with water.
7. Bake at 170°C/340°F for 35 minutes until cooked.
8. Once baked, turn the sticky bun upside down and serve slightly warm.

# Swiss Braided Bread

### Ingredients

- 680 grams bread flour
- 15 grams fresh yeast
- 430 grams lukewarm milk
- 1 teaspoon castor sugar
- 2 teaspoon salt
- 30 grams butter
- 1 egg, lightly beaten

- corn oil + 1 egg to glaze
- 2 tablespoons sesame seeds, to decorate

### Method

1. Place 170 grams of bread flour in a bowl. Make a well in the centre.
2. Dissolve yeast in lukewarm milk. Pour into the flour and mix well. Cover and leave to rise for half an hour.
3. In a separate bowl mix together the remaining flour, sugar and salt. Cut in the butter until the mixture resembles breadcrumbs.
4. Add the beaten egg to the yeast mixture and immediately add this to the butter mixture. Mix until the dough becomes sticky.
5. Transfer to a floured surface and knead for 10 minutes until silky smooth and elastic.
6. Place the dough in a greased bowl and brush evenly with corn oil. Cover with a damp cloth and leave to rise for 1 to 1 1/2 hours until double in bulk.
7. Punch down the dough, knead for a while and divide into three equal parts. Roll each portion into a 40-cm strand. Place the strands side by side on a greased baking tray and plait them together. Neaten the edges. Do not plait the strands too tightly.
8. Cover with a damp towel and leave to rise for an hour until double in bulk.
9. Glaze with egg, sprinkle with sesame seeds and bake for 15 to 20 minutes at 230°C/450°F until golden brown. Lower the temperature to 200°C/390°F and bake for another 20 minutes. Cool on a wire rack.

# Carrot Cheese Bread

### Ingredients

- 4 eggs, separated
- 3 cups carrots, coarsely grated
- 1 cup heavy cream
- 3/4 cup cheddar cheese, grated
- 1 cup cream cracker crumbs
- 2 tablespoons butter, melted
- 1 onion, finely diced
- 1/2 teaspoon fresh basil, finely chopped
- 2 tablespoons parsley, finely chopped
- 3/4 teaspoon salt
- 1/4 teaspoon pepper

### Method

1. Whisk egg whites until fluffy.
2. In another bowl beat egg yolks. Gradually add the remaining ingredients until well mixed. Fold in the egg whites.
3. Pour the batter into a greased standard-size loaf pan and bake at 170°C/340°F for 40 to 45 minutes. Serve warm.

*Opposite: Swiss Braided Bread (left) and Prune and Pecan Sticky Buns (right).*

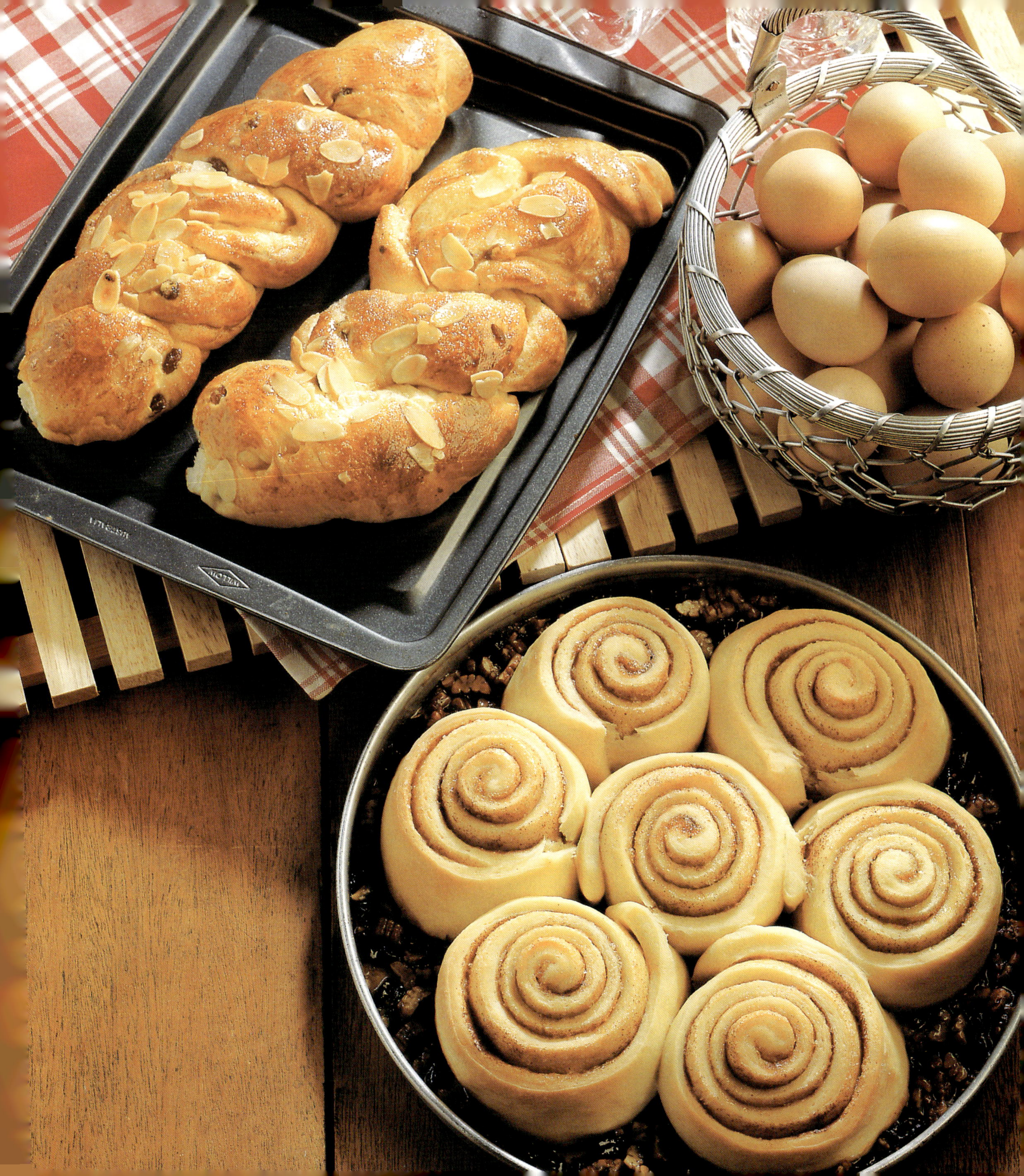

# Cakes

The Art of Baking Cakes, p138  1 Apple and Date Princess Cake, p140  2 All-American Chocolate Cake, p140  3 Apple and Date Harvest Cake, p140  4 Chocolate Brownies, p140  5 Apple Hazelnut Torte, p142  6 Apricot Cake, p142  7 Evelyn Orange Tea Loaf, p142  8 Fruit Chiffon Cake, p142  9 Maria's Apricot Gugelhupf, p144  10 Apricot Jelly Roll, p144  11 Chocolate Gingerbread Cake, p144  12 Cherry Almond Cake, p144  13 Carrot Walnut Cake with Orange Frosting, p146  14 Banana Cake with Cream Cheese Frosting, p146  15 Apricot Prune Gugelhupf, p146  16 Fruity Tangerine Tea Cake, p148  17 Apricot Tea Cake, p148  18 Walnut Prune Cake, p148  19 Coconut Carrot Cake, p148  20 Bittersweet Chocolate Date Cake, p150  21 Blueberry Cake, p150  22 Swiss Carrot Cake, p150  23 Chocolate Gugelhupf, p152  24 Hot Apple Cake with Caramel Pecan Sauce, p152  25 Chocolate Potato Cake, p152  26 Chocolate Cake, p152  27 Boiled Fruitcake, p154  28 Cinnamon Walnut Coffee Cake, p154  29 Prune and Lemon Cake, p154  30 Orange Sponge Cake, p154  31 Chocolate Valentino, p156  32 Caramelised Pineapple Cake, p156  33 Lemon Ginger Tea Cake, p156  34 Chocolate Orange Bavaroise, p158  35 Chocolate Paradise, p158  36 Persimmon Cake, p158  37 Pineapple Upside-Down Cake, p160  38 Lemon Tea Cake, p160  39 Cherry Butter Cake, p160  40 Victoria Sponge Sandwich, p160  41 Fresh Ginger Cake, p162  42 Madeleines, p162  43 Ginger, Peaches and Pineapple Cake, p162  44 Visitandine, p162  45 Crispy Cornflake Cake, p164  46 La Tropicana Cake, p164  47 Fruit Cobbler, p164  48 Lemon Poppy Seed Cake, p166  49 Plum Tea Cake, p166  50 Mississippi Mud Cake, p166  51 Chocolate Rehrucken, p168  52 Tiramisu, p168

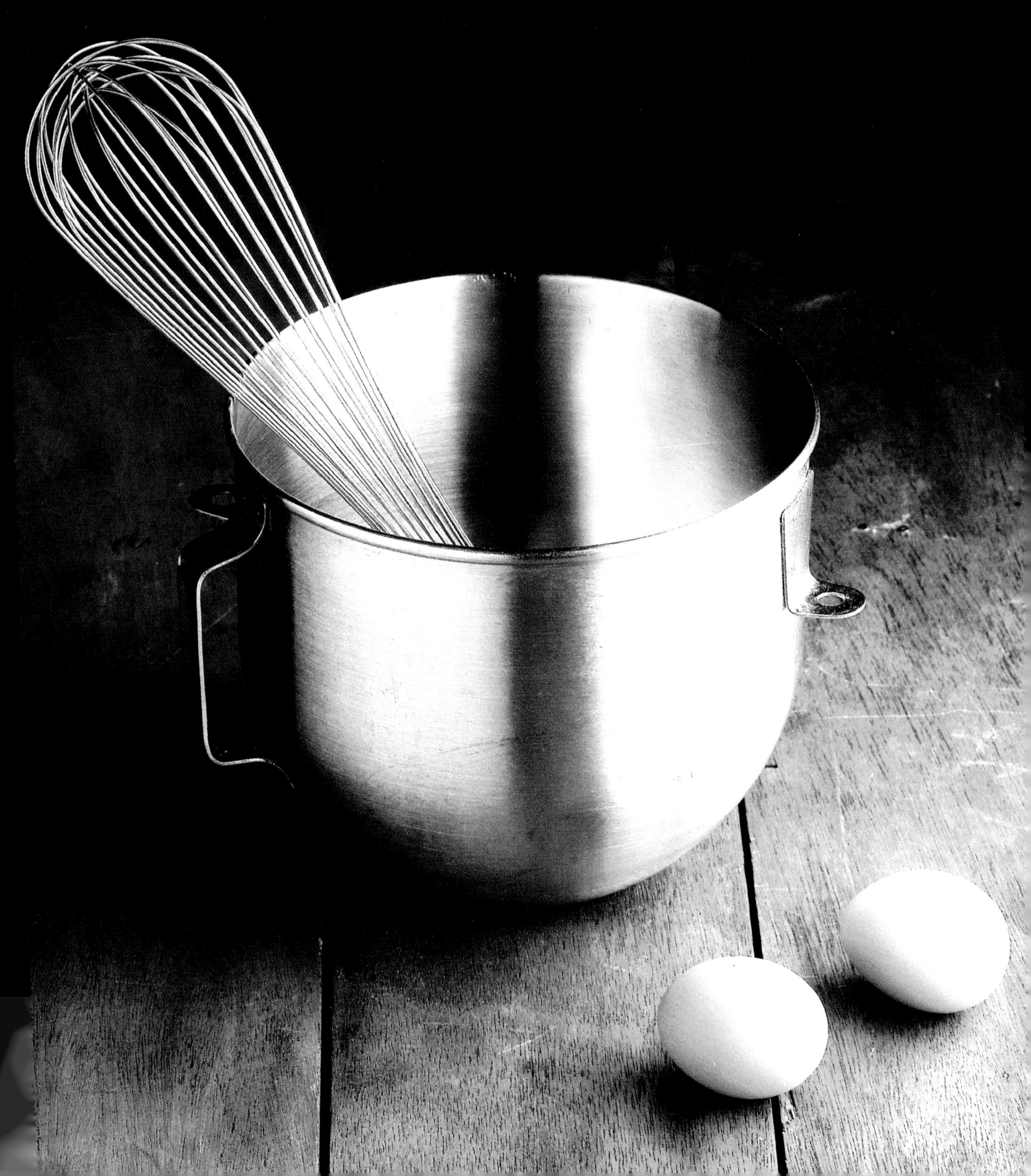

# The Art of Baking Cakes

Cake making is a precise art. The ingredients and their relationship with each other are balanced like a chemical formula. During baking a chemical process takes place, transforming the raw ingredients into a delicious new entity.

The basic ingredients for a cake are eggs, flour, sugar and some fat, most often butter, margarine, shortening or cooking oil. The English sponge cake, French genoise and American layer cake use these basic ingredients. Variations are achieved by changing the flavour, texture and shape of the cake.

There are three basic cake-mixing methods, each producing a different kind of cake: whisking creates sponge cakes like the genoise, creaming produces pound cakes and fruitcakes that require leavening, and melting creates heavier cakes such as gingerbread.

## SELECTING CAKE PANS

The use of different cake pans affects baking time and gives character to the finished cake. It is important to use the correct size and type of pan stated in the recipe. For example a springform pan with a removable bottom is useful for fragile cakes that need careful unmoulding. In general a dense, long-cooking cake such as fruitcake needs a thicker pan to prevent scorching.

Cake pans should be coated with fat, flour, or a combination of the two to give the cake a smooth, golden finish.

Lining the pan with parchment or wax paper also makes cakes easier to unmould and protects the batter from oven heat. For cakes made with egg white, the pan is left ungreased as the batter is meant to cling to the pan.

Nonstick pans are particularly helpful for moist batters and do not need greasing except in special cases where a light coating or a protective paper lining is used.

The fat used for greasing should be the same as that used in the batter. Melt or soften the fat and use a pastry brush to apply a thin, even coating to the pan, taking care to brush the corners and rim.

## PREPARING YOUR OVEN

Most ovens take 10 to 15 minutes to reach the correct temperature and should therefore be heated in advance. Precision is important, so check the temperature of the oven with a thermometer if possible.

Position the shelf so that the cake will fit in the centre of the oven or slightly lower. Deep cakes should be placed lower in the oven than shallow ones.

When baking more than one cake at a time, stagger the pans so that one is not directly above the other. If the oven temperature is uneven, rearrange the pans when the cakes start to brown so that the heat circulates freely. The edges of a cake pan or baking tray should never be less than 2.5 cm from the sides of the oven.

Cakes often need turning during baking so that they brown evenly. However do not open the oven door until a cake is set and lightly browned otherwise the centre will sink.

# INGREDIENTS

### Eggs
Most recipes assume that an egg weighs 60 grams, graded "large". Eggs should be at room temperature before use.

### Sugar
Castor sugar is commonly used in cakes. Coarser sugar does not blend as well and gives cakes a spotted surface. Brown sugar gives cakes added colour and a heavier texture. Powdered sugar makes for lightness.

### Salt
A pinch of salt adds flavour to any sweet mixture.

### Flour
Most cake recipes use all-purpose flour, also known as plain flour. All-purpose flour gives the cake a very light texture, while other flours such as wholemeal, semolina or rye produce heavier cakes. Cornflour, potato starch, arrowroot and rice flour are often used for extra lightness. Self-raising flour contains leavening and must not be substituted for all-purpose flour. Flour is most accurately measured by weight but if you are measuring by volume sift the flour after measuring unless otherwise specified. Sifting is particularly important for giving lightness to whisked cakes.

### Fat
Butter adds flavour to a wide variety of delicate cakes. Salted butter contains enough salt to alter the flavour of pastries, so I like to use unsalted butter, also known as sweet butter. Firm margarine may be substituted for butter, but margarine lacks flavour. Shortening produces a light cake, but has no flavour. Oil is a light alternative for such cakes as chiffon. Fat also improves the shelf-life of cakes and keeps them moist.

# MIXING THE BATTER

There are several common terms in cake-mixing:

1. To stir or combine calls for mixing ingredients thoroughly in a circular, scooping motion. Often a wooden spoon or spatula is used, but for large quantities your cupped hand is more effective.
2. To cream fat and sugar is to combine until smooth. Sugar is beaten at a high speed until it is dissolved in the fat. The air incorporated in the batter while creaming results in a light, fluffy batter.
3. To fold is the lightest way of combining ingredients. Fold with a spatula.
4. To whisk means to incorporate air, usually in eggs. A balloon whisk, either hand-held or electric, is used. To whisk to the ribbon stage means to combine eggs and sugar by beating until a light mousse is formed.
5. To beat means to work ingredients thoroughly so that a change takes place, for example beating yolks and sugar to the ribbon stage. Often air is incorporated during beating.

# CHECKING FOR DONENESS

All cakes shrink slightly from the sides of the pan when done. For whisked cakes, test by pressing the centre of the cake lightly with your fingertips. The cake should spring back if it is done. For creamed and melted cakes, insert a wooden toothpick in the centre of the cake. If it comes away cleanly, the cake is ready.

# TROUBLESHOOTING

### Sunken Centre
- Too much sugar, resulting in a dark brown crust and sticky centre;
- Too much baking powder or other leavening;
- Too much liquid, causing a sticky layer above the bottom crust;
- Oven temperature is too low, causing the cake to be undercooked;
- Oven door is opened unnecessarily, exposing the cake to a draught before it sets.

### Peaked Top
- Gluten is overdeveloped, due either to flour that is too hard or by overbeating;
- Oven temperature is too high.

### Tough Cake
- Batter is insufficiently beaten or whipped;
- Not enough rising agent;
- Not enough sugar;
- Batter is overmixed;
- Eggs or butter is too cold.

For all cakes, success depends on your following a recipe precisely.

# Apple and Date Princess Cake

## Ingredients

- 1¼ cups all-purpose flour
- 2 tablespoons ground cinnamon
- a pinch of salt
- 1 tablespoon baking soda
- grated zest of 2 lemons
- 2 tablespoons lemon juice
- ½ cup vegetable oil
- 1 teaspoon vanilla essence
- ½ cup castor sugar
- 2 eggs
- 1 cup walnuts, toasted, coarsely chopped
- ½ cup dates, chopped
- 2 green apples, peeled and grated

## Method

1. Sift together flour, cinnamon, salt and baking soda.
2. In another bowl mix together lemon zest, lemon juice, vegetable oil, vanilla essence, sugar and eggs. Fold the flour mixture into the egg mixture and add walnuts, dates and grated apples.
3. Grease small paper cups and place them in a muffin tray. Fill one-quarter of each cup with batter. Bake at 175°C/350°F for about 20 minutes until a skewer inserted in the centre of the cake comes away cleanly.

# All-American Chocolate Cake

## Cake

- 230 grams unsalted butter
- 300 grams castor sugar
- 2 teaspoons vanilla essence
- 3 eggs
- ½ cup unsweetened cocoa powder, sifted
- 1 cup hot water
- 235 grams cake flour or all-purpose flour
- 1 tablespoon baking powder
- ¾ teaspoon salt
- ½ cup walnuts, chopped

## Method

1. Cream butter and sugar until light and fluffy. Add vanilla essence and eggs one at a time.
2. Dissolve cocoa in hot water. In a separate bowl sift together flour, baking powder and salt. Alternately add cocoa and sifted flour to the butter mixture. Fold in walnuts.
3. Bake in a greased 20-cm cake pan lined with parchment paper for 35 minutes at 170°C/340°F until cooked. Cool overnight.

## Chocolate Ganache

- 150 grams bitter chocolate or semisweet chocolate, chopped
- 3 tablespoons heavy cream
- 3 tablespoons unsalted butter

## Method

Combine all ingredients in a saucepan and melt over medium heat. Cool slightly before pouring over the cake.

# Apple and Date Harvest Cake

## Ingredients

- 2 teaspoons unsalted butter
- 4 cups green apples, peeled and diced
- 1 cup walnuts, coarsely chopped
- 1½ cups castor sugar
- 2 cups all-purpose flour
- 2 teaspoons ground cinnamon
- 1½ teaspoons baking soda
- ½ teaspoon salt
- 2 large eggs, well beaten
- ¼ cup vegetable oil
- 2 teaspoons vanilla essence
- ½ cup dates, pitted and chopped

powdered sugar for dusting

## Method

1. Preheat the oven to 175°C/350°F. Lightly grease a cake pan with butter.
2. Toss apples and nuts with sugar in a large bowl. In another bowl sift together flour, cinnamon, baking soda and salt. Beat in eggs, oil and vanilla essence until the batter is thoroughly moistened. Pour over the apples. Add dates and without overmixing, stir with a wooden spoon to evenly distribute the fruit. Pour into the cake pan.
3. Bake for 45 minutes or until a skewer inserted in the centre comes away cleanly. Cool in the pan for 15 minutes. Remove to a wire rack and dust with powdered sugar.

Chef's Note: This cake is best eaten after a day or two as the flavour mellows.

# Chocolate Brownies

## Ingredients

- 150 grams unsalted butter
- 340 grams semisweet chocolate, chopped
- 1 cup castor sugar
- 2 eggs, beaten
- 1 teaspoon vanilla essence
- ½ cup all-purpose flour
- ½ cup walnuts, chopped
- ¼ teaspoon salt

## Method

1. Melt butter and chocolate until smooth. Cool slightly, add sugar, eggs and vanilla essence. Whisk until smooth. Fold in flour, walnuts and salt.
2. Pour the mixture into a baking tray lined with parchment paper and bake at 175°C/350°F for 25 to 30 minutes.

Chef's Note: Use ½ cup ground hazelnuts in place of walnuts if preferred.

*Opposite: All-American Chocolate Cake (above) and Chocolate Brownies (below).*

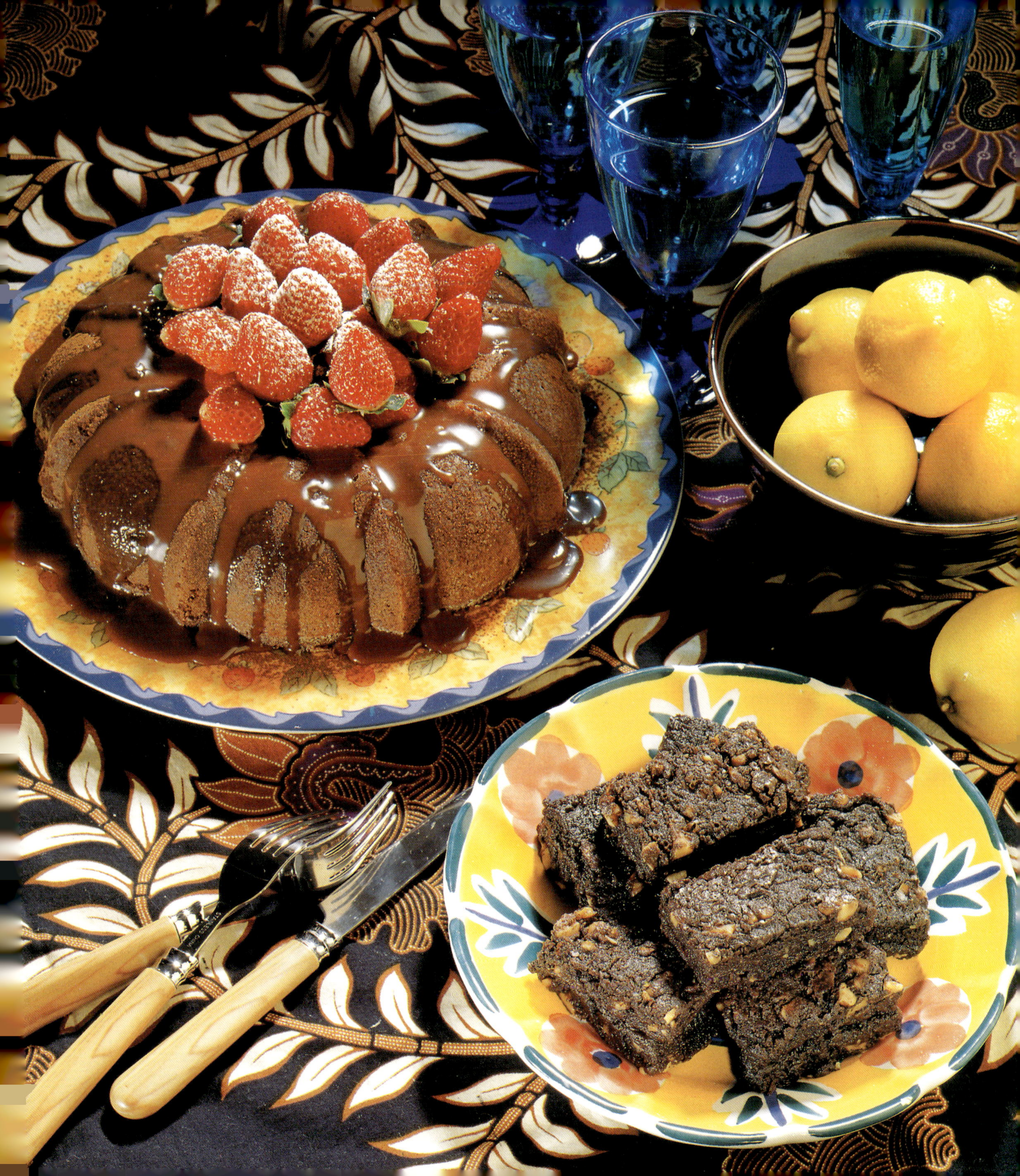

## Apple Hazelnut Torte

*Ingredients*

70 grams breadcrumbs
250 grams green apples, peeled and grated
200 grams powdered sugar
6 eggs, separated
1 tablespoon unsweetened cocoa powder
150 grams ground hazelnuts

apricot jam to glaze
150 grams unsalted butter, melted with 150 grams semisweet chocolate
ground hazelnuts to decorate
cocoa powder for dusting

*Method*

1. Mix together breadcrumbs and apples and set aside for 20 minutes.
2. With an electric mixer beat sugar and egg yolks until light and fluffy. Gradually add cocoa powder and ground hazelnuts. Add apples.
3. Meanwhile beat the egg whites until stiff and slowly fold into batter. Bake in a buttered 23-cm pan lined with parchment paper for 55 minutes at 170°C/340°F. Cool.
4. Glaze the top of the cake with apricot jam. Melt butter together with the chocolate and pour over the cake. Sprinkle with ground hazelnuts and dust with cocoa powder.

## Apricot Cake

*Ingredients*

240 grams all-purpose flour
2½ teaspoons baking powder
170 grams butter
6 tablespoons ground almonds
160 grams brown sugar
2 eggs, beaten
1 teaspoon vanilla essence
80 grams dried apricots, chopped
150 ml UHT milk

*Method*

1. Sift together flour and baking powder. Cut butter into the sifted flour until the mixture resembles breadcrumbs.
2. Add ground almonds and brown sugar and mix well. Add eggs, vanilla essence, apricots and milk and slowly mix to a consistency where the batter can be dropped. Pour into a well-greased and parchment-lined 22-cm baking pan.
3. Bake at 180°C/360°F for about 45 minutes until cooked all the way through.

## Evelyn Orange Tea Loaf

*Ingredients*

230 grams unsalted butter
1½ cups castor sugar
grated zest and juice of 2 oranges
4 eggs, separated
2 cups self-raising flour, sifted
a pinch of salt
2 tablespoons Grand Marnier, or other orange liqueur, optional

*Method*

1. Cream butter and sugar until light and fluffy. Add orange zest and egg yolks one at a time.
2. Sift together flour and salt. Alternately fold in flour and orange juice to the batter. Add orange liqueur.
3. In another bowl beat egg whites until fluffy and slowly fold into the batter. Pour into a greased and parchment-lined standard-size loaf pan. Bake at 175°C/350°F for 35 to 40 minutes until the cake is done.

## Fruit Chiffon Cake

*Ingredients*

8 eggs, separated
½ teaspoon cream of tartar
150 grams castor sugar
¾ teaspoon salt
230 grams all-purpose flour, sifted
2 teaspoons baking powder
2 bananas, mashed
125 ml corn oil
150 grams castor sugar
½ teaspoon vanilla essence
120 grams raisins
7 glace cherries, quartered

*Method*

1. Beat egg whites with cream of tartar and sugar at high speed until a stiff meringue forms. Combine salt, flour, baking powder, bananas, oil, egg yolks, sugar and vanilla essence and mix with one-third of the meringue. Fold the batter into remaining meringue.
2. Pour one-third of the batter into a large chiffon pan. Combine raisins and cherries and sprinkle over the batter. Repeat the layering until all the ingredients are used up. Bake the cake at 180°C/360°F for 45 minutes.

*Opposite: Apple Hazelnut Torte (left) and Evelyn Orange Tea Loaf (right).*

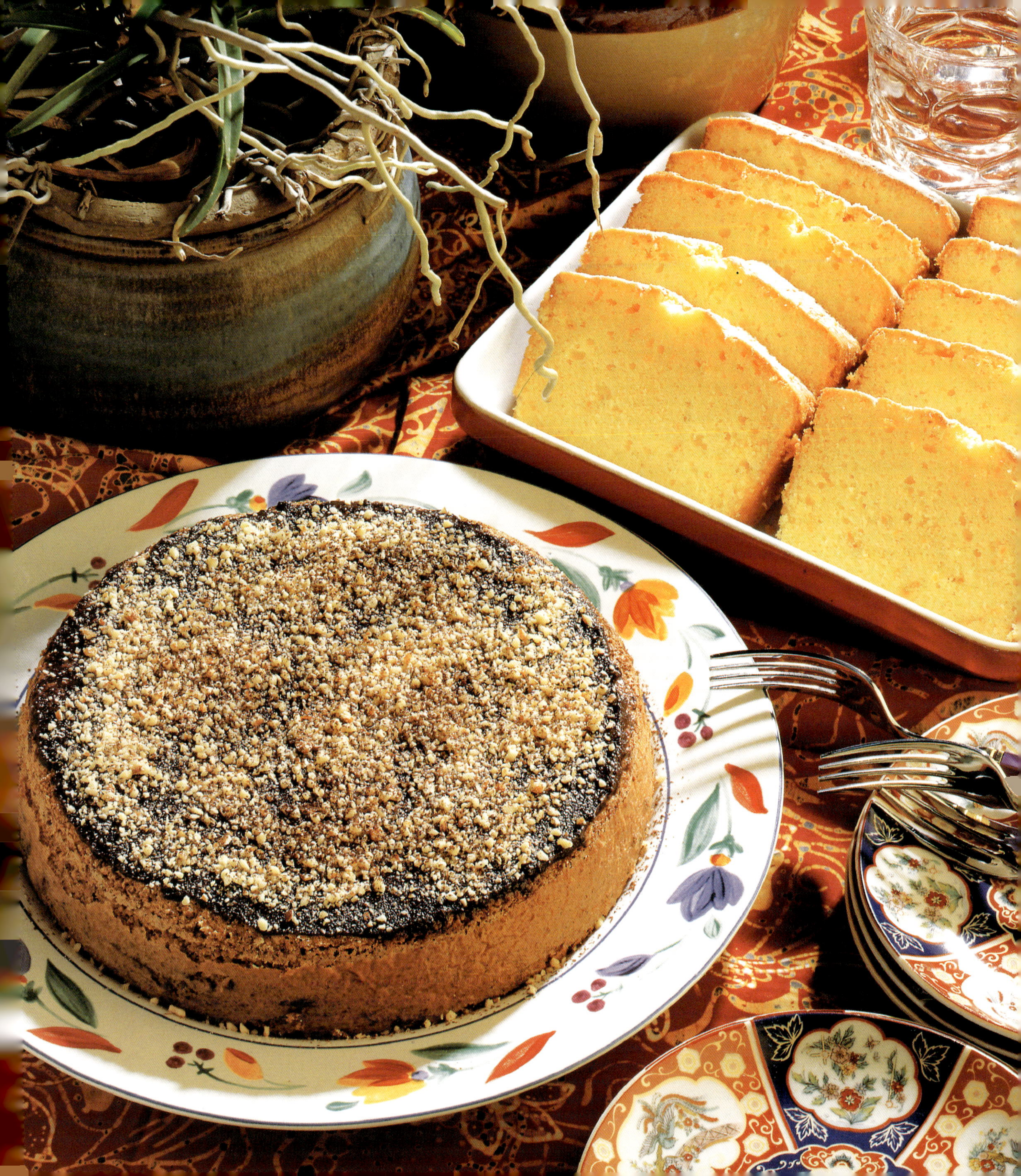

## Maria's Apricot Gugelhupf

*Ingredients*

    200 grams dried apricots, finely chopped
    juice of 1 orange
    2 tablespoons Grand Marnier
    200 grams unsalted butter
    200 grams castor sugar
    a pinch of salt
    4 eggs, separated
    grated zest and juice of 1 lemon
    150 grams yoghurt, preferably apricot-flavoured but plain is fine
    300 grams all-purpose flour
    18 grams baking powder
    2 green apples, peeled and finely diced

*Method*

1. Soak apricots in orange juice and Grand Marnier, preferably overnight or for at least 3 hours.
2. Cream butter, sugar and salt until fluffy. Add egg yolks, lemon juice, lemon zest and yoghurt. Combine soaked apricots with the butter mixture.
3. Sift together flour and baking powder and add to the batter. Gently fold in apples.
4. In a separate bowl beat egg whites until stiff. Gently fold into the batter mixture.
5. Pour into a greased and floured gugelhupf mould. Bake at 180°C/360°F for about 1 hour 15 minutes.

## Apricot Jelly Roll

*Ingredients*

    6 eggs, separated
    a pinch of salt
    4 tablespoons + 100 grams castor sugar
    80 grams ground almonds
    80 grams all-purpose flour
    powdered sugar for dusting
    1/2 cup apricot jam, warmed with a few tablespoons of water

*Method*

1. Beat egg whites and salt until slightly stiff and slowly add 4 tablespoons sugar. Continue beating until stiff and glossy. Set aside.
2. In another bowl beat egg yolks with the remaining 100 grams sugar until light and creamy.
3. In a separate bowl sift together almonds and flour. Slowly add to egg yolks and gently fold before adding egg whites.
4. Pour the batter into a greased, parchment-lined jellyroll pan measuring 30 cm long. Dust with powdered sugar and bake for 7 to 10 minutes at 205°C/400°F. The cake is done when a skewer inserted in the centre comes away cleanly. As soon as the cake is removed from the oven, immediately turn it upside down. Spread apricot jam over the entire cake and roll tightly. Wrap in foil for a few hours before cutting.

## Chocolate Gingerbread Cake

*Ingredients*

    a little butter and fine, dry breadcrumbs
    250 grams unsalted butter, cut into small pieces
    1 tablespoon instant coffee, dissolved in 1 cup boiling water
    1 cup dark brown sugar
    56 grams unsweetened chocolate, finely chopped and melted
    2 1/2 cups all-purpose flour
    1 1/2 teaspoons baking soda
    1 teaspoon salt
    1 teaspoon ground ginger
    1 teaspoon ground cinnamon
    1 teaspoon allspice
    1/3 cup candied ginger, finely chopped
    1 cup light molasses
    4 whole eggs, beaten

*Method*

1. Preheat the oven to 170°C/340°F. Butter a 22-cm cake pan and dust with fine dry breadcrumbs. Shake out the excess crumbs.
2. With an electric mixer beat butter and hot coffee, slowly mixing until the butter melts. Add brown sugar and mix well. Add melted chocolate, molasses and beaten eggs.
3. Sift together flour, baking soda, salt, ginger, cinnamon and allspice. Gradually add the sifted ingredients to the butter mixture to form a thin batter. Stir in candied ginger. Pour into pan and bake for 50 minutes until the top of the cake springs back when gently pressed. Cool the cake before removing from the pan. Serve plain or with chocolate sauce.

## Cherry Almond Cake

*Ingredients*

    275 grams red glace cherries
    225 grams butter, softened
    225 grams castor sugar
    6 eggs, separated
    65 grams self-raising flour
    a pinch of salt
    175 grams ground almonds
    1/2 teaspoon almond essence

    powdered sugar for dusting

*Method*

1. Grease a 22-cm cake pan with butter and line with parchment paper. Arrange cherries in a single layer at the base of the pan.
2. Beat butter and sugar until fluffy. Add egg yolks one at a time.
3. In a separate bowl beat egg whites until stiff.
4. Mix together flour, salt and ground almonds. Fold into the batter. Stir in almond essence. Fold in egg whites. Pour the batter into a cake pan and bake at 180°C/360°F for one hour. If the top browns too quickly, cover the pan with foil. Dust with powdered sugar.

*Opposite: Cherry Almond Cake (left) and Maria's Apricot Gugelhupf (right).*

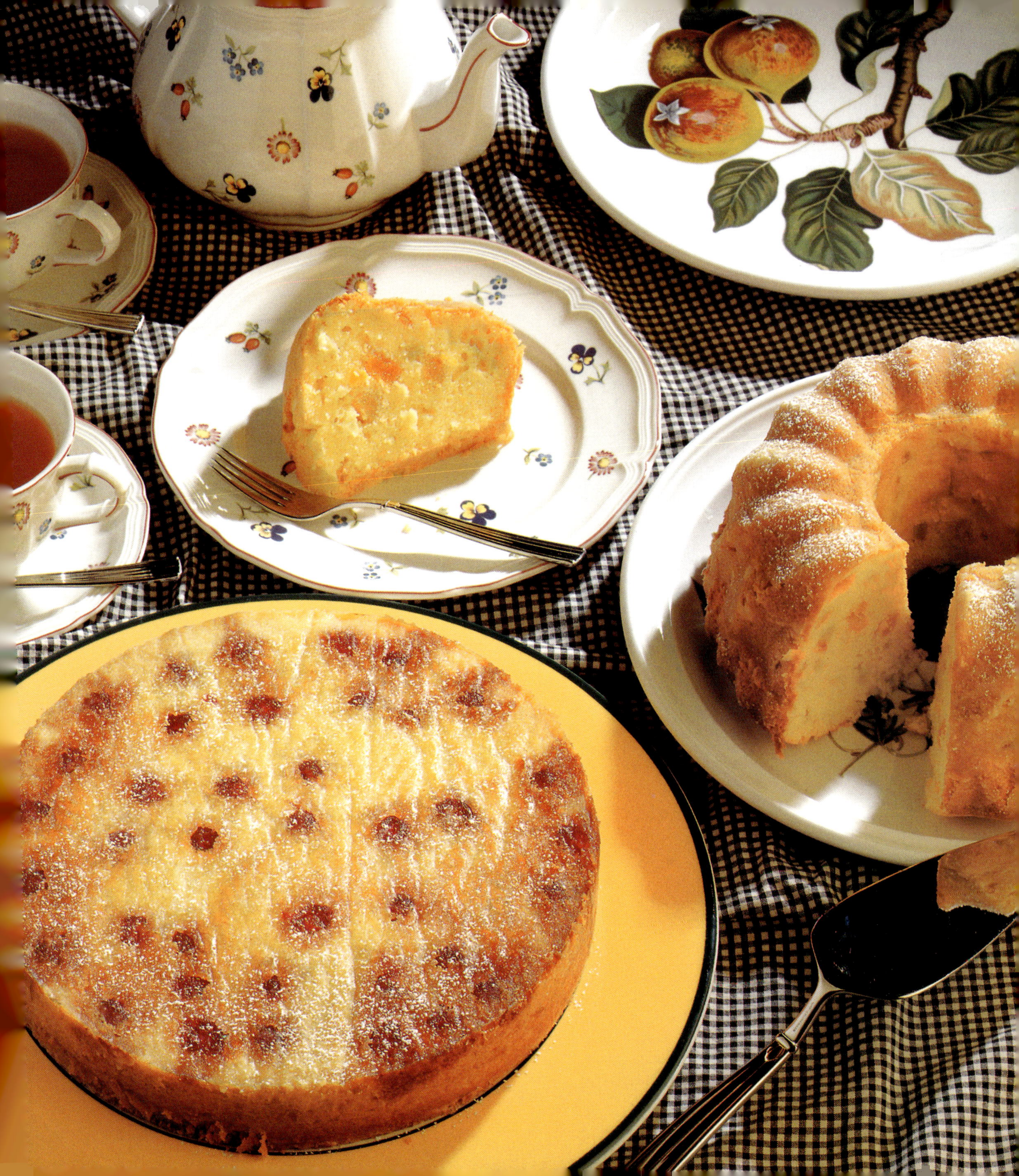

# Carrot Walnut Cake with Orange Frosting

*Cake*

- 4 eggs
- 3/4 cup corn oil
- 390 grams castor sugar
- 255 grams bread flour
- 1/2 teaspoon salt
- 1 teaspoon ground cinnamon
- 3/4 teaspoon baking soda
- 1/4 teaspoon baking powder
- 455 grams grated carrots
- 75 grams walnuts, chopped

*Method*

1. With an electric mixer whip eggs until light and frothy, then gradually add oil. Reduce the speed to low and add sugar. Continue beating on high speed for another 3 to 4 minutes until mixture has doubled its volume.
2. Sift together flour, salt, cinnamon, baking soda and baking powder. Add to the batter. Fold in carrots and walnuts, distributing them evenly.
3. Pour the batter in a greased and floured 25-cm cake pan. Bake at 190°C/375°F for about 50 minutes.

*Orange Cream Cheese Frosting*

- 220 grams cream cheese
- 60 grams unsalted butter, softened
- 1 teaspoon vanilla essence
- 130 grams powdered sugar
- grated zest of 1 orange
- juice from 1 orange, reduced to 1 teaspoon by heating it
- 3 tablespoons Grand Marnier

grated carrots to decorate

*Method*

1. Set an electric mixer at low speed and blend cream cheese. Gradually mix in butter. Add vanilla essence and powdered sugar, orange zest, orange juice and Grand Marnier. Without overmixing, blend until smooth and spreadable.
2. Frost the cake and top with grated carrots or marzipan shapes.

Chef's Notes: (1) Baking powder and baking soda stop working at approximately 77°C/170°F. The batter around the sides of the pan tends to heat up faster, so a heavy sponge cake like this will be higher in the middle. (2) If you find that the frosting is too soft, leave it in the refrigerator to firm up for a few hours before spreading.

# Banana Cake with Cream Cheese Frosting

*Cake*

- 225 grams unsalted butter
- 1 cup castor sugar
- 2 eggs
- 1 cup bananas, mashed
- 1/3 cup yoghurt
- 1 teaspoon vanilla essence
- 1 3/4 cups all-purpose flour
- 1/4 teaspoon salt
- 1 teaspoon baking soda

*Method*

1. Beat butter and sugar until light and fluffy. Add eggs one at a time followed by mashed bananas. Add yoghurt and vanilla essence. Sift together flour, salt and baking soda and fold into the batter.
2. Pour into a greased and floured 22-cm cake pan. Bake at 180°C/360°F for about 50 minutes. Cool.

*Banana Cream Cheese Frosting*

- 340 grams cream cheese, softened at room temperature
- 1/4 cup bananas, mashed
- 1 cup powdered sugar
- 1/2 cup walnuts, toasted and chopped

*Method*

Beat cream cheese until smooth before adding the remaining ingredients. Frost the cooled cake.

Chef's Note: As an option, divide the cake batter between two pans measuring 20 cm by 5 cm. When the cakes are cooked and cooled, sandwich them together and fill with frosting. You can also use a loaf pan instead.

# Apricot Prune Gugelhupf

*Cake*

- 3 eggs
- 1/3 cup castor sugar
- 1 cup fresh milk
- 1/2 cup butter, melted
- 2 cups all-purpose flour
- 1 tablespoon baking powder
- 1/2 teaspoon salt
- 1 cup dried apricots, chopped
- 1 cup prunes, chopped

powdered sugar for dusting

*Method*

1. Grease and flour a gugelhupf mould.
2. Beat eggs and sugar until just mixed. Add milk and melted butter.
3. Sift together flour, baking powder and salt. Fold into the batter, followed by dried fruit.

*Filling*

- 1/4 cup brown sugar
- 1 teaspoon ground cinnamon
- 1/2 cup walnuts, chopped

*Method*

1. Combine all the ingredients for the filling.
2. Transfer one-third of the cake batter into the prepared mould and sprinkle with one-third of the walnut filling. Continue the layering process until all the ingredients are used up.
3. Bake at 175°C/350°F for one hour. Dust with powdered sugar.

Chef's Note: It is important to cool the cake totally before you make any attempt to remove it from the pan. As an option add 2 tablespoons of apricot brandy to the filling for flavour. The cake is best eaten the day after baking.

*Opposite: Banana Cake with Cream Cheese Frosting (above left) and Carrot Walnut Cake with Orange Frosting (below).*

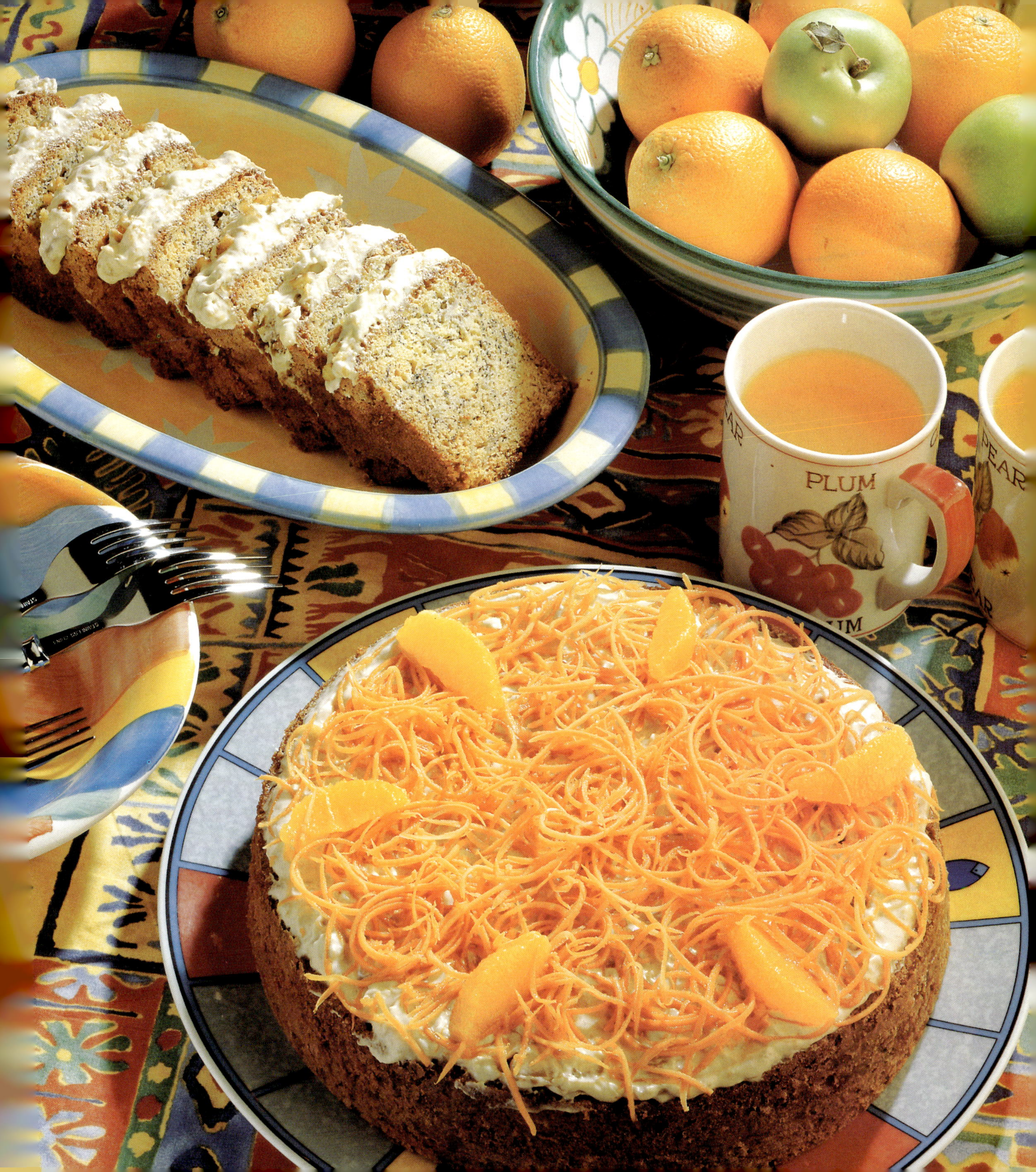
PLUM
PEAR

## Fruity Tangerine Tea Cake

### Ingredients

- 455 grams dried mixed fruit
- 150 grams unsalted butter
- 1 tablespoon earl grey tea flavoured with tangerine, steeped in 1 cup hot water
- 1 cup castor sugar
- 1½ cups all-purpose flour
- 1 cup self-raising flour
- ½ teaspoon bicarbonate of soda
- 1 teaspoon mixed spice
- 2 eggs, beaten
- 140 grams dates, chopped
- 100 grams walnuts, chopped

almonds and cherries to decorate

### Method

1. In a heavy saucepan combine mixed fruit, butter, strained tea and sugar. Bring to a simmer until the sugar dissolves.
2. Sift both types of flour with bicarbonate of soda and mixed spice.
3. In a separate bowl beat eggs and mix with the fruit. Fold in the sifted ingredients, dates and walnuts. Pour the batter into a 22-cm cake pan greased with butter and lined with parchment paper. Decorate with almonds and cherries. Bake at 170°C/340°F for 1¼ to 1½ hours until a skewer inserted in the centre comes away cleanly.

## Apricot Tea Cake

### Ingredients

- 1½ cup self-raising flour
- ½ cup ground almonds
- ½ teaspoon salt
- ¾ cup + 1 tablespoon castor sugar
- 120 grams cold, unsalted butter, cut into small pieces
- 3 eggs
- ½ cup milk
- 1 teaspoon almond essence or 2 tablespoons apricot brandy
- 2 medium-sized cans apricot, drained
- 3 tablespoons sliced almonds

½ cup powdered sugar for dusting

### Method

1. Sift together flour, almonds and salt. Combine with ¾ cup sugar and cut in butter until the mixture resembles breadcrumbs.
2. In a separate bowl beat eggs. Add milk, almond essence and combine with the flour mixture.
3. Grease a 22-cm springform pan with butter and sprinkle with the remaining 1 tablespoon castor sugar. Arrange a single layer of apricots at the base of the pan. Spread half of the cake batter over the apricots. Repeat the layering process, ending with apricots. Sprinkle with sliced almonds. Bake at 180°C/360°F for 40 to 45 minutes. When cool dust with powdered sugar.

## Walnut Prune Cake

### Ingredients

- 250 grams prunes, pitted
- juice of ½ orange
- 3 tablespoons sliced almonds
- 4 eggs
- 1¼ cup castor sugar
- 1 tablespoon grated lemon zest
- 1¼ cup whipped cream, whisked lightly for about 1 minute
- 2 cups self-raising flour
- 3 tablespoons apricot jam
- 1 cup walnuts
- ¼ cup cocoa powder

melted chocolate to decorate

### Method

1. Steep prunes in orange juice for 3 hours.
2. Grease a gugelhupf pan and sprinkle sliced almonds in the base.
3. In a separate bowl beat eggs, sugar and lemon zest until stiff. Gradually add whipped cream. Fold in flour. Divide the batter into portions of one-third and two-thirds. Pour two-thirds of the batter in a baking pan.
4. Mix together the jam, walnuts, marinated prunes and cocoa powder with the remaining one-third of the batter. Pour in the pan. Create a marbled effect with the tip of a knife. Bake at 170°C/340°F for 1 to 1¼ hours. When cooled, pour melted chocolate over the cake to decorate.

## Coconut Carrot Cake

### Ingredients

- 6 eggs, separated
- 150 grams castor sugar
- 230 grams sweetened coconut flakes, finely ground
- 150 grams ground almonds
- 230 grams grated carrots
- a pinch of salt
- 2 tablespoons castor sugar
- 4 tablespoons apricot jam to glaze
- 1 cup sweetened coconut flakes to decorate

### Method

1. Beat egg yolks and sugar until light and fluffy. Fold in coconut flakes, ground almonds and grated carrots.
2. Meanwhile beat egg whites with salt until fluffy and slowly add sugar. Beat mixture until stiff and glossy. Fold into the batter without overmixing.
3. Bake in a greased 22-cm cake pan at 180°C/360°F for about 45 minutes. Cool the cake before glazing the top and sides with warm apricot jam. Decorate with coconut flakes pressed into the sides.

*Opposite: Walnut Prune Cake.*

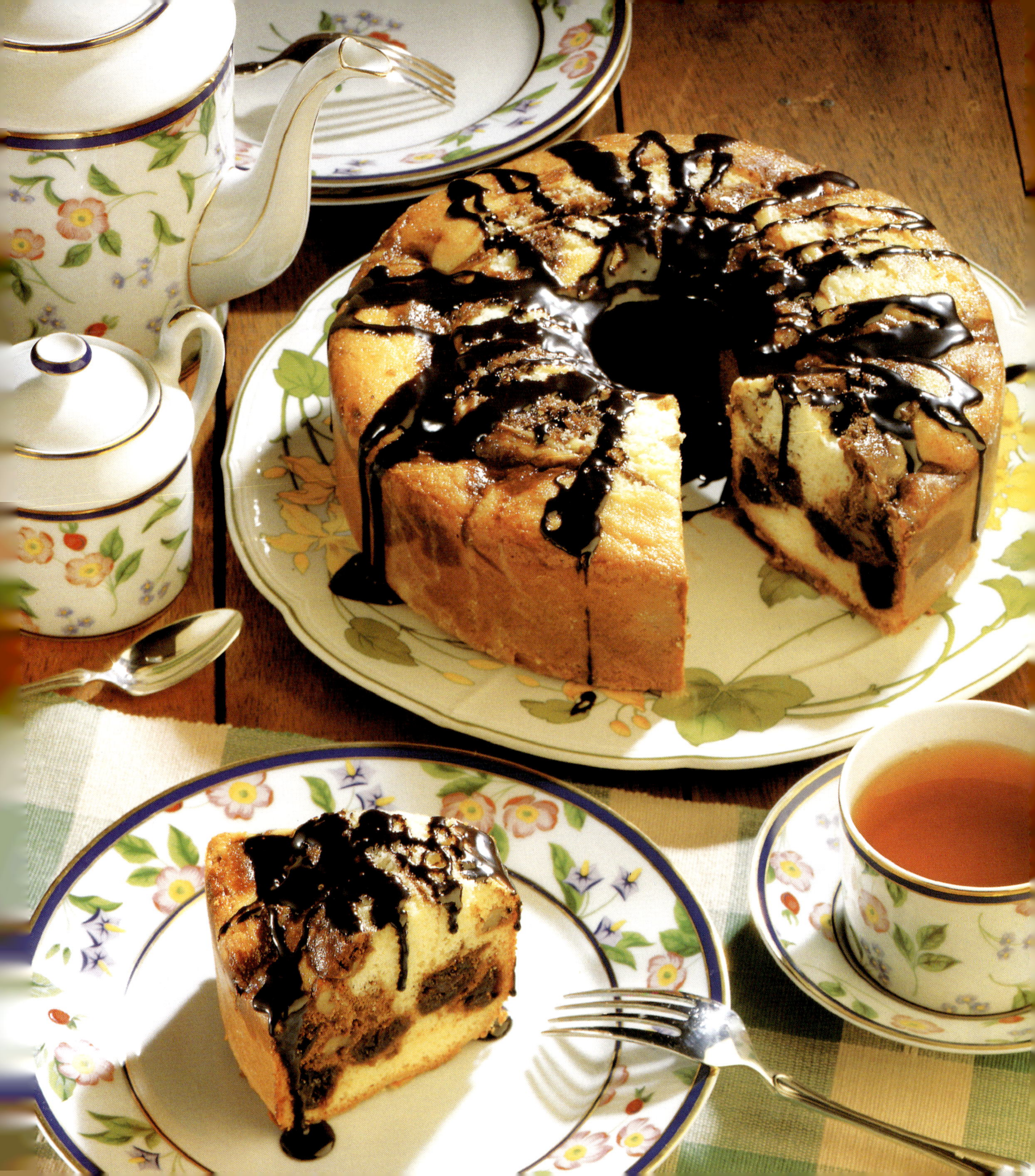

# Bittersweet Chocolate Date Cake

*Cake*

- 60 grams unsweetened chocolate, chopped
- 170 grams bittersweet chocolate, chopped
- 1/2 cup unsalted butter, softened
- 3/4 cup castor sugar
- 6 large eggs, separated
- 1/4 cup bourbon
- 1 tablespoon all-purpose flour
- 1/2 cup pecans, lightly toasted and finely chopped
- 1/2 cup dates, chopped

*Method*

1. Line the base of a greased 22-cm springform pan with parchment paper. Grease the paper and dust the pan with flour, shaking out the excess.
2. In a heatproof bowl set over a saucepan of simmering water, melt both types of chocolate, stirring until smooth. Remove the bowl and cool.
3. Meanwhile cream butter and sugar until pale and fluffy. Add the melted chocolate and beat well. Beat in egg yolks one at a time and add bourbon and flour.
4. In another bowl beat egg whites until stiff peaks form. Stir one-third of the egg whites into the batter, then gently fold in the remaining egg whites, chopped pecans and dates until well-mixed.
5. Pour the batter into the pan and bake for 35 to 40 minutes at 175°C/350°F until a skewer inserted 5 cm from the rim comes away cleanly. The centre of the cake will remain moist. When the cake is done, remove it from the pan and cool.

*Glaze*

- 170 grams bittersweet chocolate
- 1/2 cup heavy cream

whipped cream to serve

*Method*

Place chocolate in a bowl. In a saucepan bring cream to a boil and pour over the chocolate. Stir until the chocolate is smooth and melted. Pour over the chocolate cake and smoothen with a spatula. Let the cake stand for two hours until the glaze sets. Serve with whipped cream

Chef's Note: Substitute bourbon with heavy cream if you prefer. The walnuts may also be substituted with pecans.

# Blueberry Cake

*Cake*

- 1/4 cup unsalted butter
- 3/4 cup castor sugar
- 2 eggs
- 2 cups all-purpose flour
- 2 teaspoons baking powder
- 1/2 teaspoon salt
- 1/2 cup fresh milk
- 1 500-gram can blueberries, drained

*Method*

1. Beat butter and sugar until fluffy. Add eggs one at a time.
2. In a separate bowl sift together flour, baking powder and salt. Fold into the egg mixture alternately with milk.
3. Stir in blueberries. Pour the batter into a 20-cm springform pan.

*Topping*

- 1/4 cup butter
- 1/2 cup castor sugar
- 1/3 cup all-purpose flour
- 1/2 teaspoon ground cinnamon

powdered sugar for dusting

*Method*

Combine butter, sugar, flour and cinnamon and sprinkle over the cake. Bake at 180°C/360°F for an hour. Dust with powdered sugar.

# Swiss Carrot Cake

*Ingredients*

- 75 grams cornflour
- a pinch of ground cinnamon
- a pinch of ground cloves
- 10 grams baking powder
- a pinch of salt
- 5 large eggs, separated
- 300 grams castor sugar
- grated zest and juice of 1 lemon
- 300 grams ground almond
- 300 grams carrots, peeled and grated
- 50 ml fresh milk

- 1/2 cup apricot jam to glaze
- powdered sugar for dusting

*Method*

1. Sift together cornflour, cinnamon, cloves, baking powder and salt.
2. In a separate bowl beat egg yolks and sugar until creamy. Add lemon juice and zest followed by almonds and carrots. Fold in the sifted ingredients and add milk.
3. In another bowl whisk egg whites until stiff and fold into the batter.
4. Pour the batter into a 24-cm round cake pan lined with parchment paper. Bake at 180°C/360°F for an hour. Cool slightly before glazing with apricot jam and dusting with powdered sugar.

*Opposite: Blueberry Cake (above) and Swiss Carrot Cake (below).*

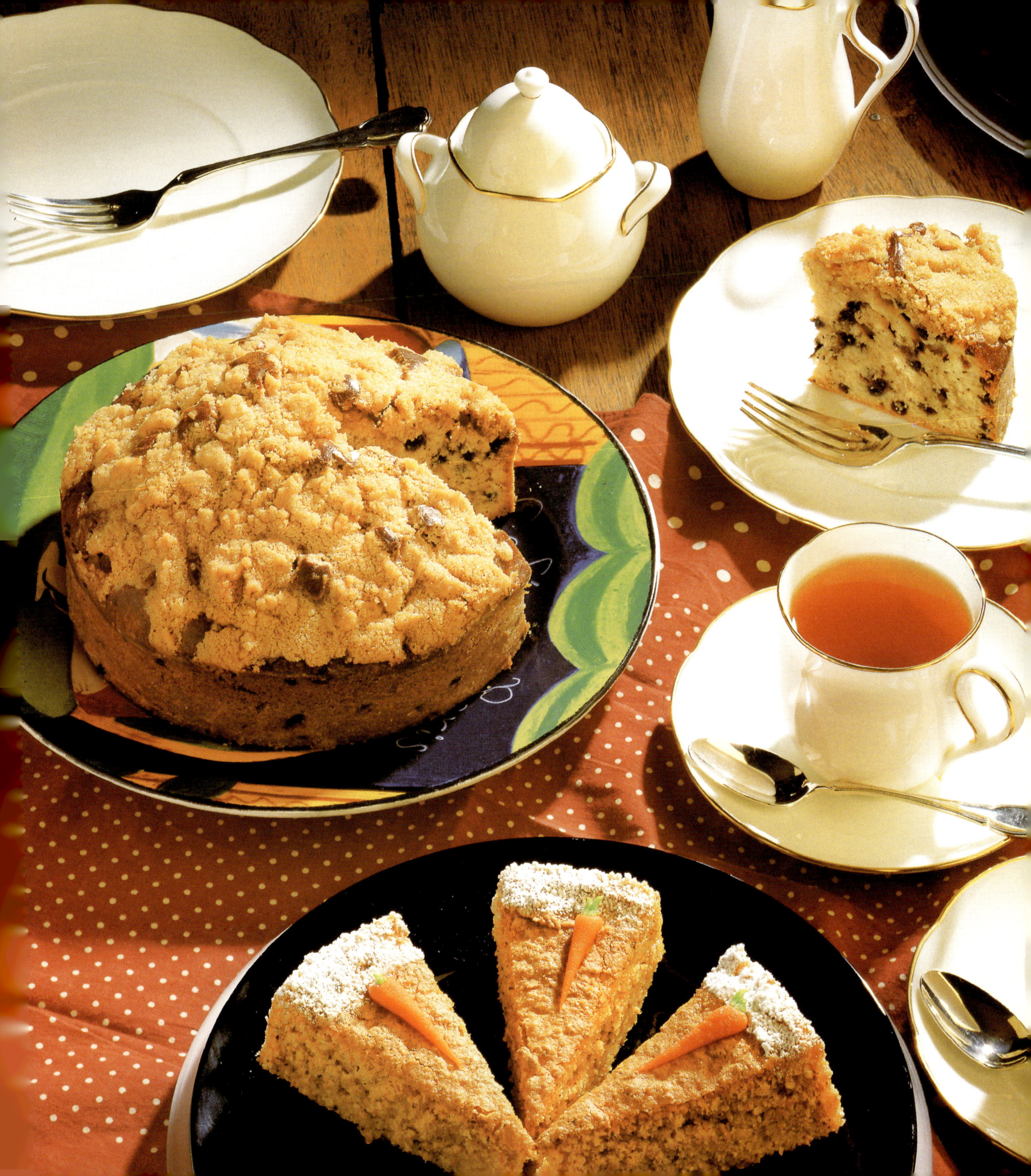

# Chocolate Gugelhupf

*Ingredients*

    170 grams all-purpose flour
    1 teaspoon baking powder
    6 eggs
    250 grams castor sugar
    200 grams semisweet chocolate, coarsely chopped
    170 grams butter, melted and cooled
    180 grams ground hazelnuts
    50 grams semisweet chocolate, chopped

*Method*

1. Sift together flour and baking powder.
2. In a separate bowl whisk eggs and sugar until light and fluffy.
3. Melt chocolate in a heatproof bowl placed over a pot of simmering water. Slowly stir melted chocolate into the egg mixture together with butter, hazelnuts and the sifted ingredients. Add chopped chocolate.
4. Pour the batter into a greased and lightly floured gugelhupf pan. Bake at 175°C/350°F for 50 minutes.

# Hot Apple Cake with Caramel Pecan Sauce

*Cake*

    226 grams butter
    1 cup castor sugar
    2 eggs
    1½ cups all-purpose flour
    ¼ teaspoon ground nutmeg
    1½ teaspoon ground cinnamon
    1 teaspoon baking soda
    ¼ teaspoon salt
    3 medium apples, peeled and diced
    ¾ cup pecans, chopped
    1 teaspoon vanilla essence

*Method*

Cream butter and sugar until fluffy. Add eggs one at a time. Fold in dry ingredients. Add apples, pecans and vanilla essence. Bake for 30 to 40 minutes at 175°C/350°F.

*Sauce*

    4 tablespoon butter
    ½ cup whole pecans
    1 cup brown sugar
    1 cup cream, bring to a simmer

*Method*

1. Melt the butter and add pecans. Add sugar and cook for a few minutes until it starts to caramelise before adding the hot cream. Bring to a boil and stir frequently.
2. Boil until the sugar is dissolved and the sauce turns golden brown.

Chef's Note: Vanilla ice-cream goes well with this cake as well.

# Chocolate Potato Cake

*Ingredients*

    220 grams unsalted butter
    2 cups castor sugar
    4 eggs, separated
    2 cups all-purpose flour
    2 teaspoons baking powder
    ½ teaspoon nutmeg
    ¼ teaspoon ground cloves
    1 teaspoon ground cinnamon
    4 teaspoons cocoa powder
    ½ teaspoon salt
    ½ teaspoon baking soda
    1 cup plain yoghurt
    2 teaspoons whipping cream
    1 cup potatoes, cooked, mashed and cooled
    1 teaspoon vanilla essence

    pecans to decorate
    chocolate sauce to serve

*Method*

1. Cream butter and sugar until fluffy. Beat in egg yolks one at a time.
2. Sift together flour, baking powder, nutmeg, cloves, cinnamon, cocoa, salt and baking soda.
3. In another bowl mix yoghurt, cream and potatoes well.
4. Add sifted ingredients and potato mixture alternately to the egg batter. Stir in vanilla essence.
5. In a separate bowl beat egg whites until stiff but not dry. Fold into the batter and pour into a 24-cm springform pan. Bake at 180°C/360°F for 45 minutes until done. Decorate with pecans and serve with chocolate sauce.

# Chocolate Cake

*Ingredients*

    1 cup boiling water
    ½ cup unsweetened cocoa powder, sifted
    227 grams unsalted butter
    300 grams castor sugar
    3 large eggs
    2¼ teaspoons vanilla essence
    235 grams cake flour or all-purpose flour
    15 grams baking powder
    ¾ teaspoon salt

    chocolate ganache* to serve

*Method*

1. Combine boiling water and cocoa powder until well mixed. Cool.
2. In a separate bowl beat butter and sugar until fluffy. Add eggs one a time. Add vanilla essence.
3. Sift together flour, baking powder and salt. Fold into the butter mixture alternately with the cocoa mixture.
4. Pour the batter into a 22-cm cake pan lined with parchment paper, greased with butter and slightly floured. Bake at 170°C/340°F for 25 to 35 minutes. Serve plain or with chocolate ganache.

*Refer to recipe for Chocolate Orange Bavaroise on page 158.

*Opposite: Chocolate Gugelhupf (above) and Hot Apple Cake with Caramel Pecan Sauce (below).*

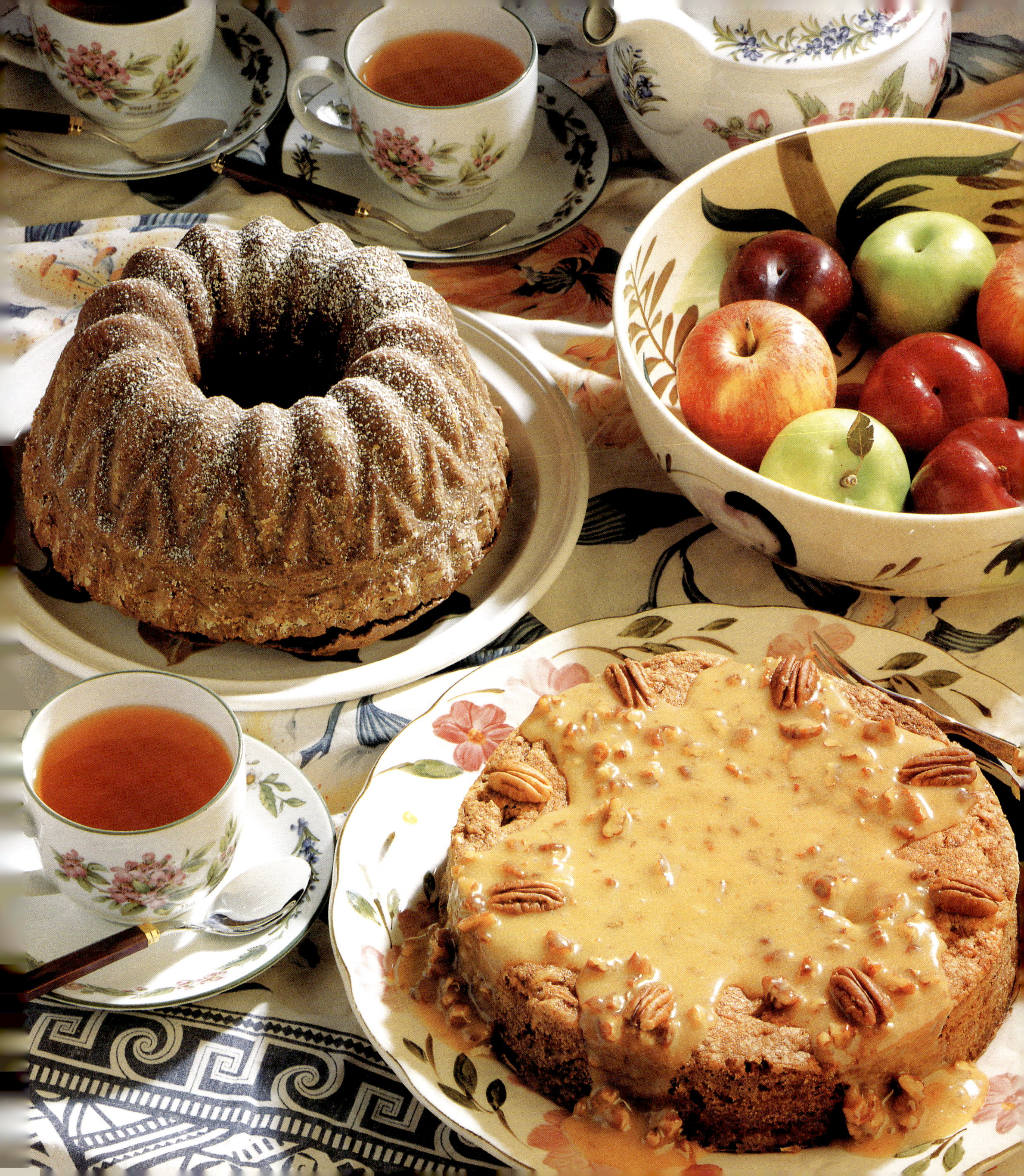

# Boiled Fruitcake

*Ingredients*

- 450 grams canned pineapple rings, diced with syrup drained and kept aside
- 3/4 cup castor sugar
- 3 tablespoons honey
- 125 grams butter, cut into small pieces
- 2 cups dark raisins
- 1/2 cup currants
- a pinch of salt
- 1/2 teaspoon ground cinnamon
- 1/2 teaspoon mixed spice
- 1 teaspoon bicarbonate of soda
- 2 eggs
- 1 cup all-purpose flour
- 1 cup self-raising flour
- 1/2 cup walnuts, chopped

*Method*

1. Place pineapples and the syrup in a saucepan with the sugar, honey, butter, raisins, currants, salt and spices. Boil gently for 12 to 15 minutes. Remove from the stove and stir in bicarbonate of soda. Cool completely.

2. Beat eggs slightly and combine with the fruit mixture.

3. In another bowl mix together both types of flour and walnuts. Add to the fruit mixture.

4. Pour the batter into a greased 20 cm cake pan. Bake at 170°C/340°F for 1 hour in the centre of the oven. The cake is done when a skewer inserted in the centre of the cake comes away cleanly. Allow the cake to cool before removing from the pan.

# Cinnamon Walnut Coffee Cake

*Cake*

- 1 tablespoon baking powder
- 2 cups all-purpose flour
- 1 teaspoon salt
- 150 grams unsalted butter
- 1 cup castor sugar
- 2 eggs
- 2 teaspoons instant coffee, dissolved slightly with a little warm water
- 1 cup fresh milk
- 1 1/2 cups walnuts, chopped

*Method*

1. Sift together baking powder, flour and salt. Set aside.

2. Cream butter and sugar until light and fluffy. Add eggs and instant coffee. Alternately fold in sifted ingredients and milk. Add walnuts, stir and pour into a greased and parchment-lined 22-cm cake pan.

*Topping*

- 1/2 cup all-purpose flour
- 3 tablespoons butter
- 1 teaspoon ground cinnamon
- 1/2 cup walnuts, coarsely ground
- powdered sugar for dusting

*Method*

1. Combine flour, butter, cinnamon and walnuts. Mix well and sprinkle over the cake.

2. Bake at 170°C/340°F for about 40 minutes. Cool before cutting. Dust with powdered sugar.

# Prune and Lemon Cake

*Ingredients*

- 1 1/2 cups prunes, pitted
- 1/4 lemon juice
- 125 grams butter
- 1 cup castor sugar
- 2 eggs
- grated zest of 1 lemon
- 1 teaspoon vanilla essence
- 2 cups all-purpose flour
- 1 teaspoon baking powder
- 1 teaspoon baking soda
- 1/4 teaspoon salt
- 1 cup fresh milk
- 1/2 cup pecans, chopped

*Method*

1. Steep prunes in lemon juice until plumped up. Set aside.

2. Beat butter and sugar until fluffy. Add eggs one at a time, followed by lemon zest and vanilla essence.

3. Sift together flour, baking powder, baking soda and salt. Fold sifted ingredients into the batter, alternating with milk. Stir in pecans and marinated prunes.

4. Pour the batter into a greased bundt pan. Bake for 40 minutes at 175°C/350°F.

# Orange Sponge Cake

*Ingredients*

- 6 eggs
- 225 grams castor sugar
- 1/2 teaspoon vanilla essence
- grated zest of 1 orange
- 1 teaspoon orange essence
- 225 grams all-purpose flour or cake flour

*Method*

1. Mix together eggs, sugar and vanilla essence in a heatproof bowl and heat to about 43°C/110°F over a pan of simmering water, stirring constantly. Remove from heat and whip at full speed until the mixture cools completely and is light and fluffy. Add zest and orange essence.

2. Sift flour and gradually fold, not stir, into the batter by hand. Pour the batter into a greased and floured 25-cm cake pan.

3. Bake at 180°C/360°F for about 20 to 25 minutes until the skewer test comes away clean.

Chef's Note: For a chocolate sponge cake, replace 30 grams of the flour with 30 grams of cocoa powder.

*Opposite: Cinnamon Walnut Coffee Cake (above) and Boiled Fruitcake (below).*

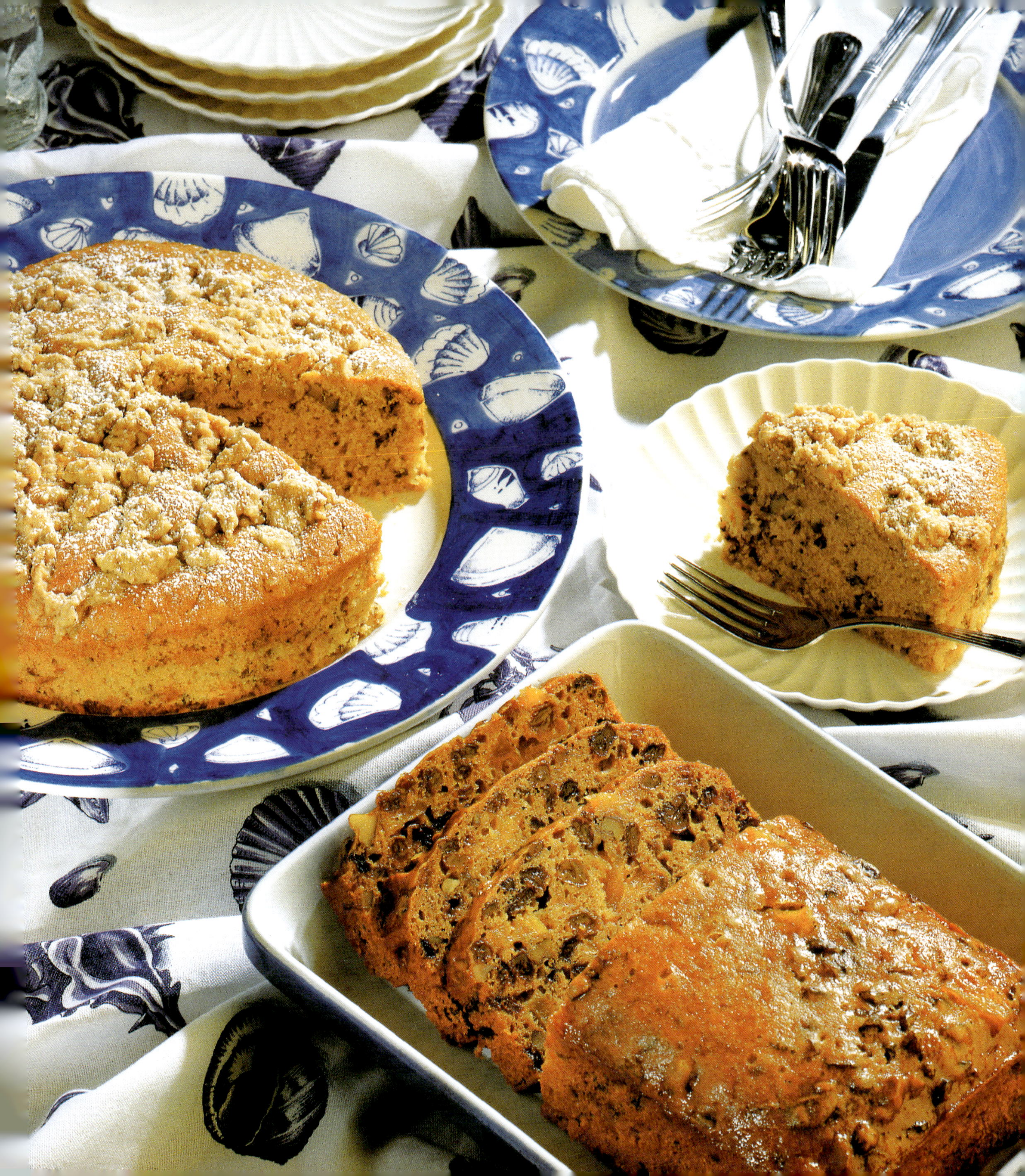

## Chocolate Valentino

*Ingredients*

    453 grams semisweet chocolate, coarsely chopped
    140 grams butter
    5 eggs, separated

*Method*

1. Melt chocolate and butter in a heatproof bowl set over a pan of simmering water. Stir until smooth. Cool.

2. Grease a 22-cm springform pan. Beat egg yolks and stir into cooled chocolate.

3. Beat egg whites until stiff peaks form. Gently fold one-quarter of the egg whites into the chocolate mixture. Fold in remaining egg whites.

4. Pour the batter into a pan and bake for 25 minutes at 190°C/375°F. Cool.

*Topping*

    3 cups whipping cream
    2 tablespoons castor sugar
    1/2 teaspoon vanilla essence

    cocoa powder for dusting

*Method*

Beat together whipping cream, sugar and vanilla essence until stiff. Spoon over the cake. Remove the springform sides and dust with cocoa. You can also decorate the cake with grated chocolate and strawberries.

Chef's Note: The valentino is a heart-shaped version of this cake. Bake a valentino in a heart-shaped pan. This is a very dense chocolate cake.

## Caramelised Pineapple Cake

*Ingredients*

    2 cups light brown sugar, divided into two equal parts
    1/3 cup butter, melted
    2 226-gram cans pineapple rings in heavy syrup, drained but reserving 2 tablespoons syrup
    1/3 cup vegetable shortening
    1 egg
    2 cups all-purpose flour
    1 1/2 teaspoons baking powder
    1/2 teaspoon baking soda
    3/4 teaspoon salt
    3/4 teaspoon ground cinnamon
    1/2 teaspoon allspice
    1 cup natural yoghurt
    1 teaspoon lemon juice

*Method*

1. In a small mixing bowl combine half of the brown sugar with melted butter and reserved pineapple syrup. Spread evenly in the base of a 22-cm cake pan.

2. Arrange 8 pineapple rings in a layer over the sugar. Cream the remaining brown sugar with vegetable shortening. Add egg and beat until light and fluffy.

3. Sift together flour, baking powder, baking soda, salt, cinnamon and allspice.

4. Blend together yoghurt and lemon juice, alternately adding this and the sifted ingredients to the shortening. Add the ingredients a little at a time and beat the batter well after each addition. Continue beating until smooth.

5. Pour the batter over the pineapples and bake at 180°C/360°F for about 50 minutes until cooked.

Chef's Note: The cake may also be decorated by sprinkling the base of the cake pan with pecans or glace cherries before the batter is poured in.

## Lemon Ginger Tea Cake

*Cake*

    226 grams butter
    1 1/2 cups castor sugar
    4 eggs
    3 cups all-purpose flour
    2 teaspoons baking powder
    1/2 teaspoon salt
    1 cup fresh milk
    grated zest of 2 lemons
    2 teaspoons grated fresh ginger

*Method*

1. Grease and flour a large loaf pan. Shake out the excess flour.

2. Cream butter and sugar until light and fluffy. Add eggs one at a time, beating well after each addition.

3. Sift together flour, baking powder and salt. Add to the batter, alternating with milk and beating at low speed until blended. Fold in lemon zest and fresh ginger. Bake for one hour at 175°C/350°F.

*Lemon Frosting*

    250 grams cream cheese
    100 grams unsalted butter, cut into small pieces
    1 cup powdered sugar, sifted
    grated zest of 1 lemon
    1 tablespoon lemon juice

    lemon slices and preserved ginger to decorate

*Method*

Beat cream cheese until smooth. Gradually beat in butter. Add powdered sugar, lemon zest and juice. Continue beating until smooth. Frost the cake and decorate with lemon slices and preserved ginger.

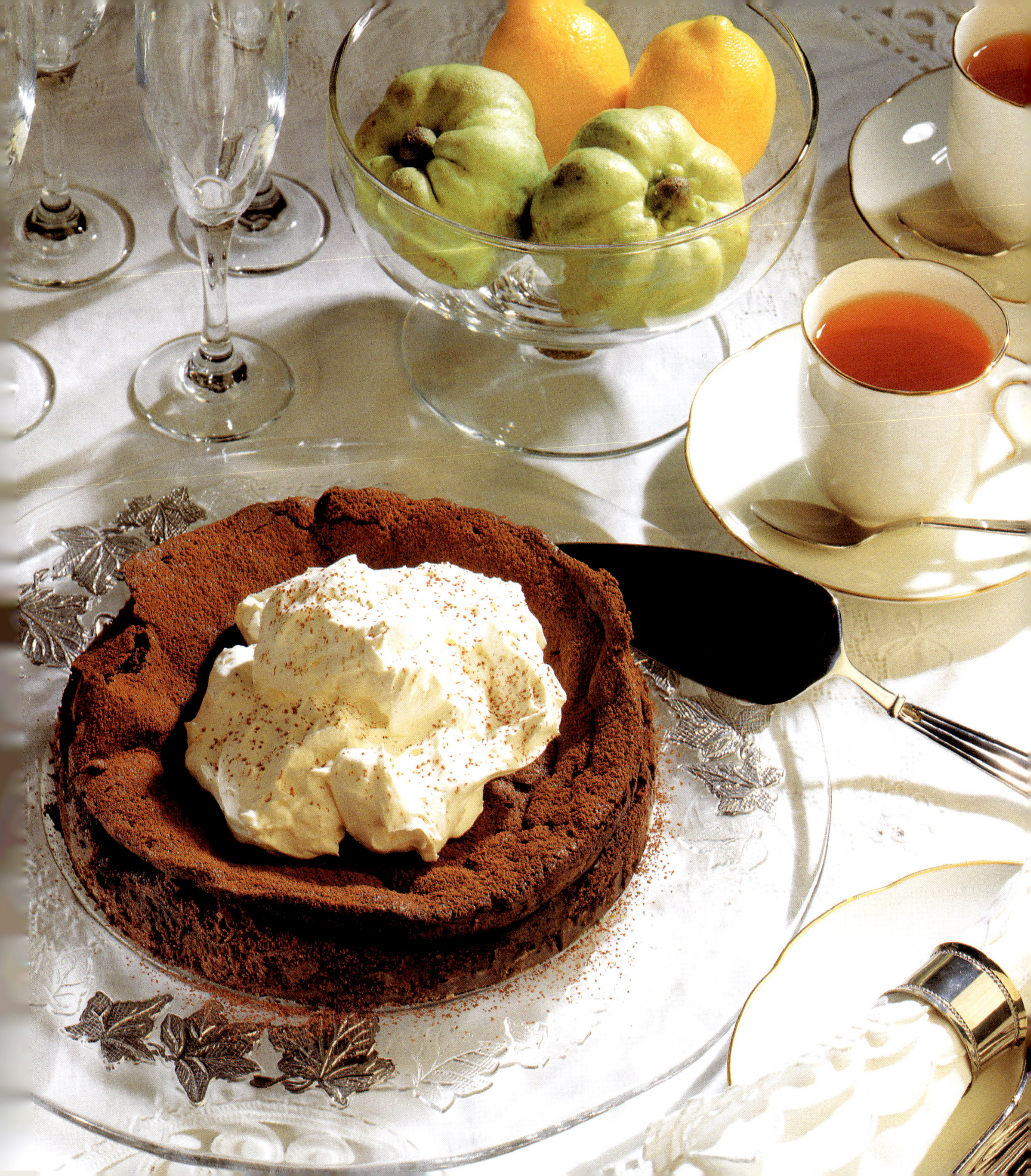

# Chocolate Orange Bavaroise

*Cake*

- 6 egg yolks
- 70 grams castor sugar
- 250 grams milk
- 3 sheets gelatine or 1 tablespoon agar-agar powder
- 250 grams orange-flavoured chocolate or semisweet chocolate, chopped
- 1 orange sponge cake 24-cm in diameter, cut into half*
- 3/4 cup sugar, heated with 1 cup of water to make syrup
- 6 slices orange, seeded
- 350 grams whipping cream

*Method*

1. Beat egg yolks and sugar until a light mousse forms.
2. Meanwhile bring milk to a boil. Remove and add the beaten egg yolk. Stir well and pour back into the milk saucepan. Continue stirring on a low flame until it coats the back of a wooden spoon. Remove from heat.
3. In another saucepan dissolve gelatine in 3 tablespoons water. Add egg yolk and milk mixture. Stir well. Add chopped chocolate and stir immediately to dissolve. Cool to room temperature.
4. Grease a 24-cm circular ring mould. Place the mould on a baking tray lined with parchment paper. Fill the base with sponge cake. Moisten with syrup and place in the refrigerator for 10 minutes. Decorate with orange slices.
5. Beat whipping cream until soft peaks form. Slowly add to chocolate mixture and pour over the cake. Chill.

*Chocolate Ganache*

- 250 grams bittersweet chocolate, finely chopped
- 70 grams unsalted butter
- 200 grams whipping cream, brought to a boil

powdered sugar and cocoa for dusting

*Method*

1. Mix together chocolate and butter, pour in hot boiling cream and stir to dissolve.
2. When the chilled cake sets, pour the melted ganache (make sure it is at room temperature) over the cake. Chill in the refrigerator again, preferably overnight. To remove the cake from the pan, run a warm knife around the rim of the cake. Dust with powdered sugar and cocoa.

* Refer to recipe for Orange Sponge Cake on page 154.

# Chocolate Paradise

*Cake*

- 200 grams bittersweet chocolate, chopped
- 250 grams unsalted butter
- 3/4 cup castor sugar
- 6 eggs, separated
- 3 tablespoons all-purpose flour
- 3 tablespoons unsweetened cocoa powder
- 1 cup almonds, finely ground
- a pinch of cream of tartar

*Method*

1. Melt chocolate in a heatproof bowl over a pan of simmering water until smooth. Cool.
2. Cream butter and sugar until light and fluffy. Add egg yolks one at a time.
3. Sift together flour and cocoa powder. Add to the batter together with the melted chocolate and ground almonds.
4. Meanwhile beat egg whites with cream of tartar and fold into the batter in three batches. Bake in a greased and floured bundt pan at 175°C/350°F for 50 minutes until the top forms a crust but the inside remains moist. Cool the cake thoroughly before attempting to remove from the pan.

*Glaze*

- 180 grams bittersweet chocolate, chopped
- 3 tablespoons whipping cream
- 1 teaspoon vanilla essence
- 2 tablespoons butter

chopped almonds to decorate

*Method*

1. Mix chocolate, cream, vanilla essence and butter over low heat until melted. Cool slightly before drizzling over the cake.
2. Sprinkle the cake with almonds.

Chef's Note: This cake normally sinks a little after it is removed from the oven.

# Persimmon Cake

*Ingredients*

- 285 grams mixed raisins, dark and golden
- 1/2 cup brandy or juice of 1 orange
- 2 cups fresh persimmon puree
- 500 grams castor sugar
- 2 teaspoons corn oil
- 1 teaspoon vanilla essence
- 225 grams all-purpose flour
- 2 teaspoons baking soda
- 1 teaspoon salt
- 1/2 teaspoon ground cloves
- 1/2 teaspoon ground nutmeg
- 215 grams walnuts, chopped
- 1 cup fresh milk

apricot jam, heated with a little water, to glaze

*Method*

1. Soak raisins in brandy or orange juice overnight until plumped up.
2. Mix persimmon puree, sugar, corn oil and vanilla essence. Sift together flour, baking soda, salt, cloves and nutmeg. Add to the persimmon mixture, followed by walnut, fresh milk and raisins.
3. Line a 22-cm cake mould with parchment paper and pour in the batter. Bake at 170°C/340°F for 1 1/4 to 1 1/2 hours. Let the cake cool completely before unmoulding. Glaze with jam.

*Opposite: Chocolate Paradise (above) and Chocolate Orange Bavaroise (below).*

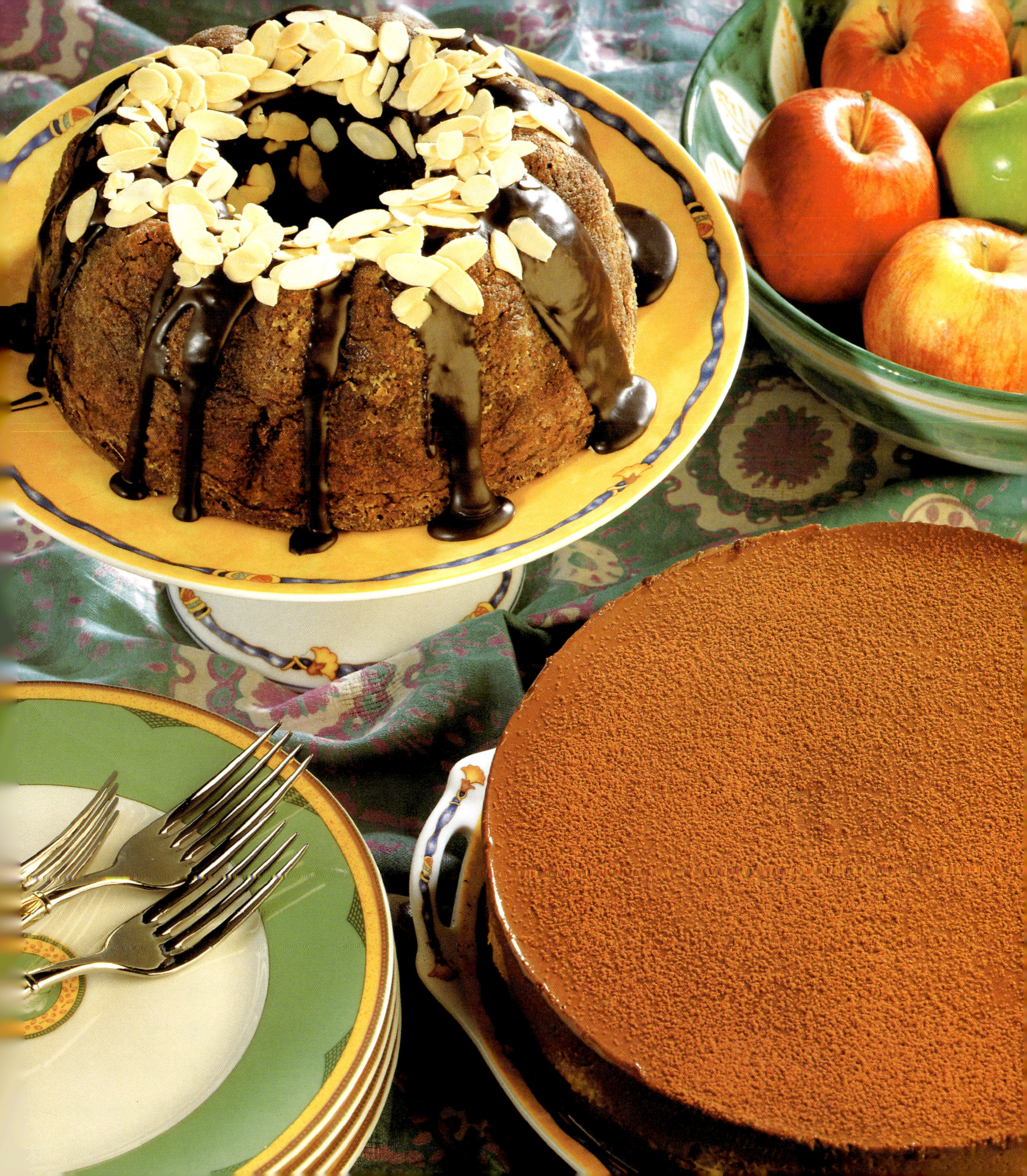

# Pineapple Upside-Down Cake

### Bottom Layer

1/4 cup butter
1/2 cup brown sugar
8 pineapple rings
6 whole glace cherries

### Top Layer

2 cups cake flour
2 teaspoon baking powder
1/4 teaspoon salt
1/2 cup unsalted butter, softened
1 cup castor sugar
2 eggs
2 teaspoons vanilla essence
1 cup pineapple juice

*Method*

1. For the bottom layer, grease a 22-cm cake pan with the butter and sprinkle brown sugar in the base. Arrange pineapple rings in a single layer over the sugar and place a cherry in the centre of each pineapple ring.
2. For the top layer, sift together flour, baking powder and salt. Set aside.
3. In another bowl beat the butter and sugar until fluffy. Beat in sifted ingredients, eggs, vanilla essence and pineapple juice.
4. Pour the batter over the bottom layer and bake for 45 minutes at 175°C/350°F. The cake is done when a skewer inserted in the centre of the cake comes away cleanly.

# Lemon Tea Cake

### Cake

226 grams unsalted butter, at room temperature
1/2 cup + 1/2 cup castor sugar
grated zest of 1 lemon
1 tablespoon lemon juice
1 cup sour cream
2 teaspoons vanilla essence
6 egg whites
a pinch of salt
2 cups all-purpose flour
1 teaspoon baking powder
1 cup ground almonds

*Method*

1. Beat butter and 1/2 cup sugar. Add lemon zest and juice followed by sour cream and vanilla essence.
2. In a separate bowl whisk egg whites and salt until soft peaks form. Do not overbeat. Gradually add the remaining 1/2 cup of sugar and beat again until fluffy.
3. Sift flour and baking powder and mix well with almonds. Fold into the butter mixture. Add one-third of the egg whites. Add the remaining egg whites and pour the batter into a standard-size loaf pan or bundt pan.
4. Bake at 175°C/350°F for one hour.

### Syrup

1/4 cup lemon juice
1/4 cup water
1/2 cup brown sugar

lemon slices to decorate

*Method*

Heat together all the ingredients for the syrup until thick. When the cake is done, pour the syrup over. Cover the cake and allow the syrup to soak in overnight. Decorate with lemon slices.

# Cherry Butter Cake

### Ingredients

2 cups all-purpose flour
2 1/2 teaspoons baking powder
1 teaspoon salt
1 egg
1/3 cup butter or margarine
1/3 cup brown sugar
1 tablespoon lemon juice
1 cup milk
1 1/2 cups dark pitted canned cherries, drained

*Method*

1. Grease a 12-cup muffin tray. Preheat the oven to 220°C/425°F. Sift together the flour, baking powder and salt.
2. In a separate bowl beat the egg and butter until fluffy. Beat in brown sugar and lemon juice. Add sifted ingredients and milk and continue beating. Gradually stir in cherries.
3. Fill muffin cups three-quarters full of batter and bake for 20 minutes or until cooked.

Chef's Note: For this recipe just about any kind of canned fruit may be used, but be sure to drain the syrup first. Try adding mashed or coarsely chopped bananas.

# Victoria Sponge Sandwich

### Ingredients

175 grams unsalted butter
200 grams castor sugar
3 eggs
280 grams all-purpose flour
4 teaspoons baking powder

250 grams strawberry or raspberry jam
2 tablespoons powdered sugar for dusting

*Method*

1. Beat butter and castor sugar until light and creamy. Add eggs one at a time.
2. Sift together flour and baking powder. Fold into the batter and bake in two separate cake pans of the same size for 25 to 30 minutes at 180°C/360°F. Cool and spread jam over one layer of the cake. Top with a second layer. Dust with powdered sugar just before serving.

Chef's Note: This sponge cake is a British favourite. It was one of the first cakes that I started baking when I was 13. Be sure to use high-quality jam for the filling. The cake will keep for a couple of days but is best eaten fresh.

*Opposite: Pineapple Upside-Down Cake.*

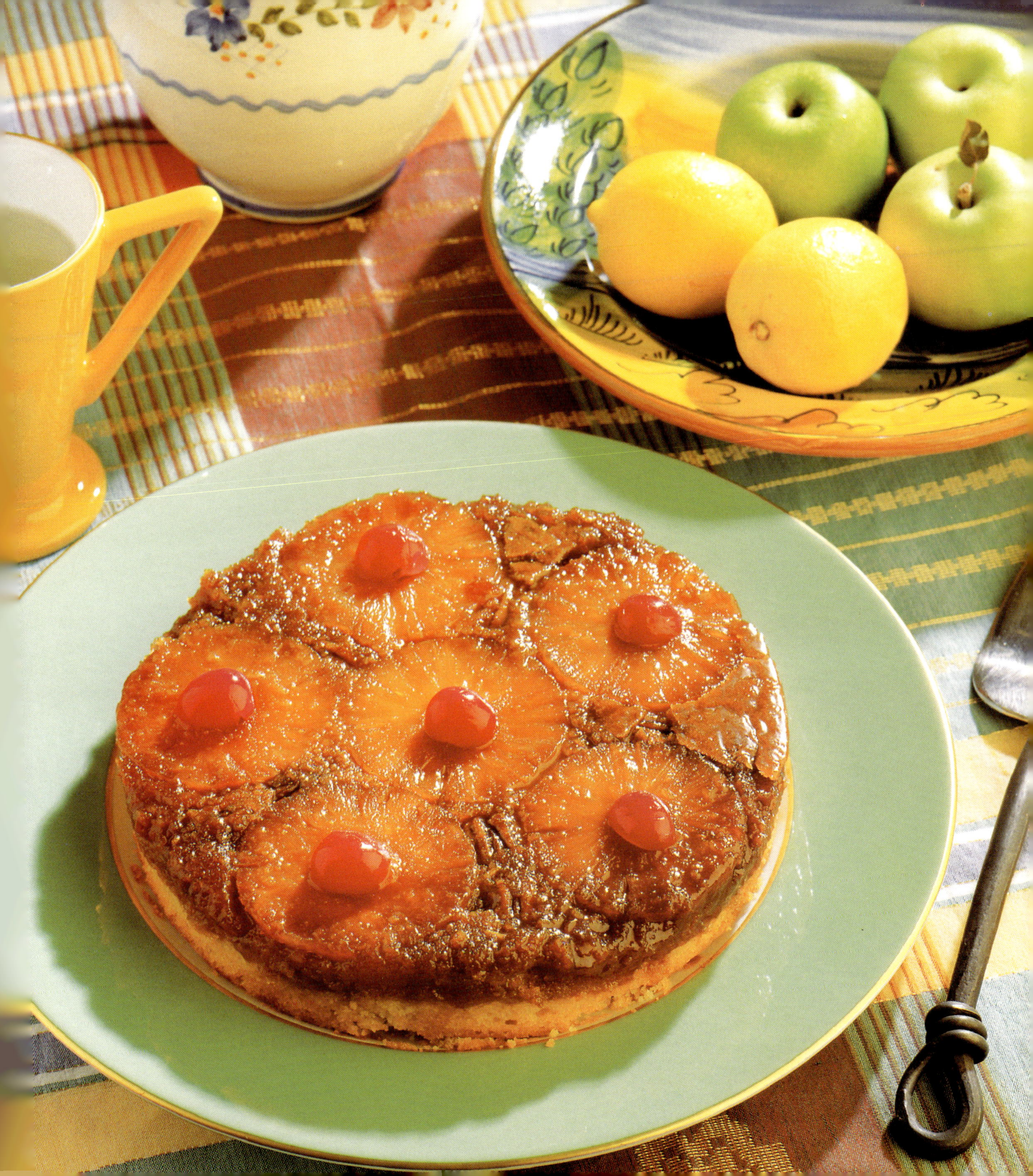

# Fresh Ginger Cake

*Ingredients*

    250 grams unsalted butter
    1 cup castor sugar
    2 eggs
    1 cup plain yoghurt
    2 cups all-purpose flour
    1/4 teaspoon salt
    3/4 teaspoons baking soda
    2 cm knob of fresh ginger, thinly shredded
    grated zest of 1 lemon
    100 grams candied ginger, chopped
    1 teaspoon ground ginger
    150 grams candied orange peel

*Method*

1. Beat butter and sugar until light and fluffy. Add eggs one at a time, together with yoghurt.
2. Sift together flour, salt and baking soda. Add to the batter with fresh ginger, lemon zest, candied ginger, ground ginger and candied orange peel.
3. Pour into a 22-cm greased loaf pan and bake at 175°C/350°F for 50 minutes.

# Madeleines

*Ingredients*

    4 eggs
    200 grams castor sugar
    grated zest of 2 lemons
    225 grams all-purpose flour
    185 grams unsalted butter, melted and cooled

*Method*

1. Beat eggs and sugar until lemon-coloured. Add zest. Fold in flour and butter. Refrigerate the batter for one hour.
2. Butter the madeleine moulds and spoon in the batter to fill three-quarters of each mould. Bake for 10 to 12 minutes at 190°C/375°F until golden brown. Remove as soon as the madeleines are baked and cool on a wire rack.

Chef's Note: While living in Paris in 1990 I discovered madeleines, the plump and golden tea cakes shaped like scallops. The best and freshest madeleines have a dry, almost dusty taste. To release the fragrance of madeleines dip them in lemon-flavoured tea.

# Ginger, Peaches and Pineapple Cake

*Bottom Layer*

    4 tablespoons unsalted butter
    1/4 cup brown sugar
    1/4 teaspoon ground cinnamon
    1/4 teaspoon ground ginger

*Top Layer*

    240 grams unsalted butter
    3/4 cup castor sugar
    4 eggs
    6 tablespoons light molasses
    2 teaspoons vanilla essence
    3 cups all-purpose flour
    2 teaspoons ground ginger
    3/4 teaspoons ground cinnamon
    1/4 teaspoon ground cloves
    a pinch of salt
    1/2 cup boiling water

    1 large can peaches, drained, and 1 cup fresh pineapple, diced, to decorate

*Method*

1. Heat butter, brown sugar and spices until melted. Pour onto the base of a 22-cm cake pan.
2. In a separate bowl beat butter and sugar until fluffy. Add eggs one at a time followed by molasses and vanilla essence.
3. Sift together flour, ginger, cinnamon, cloves and salt. Fold into the batter alternately with boiling water. Do not overmix. Pour over the bottom layer. Top with peaches and pineapples. Bake at 175°C/350°F for 40 minutes.

# Visitandine

*Ingredients*

    150 grams ground almonds
    150 grams castor sugar
    5 1/2 tablespoons all-purpose flour, sifted
    4 egg whites
    a pinch of salt
    200 grams butter

*Method*

1. Mix almonds, sugar and flour with a wooden spatula, then beat in egg whites and salt.
2. In another bowl heat butter until nut brown in colour, then strain into the batter. Stir until smooth and allow the batter to rest for 10 to 15 minutes before baking.
3. Preheat the oven to 220°C/425°F. Grease round visitandine moulds or rectangular financier moulds. Spoon in the batter to fill three-quarters of each mould and bake for four to five minutes. Lower the oven temperature to 205°C/400°F and bake for another seven to 10 minutes. Test for doneness by turning out one pastry and checking to see if the entire pastry is evenly browned. When the pastries are done, turn them out onto a wire rack to cool.

Chef's Note: This wonderful almond pastry originates from the cooking school in the Ritz Hotel, Paris, and is sold in pastry shops and sidewalk cafés all over Paris. Visitandine is rich and addictive. It can be kept for four to five days in an airtight container. The pastry is ready when the butter stops crackling.

*Opposite: Visitandine (above right), Madeleines (centre) and Fresh Ginger Cake (below).*

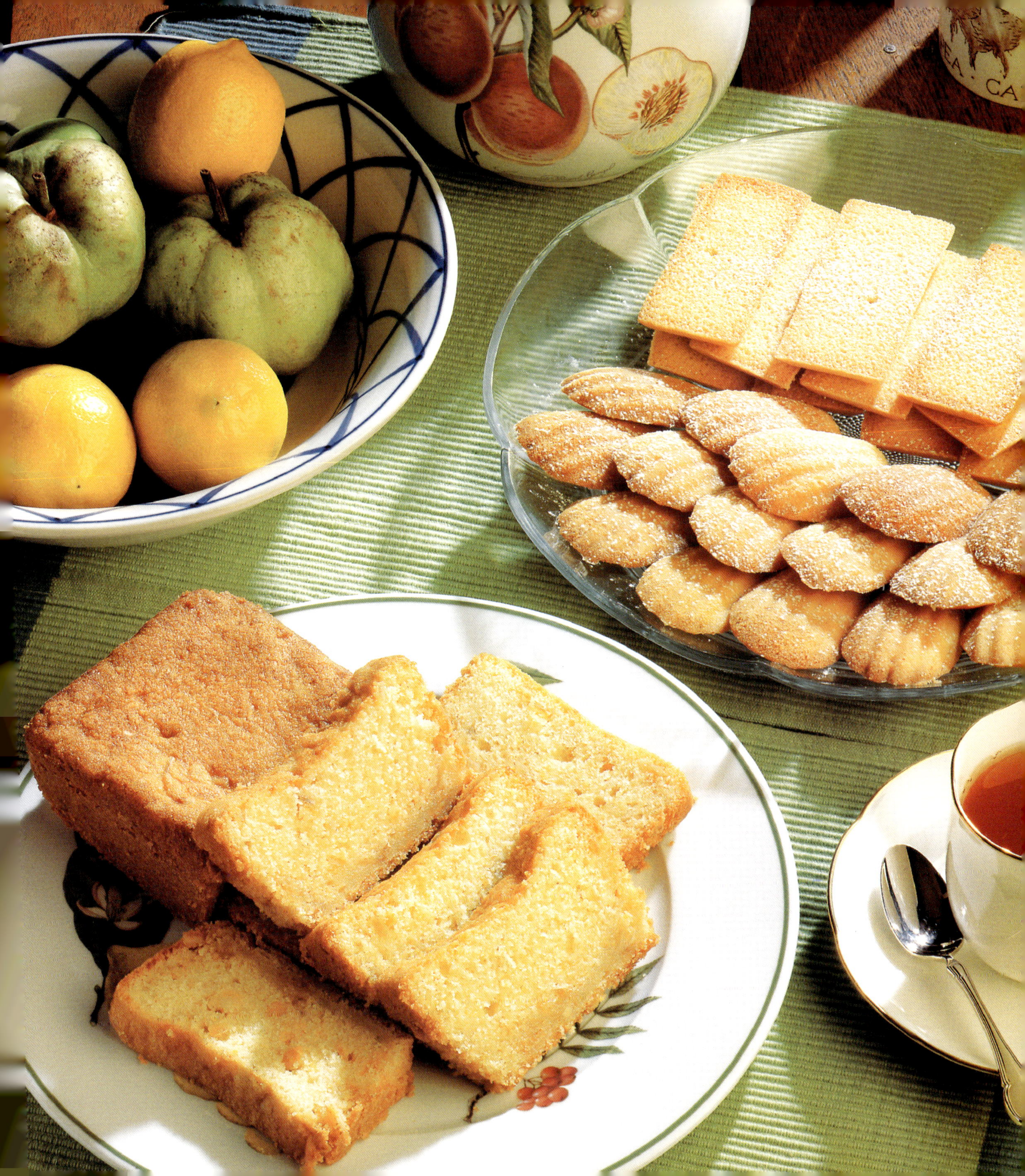

## Crispy Cornflake Cake

*Ingredients*

    250 grams butter
    1 tablespoon condensed milk
    6 cold eggs
    100 grams castor sugar
    ½ cup orange juice
    150 grams self-raising flour
    30 grams cornflour
    50 grams cornflakes, crushed
    50 grams walnuts, shelled
    1 teaspoon orange zest

*Method*

1. Beat together butter and condensed milk for 10 minutes. Set aside.
2. In another bowl whisk eggs and sugar for eight minutes. Stir in orange juice.
3. Combine flour, cornflour, cornflakes, walnuts and orange zest, and gradually fold into the egg mixture. Gradually add butter-and-milk mixture. Pour into a greased 22-cm cake pan and bake at 180°C/360°F for about 30 minutes until half-cooked.

*Topping*

    2 egg yolks
    50 grams castor sugar
    80 grams cornflakes
    50 grams desiccated coconut

    whipped cream to serve

*Method*

Beat egg yolks and sugar for two minutes. Stir in cornflakes and coconut. Sprinkle the topping over the cake and continue baking until cooked. Cool and top with whipped cream.

## La Tropicana Cake

*Cake*

    3 eggs
    1¼ cup castor sugar
    1 cup vegetable oil
    1 teaspoon vanilla essence
    250 grams canned pineapples in syrup, undrained and chopped into small pieces
    4 small bananas or 1 large banana, chopped
    2 cups all-purpose flour
    ¼ teaspoon salt
    1 teaspoon bicarbonate of soda
    1 teaspoon ground cinnamon

*Method*

1. Beat eggs, sugar and oil until just mixed. Add vanilla essence and mix in chopped pineapple, syrup and bananas.
2. Sift together flour, salt, bicarbonate of soda and cinnamon. Add to the batter.
3. Pour the batter into a greased 25-cm cake pan and bake at 175°C/350°F for about 45 minutes. Cool before unmoulding.

*Cream Cheese Frosting*

    375 grams cream cheese, softened
    120 grams butter, softened
    ¾ cup powdered sugar, sifted
    1 tablespoon lemon juice
    ½ teaspoon vanilla essence

    mango slices and mint leaves to decorate

*Method*

Cream cheese, butter, sugar, lemon juice and vanilla essence. Chill in the refrigerator before frosting the cake. Decorate with mango slices and mint leaves.

Chef's Note: Passion fruit can also be included in the batter.

## Fruit Cobbler

*Ingredients*

    ½ cup unsalted butter
    ¼ cup castor sugar
    2 eggs
    ½ cup fresh milk
    1½ teaspoons vanilla essence
    1 cup all-purpose flour
    1 teaspoon baking powder
    ¼ teaspoon salt
    3 cups mixed fruit such as black cherries, apricots, plums and bananas, chopped
    juice from ½ lemon
    ¼ cup castor sugar, mixed with 1 teaspoon ground cinnamon, for sprinkling
    2 tablespoons powdered sugar for dusting

*Method*

1. Beat butter and sugar until fluffy. Add eggs one at a time.
2. Combine milk and vanilla essence.
3. In a separate bowl sift together flour, baking powder and salt. Fold into the egg mixture alternately with the milk.
4. Grease a rectangular baking dish of about 15 cm length and arrange a layer of fruit at the base. Drizzle with lemon juice and lightly press down the fruit using the back of a spoon. Sprinkle with a mixture of sugar and cinnamon. Pour the batter over the fruit and bake at 175°C/350°F for 40 minutes. Dust with powdered sugar when cool.

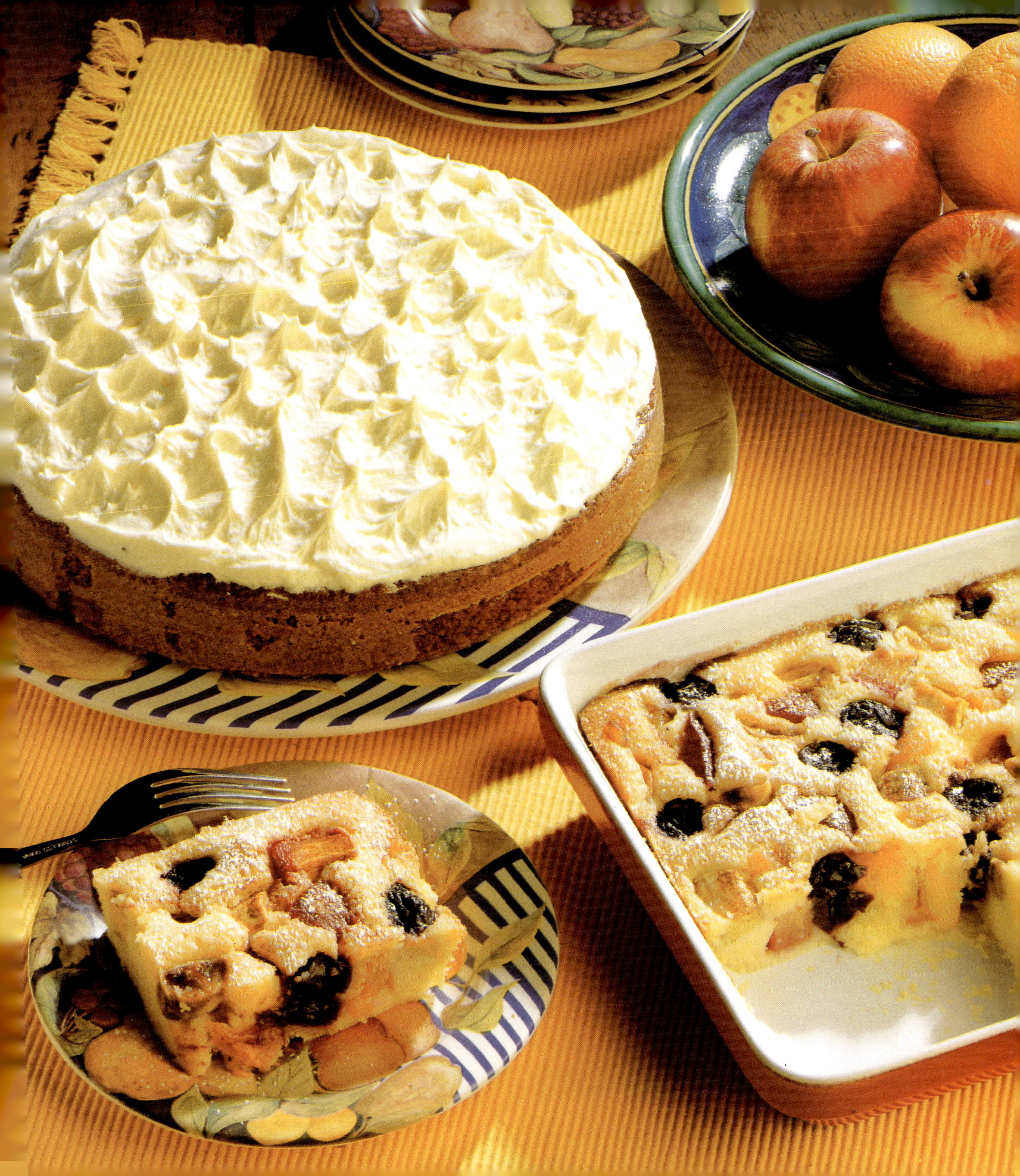

# Lemon Poppy Seed Cake

## Cake

- 1/2 cup dark poppy seeds
- 1/2 cup fresh milk
- 340 grams unsalted butter, softened
- 1 1/4 cups + 1/4 cup castor sugar
- 2 tablespoons lemon juice
- 1 tablespoon grated lemon zest
- 8 eggs, separated
- 2 cups cake flour, sifted
- 3/4 teaspoon salt

## Method

1. Soak poppy seeds in milk for a minimum of four hours. Rinse seeds under cold running water and drain well.
2. Cream butter and gradually beat in 1 1/4 cups of castor sugar. Beat in lemon juice and zest as well as poppy seeds.
3. Add egg yolks one at a time, beating well after each addition. Continue beating until light and creamy.
4. In another bowl beat egg whites until soft peaks form. Slowly add the remaining 1/4 cup castor sugar and beat until stiff peaks form.
5. Sift together flour and salt. Gently fold into the batter in three batches, alternating with the egg whites.
6. Pour the batter in a greased and floured 30-cm cake pan and bake for one hour at 175°C/350°F.

## Syrup

- 1/4 cup fresh lemon juice
- 1/4 cup fresh orange juice
- 1/3 cup powdered sugar

## Method

For a tangy cake, make a syrup by combining lemon juice and orange juice. Stir in powdered sugar until dissolved. When the cake has cooled, make several holes on the surface with a fork and pour syrup over to completely cover the cake. Cool the cake in its pan to allow the syrup to soak in.

# Plum Tea Cake

## Ingredients

- 2 cups self-raising flour
- 1 teaspoon ground cinnamon
- 1/4 teaspoon mixed spice
- 100 grams cold, unsalted butter, cut into small pieces
- 1/2 cup castor sugar
- 3 eggs, lightly beaten
- 1/2 cup fresh milk
- 10 plums, seeded and halved
- 30 grams butter, melted
- 2 teaspoons castor sugar
- 3 tablespoons almond flakes

1/2 cup powdered sugar for dusting

## Method

1. Grease a round 22-cm cake pan. Sift together flour, cinnamon and mixed spice. Cut in butter until the mixture resembles breadcrumbs. Add sugar, eggs and milk. Mix well.
2. Pour half of the mixture into the cake pan. Arrange plums on the top. Pour in the remaining mixture and layer on the remaining plums.
3. Spread top with melted butter and sprinkle with sugar and almond flakes. Bake for 45 minutes at 170°C/340°F. Dust with powdered sugar when cooled.

# Mississippi Mud Cake

## Ingredients

- A few tablespoons unsweetened cocoa powder for dusting
- 1 1/4 cups strong brewed coffee
- 1/4 cup bourbon or milk
- 155 grams unsweetened chocolate
- 1 cup unsalted butter, cut into pieces
- 2 cups castor sugar
- 2 cups all-purpose flour
- 1 teaspoon baking soda
- 1/8 teaspoon salt
- 2 eggs, lightly beaten
- 1 teaspoon vanilla essence

powdered sugar for dusting
sweetened whipped cream to serve

## Method

1. Butter a 22-cm cake pan and dust the bottom and sides with cocoa.
2. Heat coffee and bourbon in a heavy saucepan over low heat. Add chocolate and butter. Cook, stirring constantly until smooth. Remove from the heat and stir in sugar. Set aside for five minutes. Transfer to an electric mixer.
3. Sift flour with baking soda and salt. With the mixer at low speed, beat flour into the chocolate mixture in four batches. Add eggs and vanilla essence. Beat until smooth. Pour into the cake pan.
4. Bake at 180°C/360°F for about 1 1/2 hours until a skewer inserted in the centre comes away cleanly. Cool completely on a wire rack before unmoulding. Dust with powdered sugar and serve with whipped cream.

*Opposite: Plum Tea Cake (left) and Lemon Poppy Seed Cake (right).*

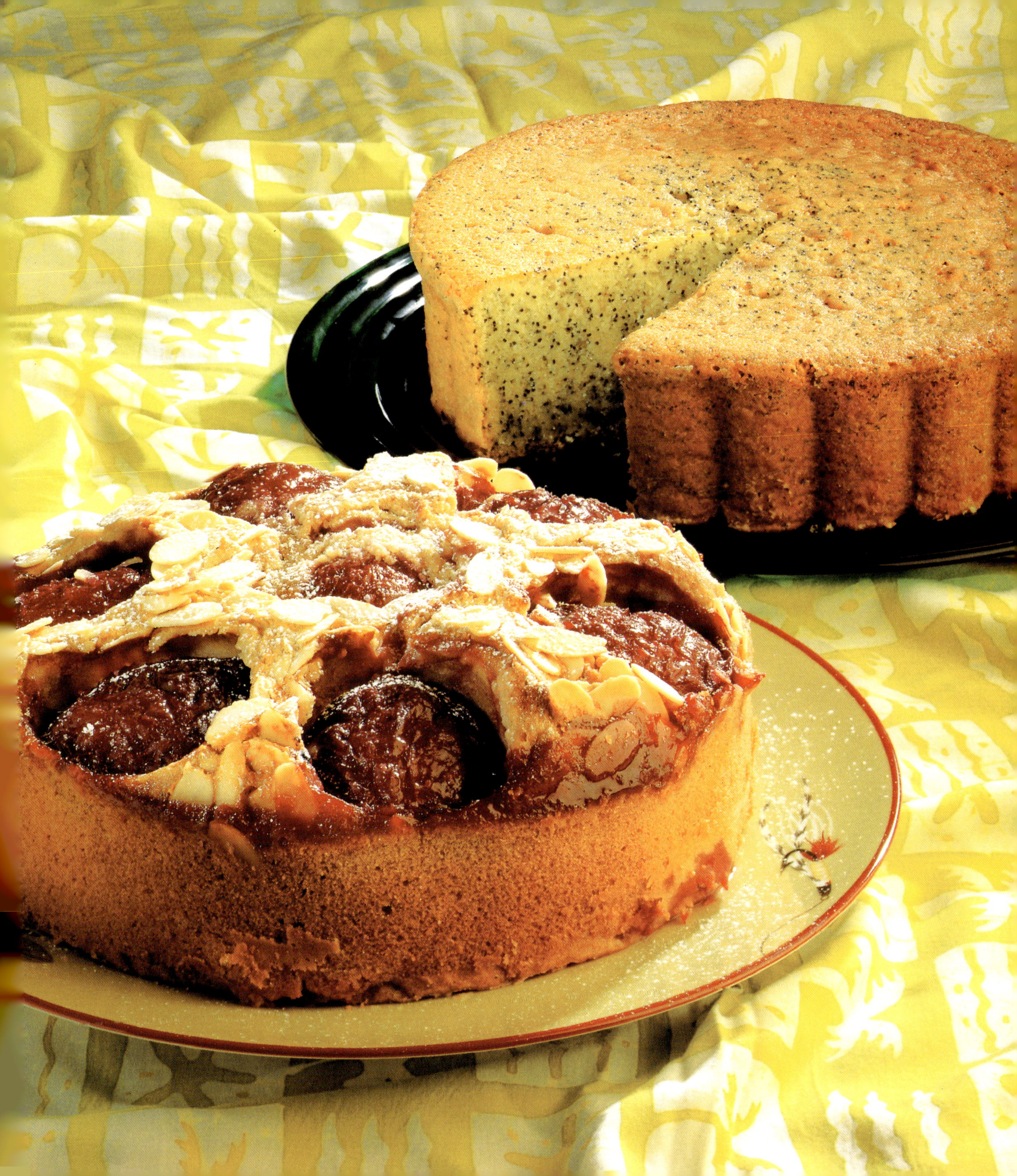

# Chocolate Rehrucken

## Ingredients

150 grams unsalted butter
150 grams castor sugar
4 egg yolks
50 grams semisweet chocolate, melted
60 grams ground almonds
5 egg whites
60 grams all-purpose flour, sifted
5 grams baking powder

100 grams semisweet chocolate, chopped, melted in 2 tablespoons water
2 tablespoons cocoa powder for dusting
¼ cup slivered almonds

## Method

1. Cream butter and sugar until light and fluffy. Add egg yolks one at a time, followed by melted chocolate and ground almonds.
2. Meanwhile beat egg whites until soft peaks form.
3. Sift together flour and baking powder and fold into the batter. Add egg whites. Pour into a greased standard-size loaf pan and bake for 45 minutes at 180°C/360°F.
4. Allow the cake to cool before spreading with melted chocolate. Dust with cocoa powder and decorate with almond slivers.

Chef's Note: This delicious chocolate log gets its name from the Porcupine, a popular Swiss Christmas cake. It is similar to the Austrian sacher torte except for its shape and the way it is presented.

# Tiramisu

## Lady Fingers

4 eggs, separated
120 grams castor sugar, divided into two equal parts
100 grams all-purpose flour, sifted

powdered sugar for dusting

## Method

1. Whip egg yolks with half of the sugar until thick.
2. In another bowl whip egg whites with the remaining sugar to form a stiff meringue. Fold flour into the egg yolks followed by the egg whites.
3. Pipe out lady fingers onto trays lined with parchment paper. Dust with powdered sugar before baking. Bake at 200°C/390°F for 10 minutes.

## White Sponge

6 eggs
170 grams castor sugar
135 grams all-purpose flour, sifted
35 grams cornflour, sifted
2 tablespoons butter, melted

## Method

1. Preheat the oven to 180°C/360°F. Line a 22-cm cake pan with parchment paper.
2. Whisk eggs and sugar until firm. Gradually fold in flour and cornflour, followed by melted butter. Bake for approximately 30 minutes.

## Coffee Syrup

100 grams castor sugar
100 ml water
2 teaspoons instant coffee powder
3 tablespoons rum

## Method

1. Mix sugar with water and boil. Remove from heat when the sugar melts.
2. Dissolve instant coffee and rum in the sugar syrup. Cool.

## Cream

4 sheets gelatine
75 grams castor sugar
4 egg yolks
400 grams mascarpone cheese
3 tablespoons rum, optional
250 grams cream, lightly whipped

## Method

1. Soften gelatine sheets in cool water and drain. Melt the gelatine with some hot water and set aside.
2. Cream sugar and egg yolks. Add mascarpone cheese. Blend well. Add rum and fold in cream. Fold in melted gelatine.

## To Assemble Tiramisu You Need:

lady fingers
white sponge cake
coffee syrup
cream

cocoa powder for dusting

## Method

1. Line the sides of a ring mould with lady fingers to a height of 2.5 cm. Slice white sponge cake into three pieces, each measuring about 1.5 cm thick. Only two slices will be used. Place a layer of sponge cake at the base of the ring mould. Brush the cake with coffee syrup.
2. Fill the ring mould with cream halfway up the sides of the mould. Top with another layer of white sponge cake and brush with coffee syrup. Fill the ring mould with the remaining cream and level with a spatula. Chill the cake until it sets. Dust with cocoa powder and remove the mould. Decorate as desired.

*Opposite: Chocolate Rehrucken.*

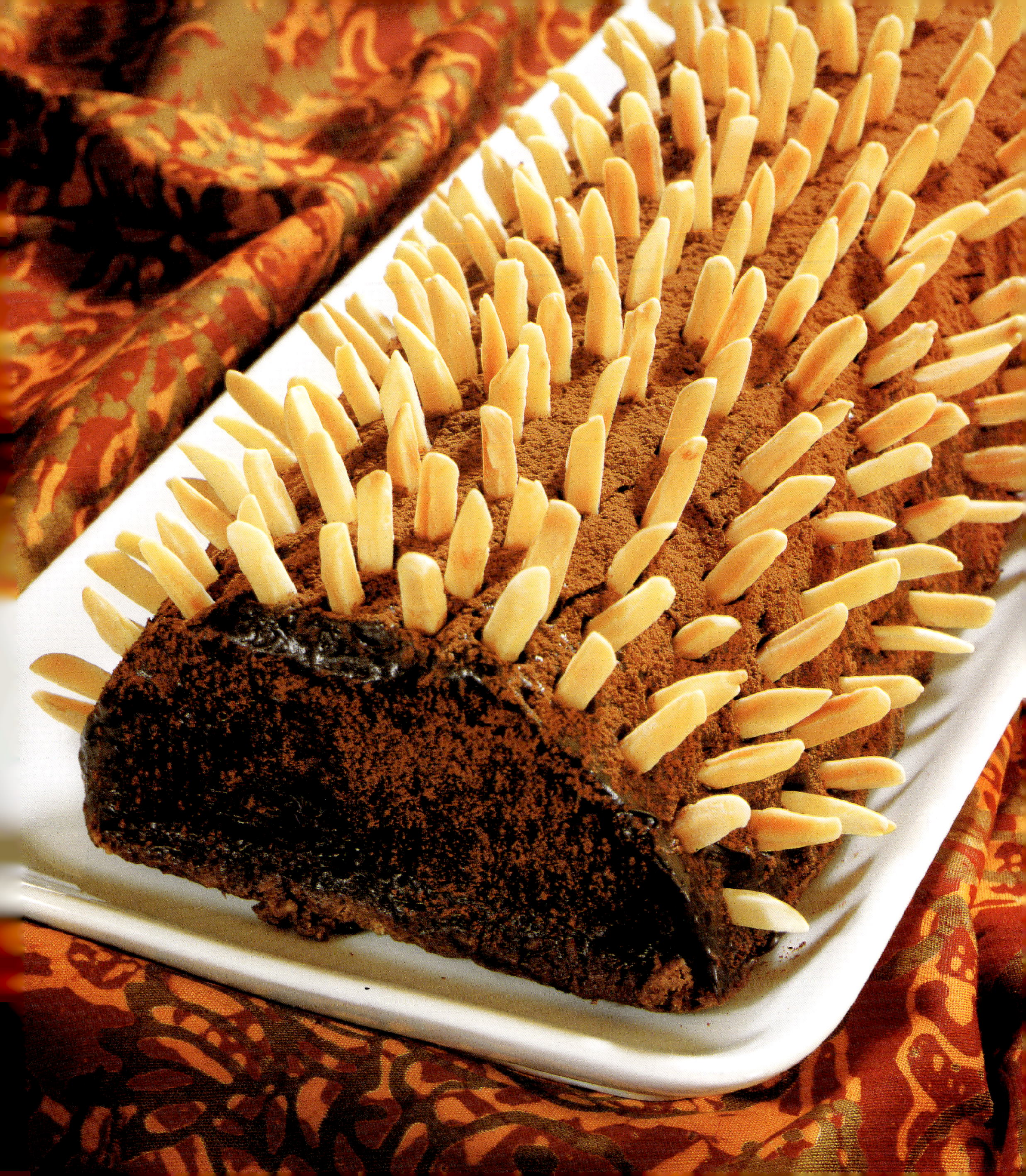

# Desserts

The Art of Making Puddings, Trifles and Other Desserts, P172  **1** Bread Pudding with Apples, P174  **2** Banana Bread Pudding, P174  **3** Chocolate Bread Pudding, P174  **4** Apple Yoghurt Pancakes, P176  **5** Banana Pudding, P176  **6** Crepes, P176  **7** Jelly with Coffee Custard, P176  **8** Chocolate Coconut Strudel, P178  **9** Sweet Potato Flan, P178  **10** Mocha Peach Trifle, P180  **11** Mango and Banana Custard Pudding, P180  **12** Pancakes, P182  **13** Persimmon Pudding, P182  **14** Pineapple Pancakes, P182  **15** English Trifle, P182  **16** Strawberry Tea Mousse, P184  **17** Belgian Waffles, P184  **18** Blackforest Cherry Pudding, P184  **19** Baked Pineapple Pudding, P184

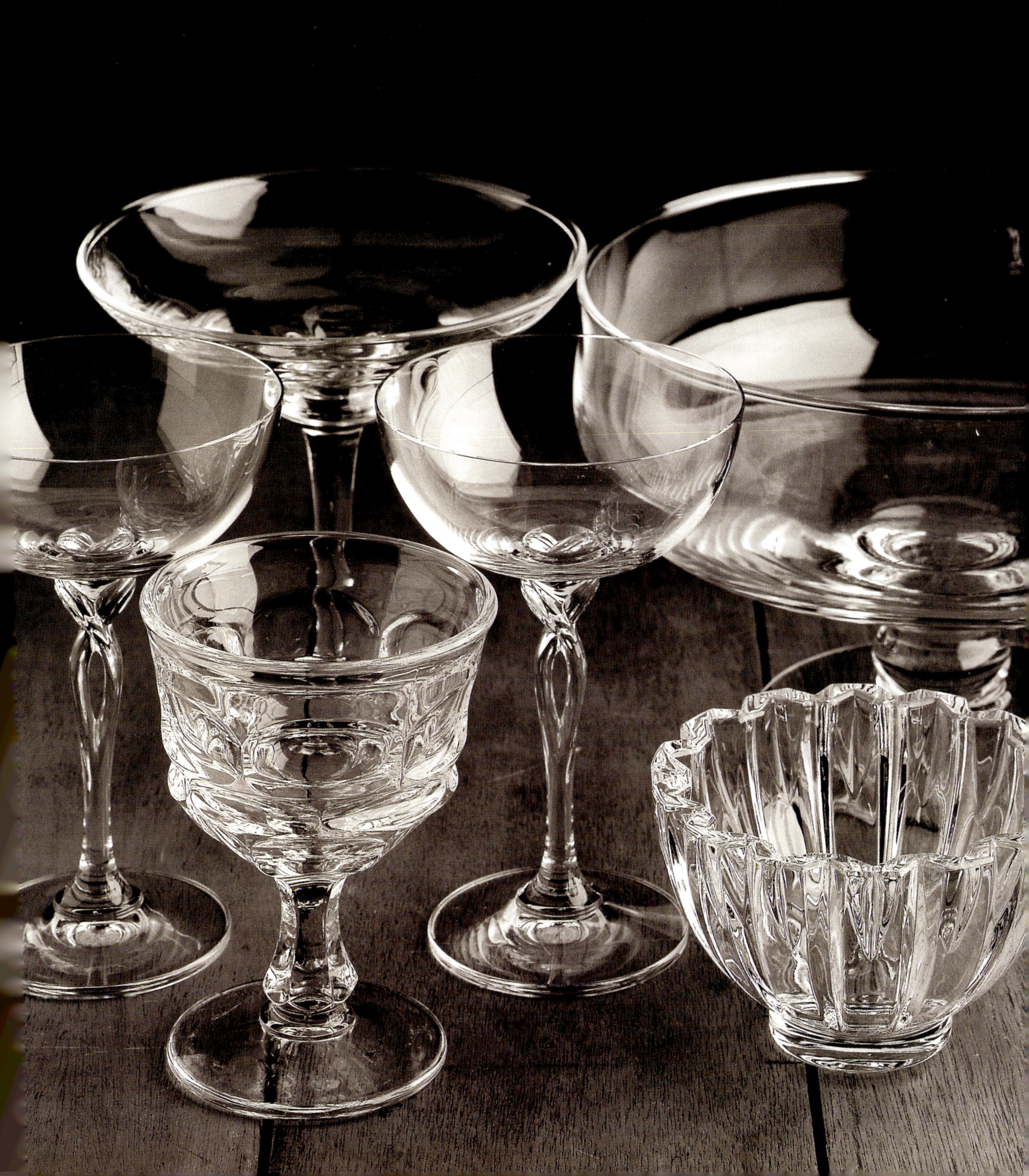

# The Art of Making Puddings, Trifles and Other Desserts

The main similarity of the desserts featured in this chapter is that they all contain eggs, cream or milk. The differences lie in the techniques used to make them and the ways in which they are presented. Charlottes, bavarois, custards, mousses and souffles are some of the desserts that fall into this category. Unfortunately, I am unable to include all of them because of space constraints.

## PUDDINGS

In England, the term "pudding" is synonymous with dessert and covers a wide range of sweet and savoury dishes. Puddings are generally steamed (as in pudding cakes, also known as sponge puddings) and served with a sauce poured over them. A moist, steamed pudding heavily flavoured with liquor (usually brandy or rum) can be stored for up to three months in a cool, dry place. Unwrap it occasionally and add more liquor if the pudding appears dry.

Some puddings are baked, as in the case of the bread pudding. This pudding is easy to make and tastes wonderful. It also gives you the chance to use up leftover bread or bread that is not very fresh. Besides the normal custard filling, you can add all sorts of fruits and nuts, or flavour with spices that lend a pleasing aroma when the pudding is served warm from the oven. Both bread and sponge puddings should be served slightly warm. Some people may find puddings slightly sticky or too sweet. You can, of course, reduce the sugar content to suit your preference.

## CUSTARDS

These are generally beaten eggs mixed with milk or cream, sugar and any of a variety of flavourings. They can be made by two methods: either baked in an oven or cooked on top of a stove. They are simple to prepare, can be made one or two days in advance, and need little or no finishing touches.

When the custard is meant to be unmoulded, a ratio of two egg yolks per cup of liquid is required. An example of this is the creme caramel. Custards are generally baked in individual earthenware cups, but can also be made in larger oven-proof dishes to be served at the buffet table. A custard should always be placed in a pan with at least $2^{1}/_{2}$ cm of hot water around it and baked at 175°C/350°F to avoid overcooking, which will result in watery and curdled custard. Custards should be smooth and the secret of success lies in quality ingredients and a low, steady heat. Eggs are an essential ingredient and it is essential that they do not curdle because of heat that is too high at any point during cooking.

For a richer baked or caramel custard, use light cream instead of milk, or use both in equal proportions to make up the original amount stated in the recipe. Canned evaporated milk can also be used to create a custard with a rich flavour. For a super-smooth custard, use sweetened condensed milk, omitting the sugar from the recipe. If you prefer a lighter custard, use low-fat milk, or combine milk with orange juice, for example. For an interesting flavour, you can add chocolate, fruit, liqueur, coffee, ginger, spice, coconut milk or grated coconut to the custard.

Classic baked custards are done when a knife inserted halfway into the centre is removed with only a small amount of the custard clinging to it. When you unmould a custard from a caramel-lined mould, it is not unusual for part of the caramel to remain hardened at the bottom of the mould.

If a custard contains a large amount of egg yolks to a small amount of liquid, cook it in a double boiler placed over simmering water. If you cook it over direct heat, you run the risk of scrambling the eggs. When making a custard base containing egg yolks that will be set with unflavoured gelatine, it is all right to undercook the custard slightly, thus avoiding any chance of scrambling the eggs. The gelatine will set the custard even if it is not as thick as it could have been.

## MOUSSES AND TRIFLES

Mousse is a term commonly used to describe almost any dessert containing whipped cream. Chocolate mousse, perhaps the most popular variety, is the easiest to prepare because chocolate is dense enough to firm up a mousse without the addition of unflavoured gelatine. Other mousses usually have a custard or cream base and need gelatine to set it.

When working with unflavoured gelatine, timing becomes a critical factor. First, the gelatine must be softened in liquid for about five minutes. Then it must be dissolved in the liquid by heat, either by being stirred into a hot mixture or by being brought to a simmer. After it is dissolved, it is stirred into the custard or cream base.

Before beaten egg whites or whipped cream can be folded together with the base, the latter must be cooled first so that the gelatine will thicken. The fastest way to cool the base is to place it in a bowl, then place this in a larger bowl of iced water. Stir the mixture occasionally until it begins to thicken and set, after which it can be folded into beaten egg whites and/or whipped cream. When whipping egg whites and cream for a mousse, they should hold soft, rounded peaks. If you beat them too stiffly, they will be difficult to fold into the mixture and the dessert will not have a soft, fluffy texture.

Commercial gelatine is available as a powder or in brittle sheets. Both are almost tasteless and easy to use. Powdered gelatine can be weighed or measured by the spoon: 1 tablespoon weighs 7 grams. It is critical to maintain the mousse at the required temperature before gelatine is added. Gelatine sets into a firm gel at 20°C/68°F. To gel 500 ml of a clear liquid such as fruit juice, 1 tablespoon/7 grams of gelatine is needed. Soft, fluffy mixtures need less while heavy, creamy ones may need more. A few fruits, notably raw pineapple, contain an enzyme that inhibits gelatine from setting. Therefore, the fruit has to be cooked first to destroy the enzyme which would otherwise break down the protein structure of the gelatine. Once set, a gelatine mixture should be left in the refrigerator for at least two hours to become firm.

A word you may come across in relation to Western desserts is "souffle". Although I have not included this in the following recipes because of limited space, you may like to know that it is closely allied with the mousse. The difference is that a souffle is lightened with egg white and prepared in such a way that the top looks as if it has puffed up in the oven.

A trifle, on the other hand, is an 18th century English dessert of custard layered with cake and fruit. Sponge cake or lady fingers are spread with jam, placed in a glass bowl, sprinkled with sherry and layered with fruit and rich custard.

## Bread Pudding with Apples

*Ingredients*

    6 green apples
    100 grams + 100 grams butter, softened
    2 tablespoons sugar
    1/4 teaspoon ground cinnamon
    2 french loaves
    1/4 cup seedless raisins
    4 eggs
    4 cups milk
    2/3 cup castor sugar
    2 teaspoons vanilla essence
    a pinch of nutmeg

    whipped cream to serve

*Method*

1. Peel, core and cut apples into large cubes. Melt 100 grams butter in a heavy skillet. Add apples, sprinkling with sugar and cinnamon. Saute over medium heat for about 10 minutes, stirring frequently.

2. Remove crusts from the bread and cut into 2-cm cubes. Liberally grease a deep 2½-quart baking dish with the remaining 100 grams butter.

3. Combine the bread, raisins, apples and pan juices in the baking dish.

4. In another bowl lightly whisk together eggs, milk, sugar, vanilla essence and nutmeg. Pour over bread and apples.

5. Set the dish in a shallow pan filled 2.5 cm high with warm water. Bake at 180°C/360°F for 1½ to 2 hours until the pudding sets. Serve hot with lightly whipped cream.

## Banana Bread Pudding

*Ingredients*

    4 cups wholewheat bread, cut into cubes
    4 cups milk
    2 tablespoons butter
    6 eggs
    1½ cups castor sugar
    2 tablespoons vanilla essence
    1 cup golden raisins
    2 cups bananas, mashed
    1/2 teaspoon ground cinnamon

    powdered sugar for dusting

*Method*

1. Soak bread in the milk for an hour. Butter a 33 cm by 22 cm by 5 cm pan and set aside.

2. Beat eggs, sugar and vanilla essence together and pour over the soaked bread cubes. Stir in raisins, bananas and cinnamon.

3. Pour the mixture into the buttered pan set in a deep baking tray half-filled with water. Bake at 170°C/340°F for about one hour or until a knife inserted in the centre of the pudding comes away cleanly. Dust with powdered sugar.

## Chocolate Bread Pudding

*Custard*

    170 grams bittersweet chocolate
    40 grams bitter chocolate
    3 whole eggs
    3 egg yolks
    1/2 cup castor sugar
    1 cup fresh milk
    1 cup whipping cream

*Method*

1. Melt both types of chocolate in a heatproof dish set over a pot of simmering water.

2. In a separate bowl beat eggs and egg yolks until thick. Beat in sugar.

3. Boil together milk and whipping cream. Gradually pour into the egg mixture. Stir in melted chocolate. Cool by setting the bowl set in a basin of iced water. Chill the cooled pudding in the refrigerator overnight.

*Bread Layer*

    1 cup fresh milk
    1/2 cup whipping cream
    1 cup castor sugar
    1/3 cup unsweetened cocoa powder
    1 loaf wholemeal bread

    cocoa powder and powdered sugar for dusting

*Method*

1. Mix the first four ingredients and heat until the cocoa dissolves.

2. Cut bread into 16 pieces using a 5-cm cookie cutter. Arrange in a baking pan and pour the cocoa mixture over. Allow the bread to absorb the liquid.

3. Meanwhile grease eight custard cups with butter. Pour one spoonful of cooled chocolate custard in each cup. Top with soaked bread pieces. Spoon in another layer of custard, top with bread pieces. Repeat the process until all the ingredients are used up, ending with a custard layer.

4. Place the custard cups on a baking tray half-filled with boiling water. Bake for 30 minutes at 170°C/340°F. Cool before chilling in the refrigerator. Dust with cocoa powder and powdered sugar.

*Opposite: Bread Pudding with Apples (above left) and Chocolate Bread Pudding (above right).*

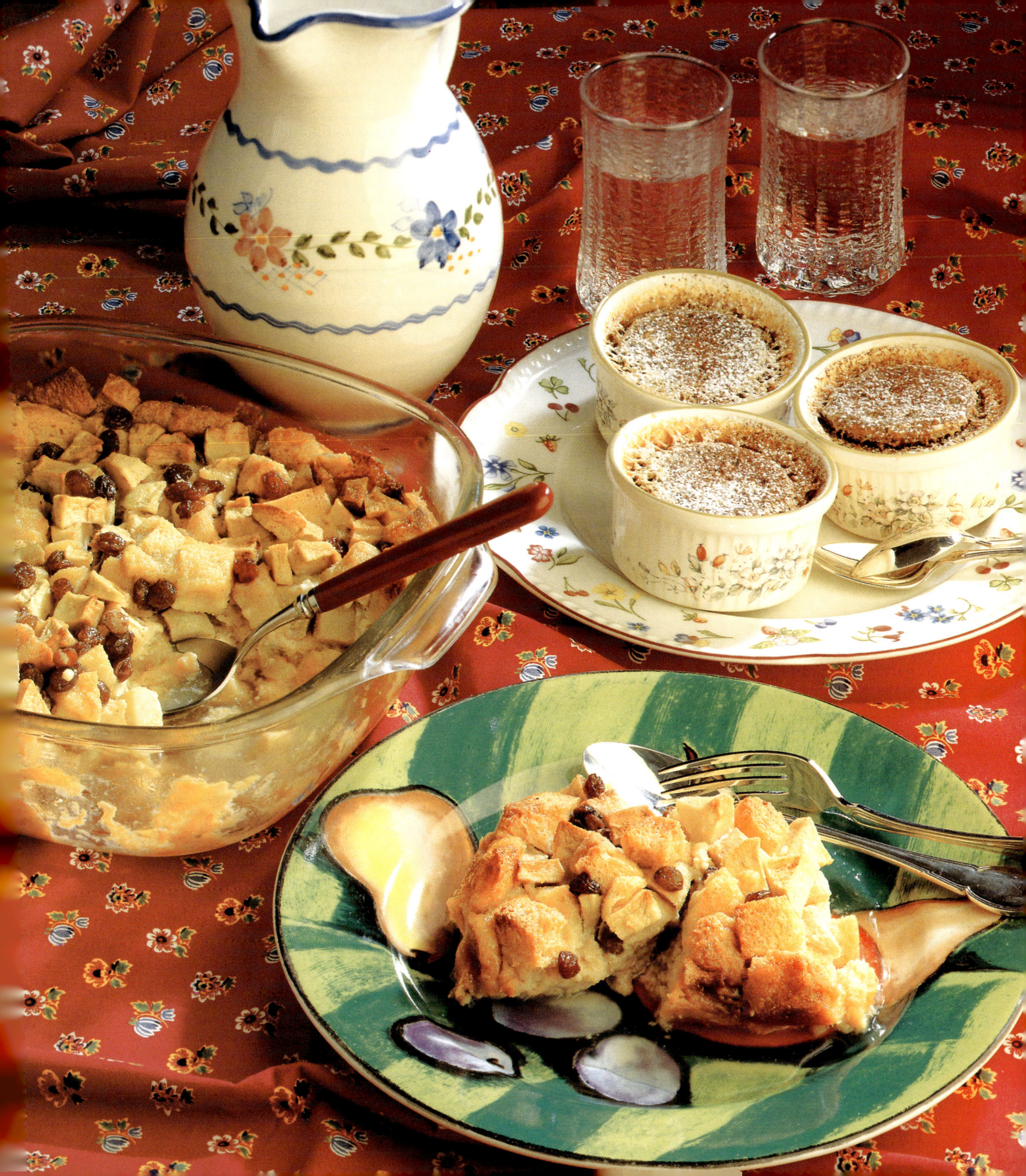

## Apple Yoghurt Pancakes

*Ingredients*

1 cup all-purpose flour
1 tablespoon castor sugar
1 teaspoon baking powder
1/2 teaspoon baking soda
1/4 teaspoon salt
a pinch of nutmeg
1 egg
1/2 cup plain yoghurt
1/2 cup milk
2 tablespoons vegetable oil
1 green apple, peeled and diced finely

butter and syrup to serve

*Method*

1. Sift together flour, sugar, baking powder, baking soda, salt and nutmeg.
2. Beat egg with yoghurt and milk in a large bowl. Beat in oil, then add sifted ingredients. Stir until just combined. The batter may still be lumpy.
3. Grease a nonstick pan and ladle in some pancake batter. Spoon a little diced apple over and cook the pancake on both sides until golden. Serve with butter and syrup.

Chef's Note: If you prefer you can substitue blueberries for the apples.

## Banana Pudding

*Ingredients*

10 bananas, sliced
6 eggs
1 cup castor sugar
4 cups coconut milk
1 cup fresh milk
a pinch of salt

*Method*

1. Butter a casserole dish and arrange sliced bananas in the base.
2. Beat eggs with sugar. Add coconut milk, fresh milk and salt. Pour over the bananas. Bake for 30 minutes at 170°C/340°F.

## Crepes

*Ingredients*

4 eggs
1 1/4 cups milk
30 grams butter, melted
115 grams all-purpose flour
1 teaspoon vanilla essence
a pinch of salt

*Method*

1. Combine all the ingredients in a food processor and blend for 30 seconds. Process until smooth and strain. If the mixture is too watery, add a little additional flour.
2. Chill the batter for 1 hour.
3. Grease a nonstick pan with a little oil and pour in a ladleful of batter. Cook on both sides over low fire. Serve warm with desired topping.

Chef's Note: The first few crepes may be pale in colour but subsequent ones should be golden brown once the heat is evenly distributed. To make sweet crepes, substitute the salt with 2 tablespoons castor sugar and add 1 teaspoon vanilla essence.

## Jelly with Coffee Custard

*Ingredients*

4 cups water
1 cup agar-agar, soaked and strained
3/4 cup castor sugar
3 teaspoons instant coffee, dissolved in a little hot water
1 cup evaporated milk

*Method*

Bring the water to a boil and dissolve agar-agar in it. Add sugar, coffee and milk and bring the mixture to a simmer. Strain the mixture into a jelly mould and chill in the refrigerator.

*Coffee Custard*

3/4 cup evaporated milk
1 cup water
4 tablespoons castor sugar
a pinch of salt
1 teaspoon vanilla essence
1 tablespoon instant coffee
2 tablespoons custard powder
1 tablespoon water

*Method*

1. In a saucepan mix all the ingredients, except for custard powder and water, and bring to a simmer.
2. Dissolve custard powder in one tablespoon water and add to the other ingredients. Stir quickly and bring to a boil.
3. Remove from heat, chill and serve cold over jelly.

*Opposite: Apple Yoghurt Pancakes (above) and Crepes (below).*

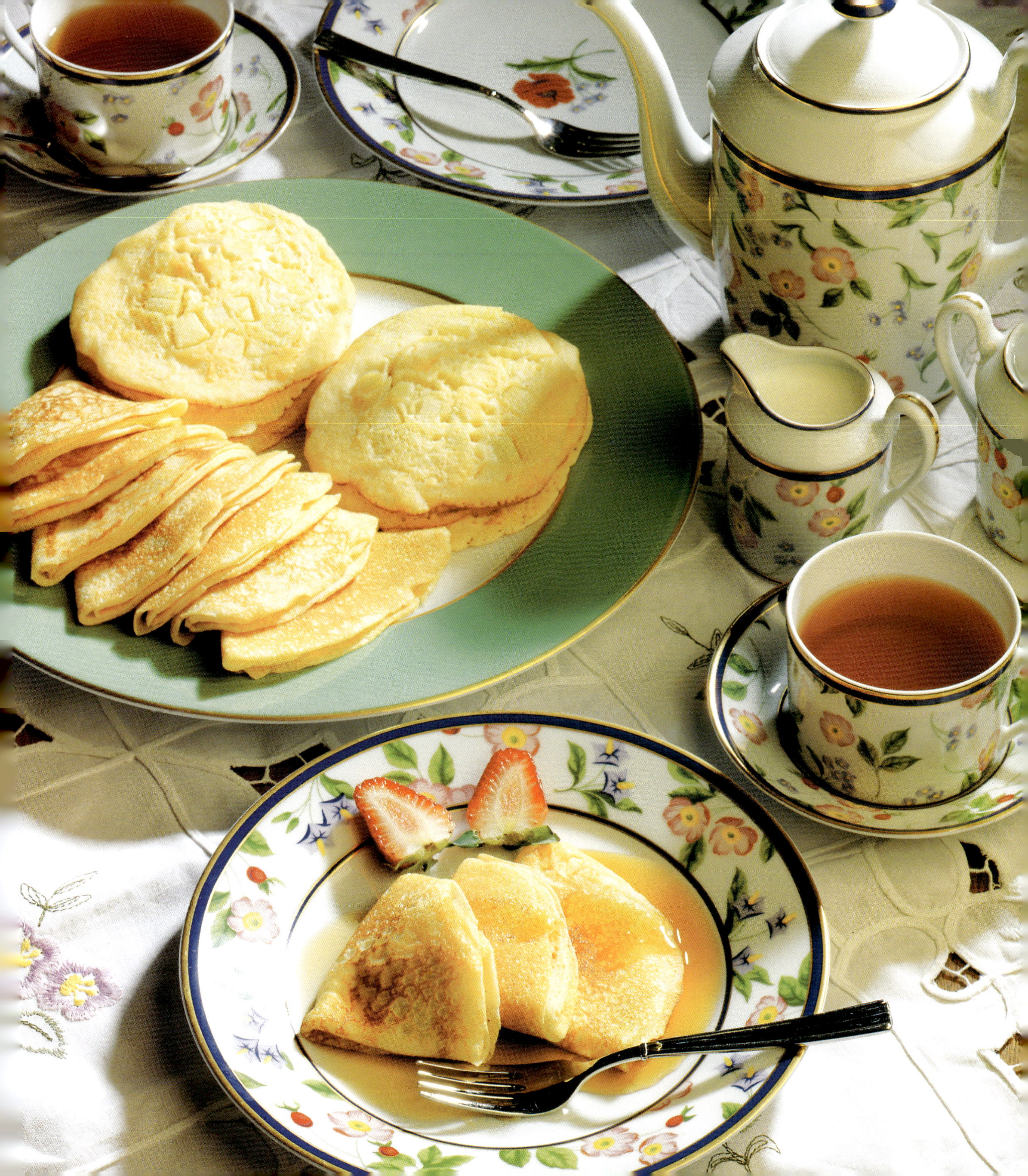

## Chocolate Coconut Strudel

### Chocolate-Coconut Filling

- 170 grams semisweet chocolate, finely chopped
- 1/2 cup sweetened flaked coconut
- 1/2 cup currants
- 3/4 cup almonds, finely ground
- 3 tablespoons unsalted butter, softened
- 1/2 cup + 1 tablespoon castor sugar
- 3 large eggs, separated

### Method

1. Stir together chocolate, coconut, currants and almonds until thoroughly blended. Set aside.
2. With a heavy duty electric mixer beat butter for 30 seconds at medium speed until creamy. Gradually add 1/2 cup sugar in a steady stream and beat at high speed for 3 to 5 minutes until light and fluffy.
3. Reduce the mixer speed to low and add egg yolks, one at a time, beating well after each addition. Add chocolate-coconut mixture and beat until just combined. Scrape the bottom and sides of the bowl and beat for another 10 seconds.
4. In a greased bowl beat egg whites at low speed until frothy. Gradually increase speed to high and beat until soft peaks form. While continuing to beat, gradually add the remaining tablespoon of sugar, one teaspoon at a time. Beat until stiff peaks form.
5. Fold one-third of the egg whites into the chocolate-coconut mixture. Fold in the remaining egg whites in two batches.

### Coconut Cream Sauce

- 1 cup heavy cream
- 1/2 cup milk
- 1 vanilla bean, split in half lengthwise
- 2 egg yolks
- 2 tablespoons castor sugar
- 1/4 cup coconut cream

### Method

1. In a saucepan bring cream, milk and vanilla bean to a gentle boil over medium-low heat. Cover the pan, remove from heat and let the mixture stand for 15 minutes. Remove vanilla bean and scald mixture again.
2. In a separate bowl whisk egg yolks and sugar. Gradually whisk about 1 cup of hot vanilla mixture into the egg mixture. Return to the saucepan and stir with a wooden spoon until the mixture is thick enough to coat the back of a spoon. Remove from the stove, strain the custard and immediately place the bowl of custard in a basin of ice water, continuing to stir until cool. Stir in coconut cream and refrigerate.

### To Assemble Strudel You Need:

- 12 sheets phyllo pastry, each measuring 30 cm by 43 cm
- 8 tablespoon unsalted butter, melted chocolate-coconut filling
- powdered sugar for dusting
- fresh strawberries, mint leaves and coconut flakes to decorate
- coconut cream sauce

### Method

1. Remove one phyllo sheet from the stack and brush lightly with melted butter. Place a second sheet of phyllo on top of the first and brush with more butter. Repeat the layering process two more times.
2. With a large spoon, spread about 1 cup of the filling onto the phyllo sheet. Roll up strudel tightly as though making jelly roll. Brush the edges with butter before tucking the ends downwards.
3. Prepare two more strudel logs with the remaining phyllo pastry and filling.
4. Bake the strudels at 170°C/340°F for 20 minutes until golden brown. Cool on a baking sheet set on a wire rack for 30 minutes.
5. To serve, cut the strudel diagonally into diamond shapes and sprinkle with powdered sugar. Top with strawberries, mint leaves and coconut flakes. Serve with coconut cream sauce.

## Sweet Potato Flan

### Ingredients

- 1 cup sugar
- 1/4 cup water
- 8 whole eggs
- 2 egg yolks
- 400 grams sweetened condensed milk
- 1 cup fresh milk
- 1 cup heavy cream
- 1 tablespoon vanilla essence
- 1 teaspoon ground nutmeg
- 1/2 teaspoon ground cinnamon
- 1/2 teaspoon ground allspice
- 600 grams sweet potatoes, cooked and mashed

### Method

1. In a heavy saucepan cook sugar with water until golden caramel in colour. Pour in a flan dish and set aside.
2. In another bowl beat eggs and egg yolks until fluffy. Add the remaining ingredients, ending with sweet potatoes. Strain into the flan dish.
3. Place the dish in a pan half-filled with boiling water. Bake for 1 hour at 170°C/340°F. To test for doneness insert a paring knife in the centre of the flan. If the knife comes away cleanly, the flan is done.

Chef's Note: If your flan batter is lumpy, run the batter in the blender for a few seconds before straining. Cooking the flan at a lower temperature of 170°C/340°F will result in a very smooth texture, but the flan may take an extra 20 minutes to cook.

*Opposite: Sweet Potato Flan (above) and Chocolate Coconut Strudel (below).*

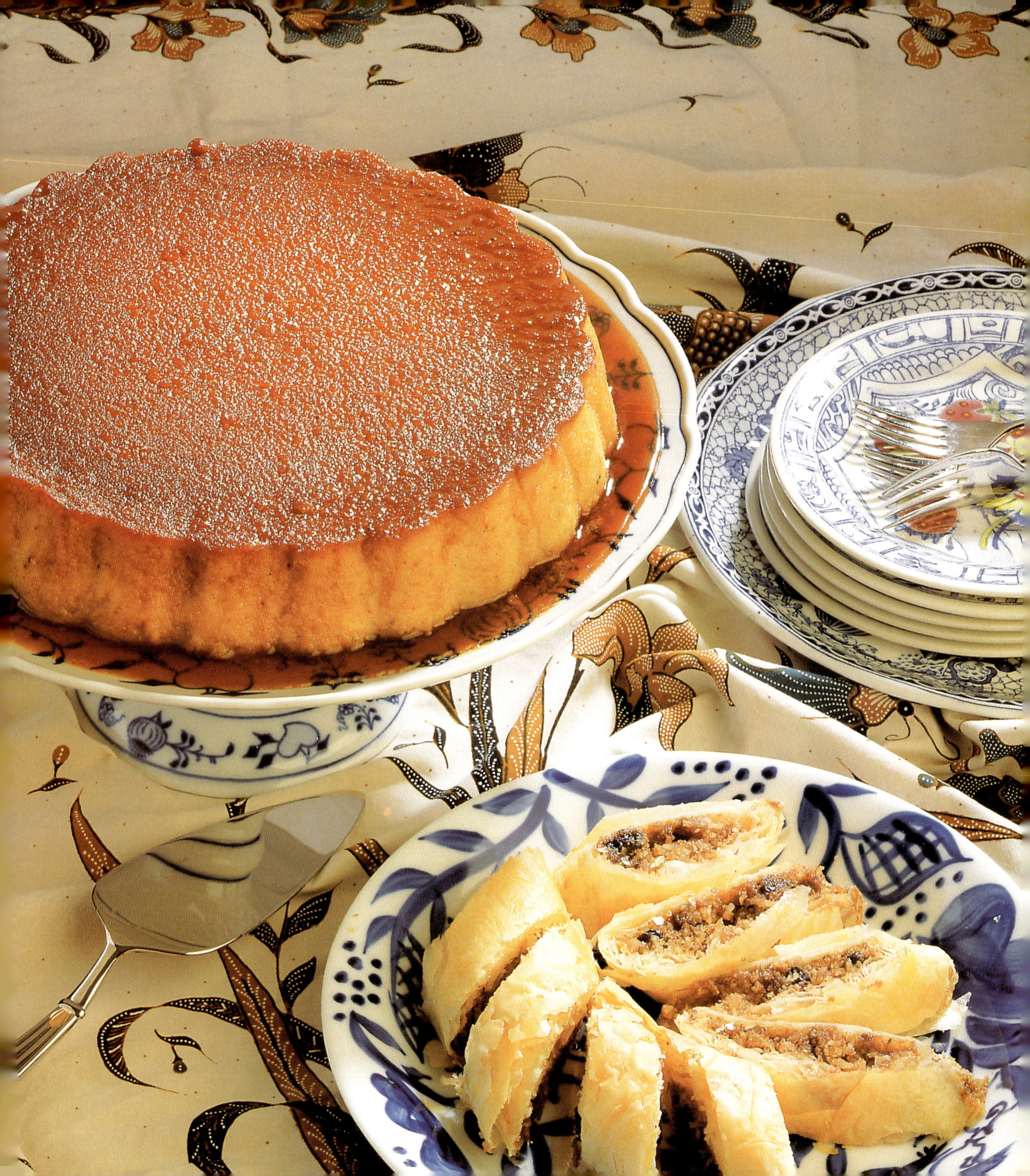

# Mocha Peach Trifle

*Coffee Sponge Cake*

    6 eggs
    225 grams castor sugar
    1/2 teaspoon vanilla essence
    1 tablespoon instant coffee, dissolved in a little hot water
    225 grams all-purpose flour

*Method*

1. In a heatproof bowl placed over a pot of simmering water beat eggs, sugar, vanilla essence and instant coffee until slightly warm, about 55°C/130°F. Transfer to a cake mixer and beat vigorously until fairly cool.
2. Sift flour into the batter in small batches and mix well. Pour the batter into a 24-cm cake pan lined with greased parchment paper and bake for 25 minutes at 185°C/365°F.

*Sugar Syrup*

    1/2 cup castor sugar
    1/4 cup water
    4 tablespoons kahlua liqueur

*Method*

Bring sugar and water to a simmer. Cool before flavouring with kahlua.

*Mocha Custard*

    4 cups fresh milk
    2 tablespoon instant coffee
    10 egg yolks
    1/3 cup castor sugar
    2 tablespoons custard powder
    100 grams butter, chilled and diced

*Method*

1. Bring milk and instant coffee to a simmer in a saucepan.
2. In a separate bowl beat egg yolks with sugar and custard powder until fluffy. Add half of the warm milk from the saucepan.
3. Stir to mix and pour back into the saucepan with the remaining milk. Stir and continue cooking until the custard boils and begins to thicken. Remove from the heat and add the chilled butter. Stir until dissolved. Chill the custard before use.

*Chocolate Cream*

    200 grams bittersweet chocolate
    1 cup whipping cream

*Method*

Place chocolate and whipping cream in a heatproof bowl over a pan of simmering water. Stir until the chocolate melts. Remove from heat.

*To Assemble Mocha Peach Trifle You Need:*

    coffee sponge cake
    sugar syrup
    1000 grams canned cling peaches, drained
    mocha custard
    chocolate cream

*Method*

1. Place slices of coffee sponge cake at the base of a trifle bowl. Drizzle with sugar syrup. Arrange a layer of peaches over the syrup, top with mocha custard and drizzle with chocolate cream. Repeat until all the ingredients are used, ending with a layer of peaches.
2. Chill overnight before serving.

Chef's Note: Trifles have been popular in England since the 18th century. Serve trifle in pretty bowls.

# Mango and Banana Custard Pudding

*Ingredients*

    45 grams all-purpose flour, sifted
    a pinch of salt
    40 grams castor sugar
    3 large eggs, beaten
    450 ml fresh milk
    1 tablespoon lemon juice
    grated zest of 1 lemon
    2–3 large bananas, peeled and thickly sliced
    1 tablespoon brown sugar
    300 grams mango, peeled and thinly sliced
    30 grams butter, softened at room temperature
    30 grams almond flakes to decorate

*Method*

1. Grease a heatproof 29 cm by 22 cm oven dish with butter.
2. Sift flour into the bowl of an electric mixer. Stir in salt and castor sugar. Beat in eggs until just blended.
3. Heat milk until almost boiling before pouring into the egg mixture.
4. In a separate bowl stir lemon juice and zest with sliced bananas and arrange at the base of the buttered dish. Sprinkle with brown sugar and top with sliced mangoes. Pour in the egg mixture and dot with butter.
5. Bake in a preheated oven at 220°C/425°F for 35 to 40 minutes until the custard sets and becomes golden brown. Sprinkle with almond flakes and serve warm.

*Opposite: Mocha Peach Trifle.*

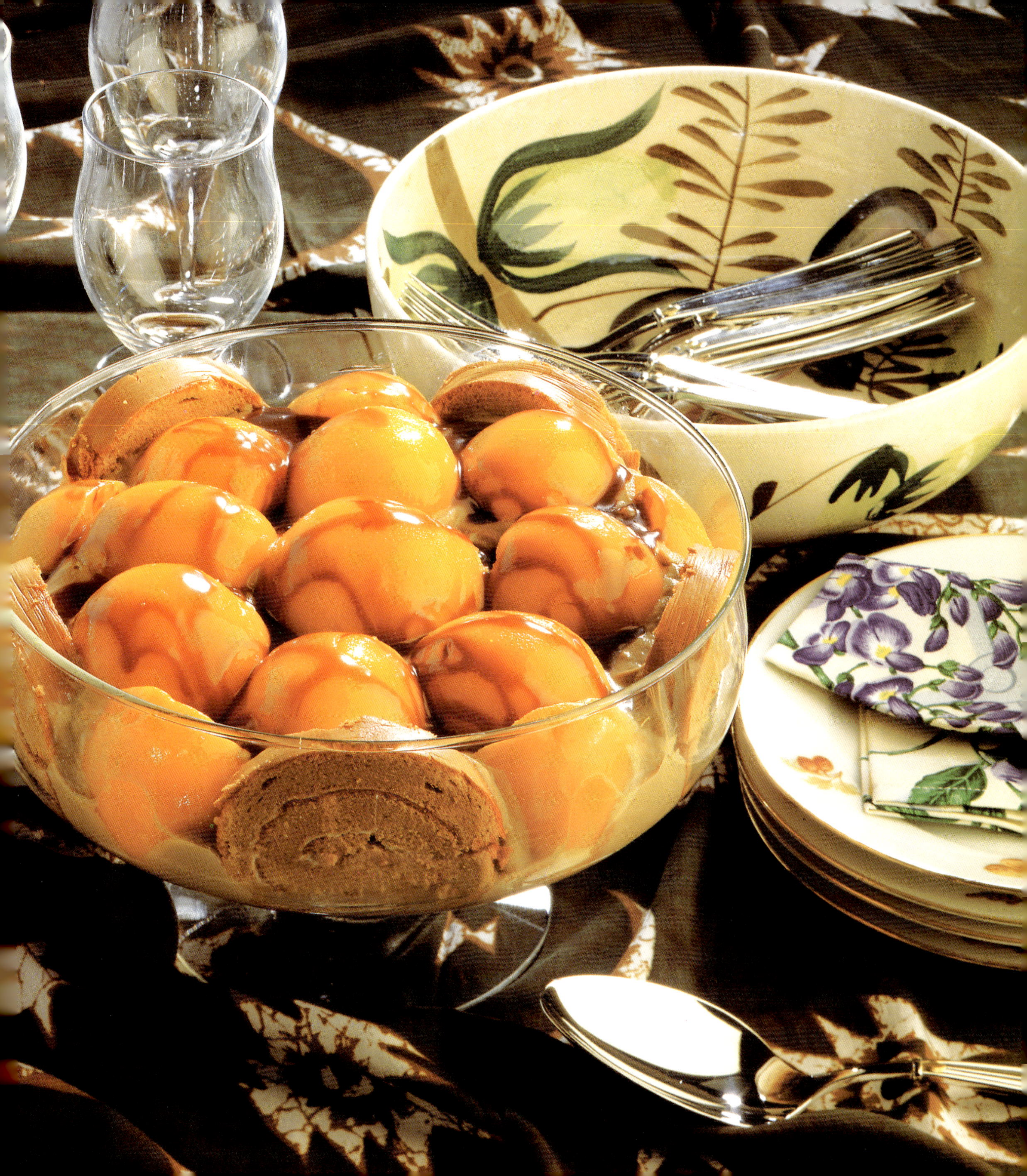

# Pancakes

### Ingredients

- 1 cup fresh milk
- 5 tablespoons butter
- 3 eggs
- 1¼ cups all-purpose flour
- 1 tablespoon castor sugar
- 4 teaspoons baking powder
- ¾ teaspoon salt
- powdered sugar for dusting
- ¼ cup mint leaves to decorate

### Method

1. Heat milk and butter until the butter melts. Do not boil the mixture. Cool for a while before adding eggs. Beat well.
2. Sift together flour, sugar, baking powder and salt. Stir into the egg mixture without overmixing. Pour a ladleful of batter into a nonstick frying pan and cook until golden. Garnish with desired topping, dust with powdered sugar and decorate with mint leaves.

### Topping Ideas

- ½ cup creamed corn
- 1½ cup fruit salad, consisting of melon, grapes, oranges, honeydew, papaya and strawberries
- 2 bananas
- ½ cup pancake syrup

# Persimmon Pudding

### Ingredients

- ½ cup castor sugar
- 6 tablespoons corn oil + a little extra for greasing the mould
- 4 eggs
- 2 teaspoons vanilla essence
- 3 to 4 very ripe, large persimmons, skinned and with the pulp mashed
- 2 cups all-purpose flour
- 1 teaspoon baking soda
- ½ teaspoon salt
- 2 teaspoons ground cinnamon

vanilla custard sauce to serve*

### Method

1. Oil a 3-litre pudding mould with a little corn oil. In a large bowl beat together sugar, corn oil, eggs and vanilla essence until fluffy. Add persimmon pulp.
2. In a separate bowl sift together flour, baking soda, salt and cinnamon. Add to the persimmon mixture and blend until smooth. Pour into the pudding mould and cover tightly with circle of parchment paper, keeping the edges down with a rubber band. Place a circle of foil over the parchment paper.
3. Place the mould on a wire rack in a large pot half-filled with water. Cover the pot, bring the water to a boil then reduce heat and simmer for 2½ hours, adding boiling water as necessary until the pudding sets. Serve warm or cold with vanilla custard sauce.

* Refer to Coconut Cream Sauce for Chocolate Coconut Strudel on page 178. But substitute ¼ cup coconut cream with ¼ cup heavy cream.

# Pineapple Pancakes

### Ingredients

- 3 eggs
- 2 tablespoons honey
- 30 grams butter, melted + 2 additional tablespoons butter
- 1¼ cups fresh milk or coconut milk
- 115 grams all-purpose flour
- ¼ cup brown sugar
- ½ ripe pineapples, diced
- ½ teaspoon ground cinnamon
- 1 tablespoon powdered sugar for dusting

### Method

1. Beat eggs and honey. Stir in 30 grams butter, milk and flour until smooth. Leave to rest for half an hour.
2. Meanwhile heat the remaining 2 tablespoons butter in a saucepan and quickly fry the brown sugar. Stir in pineapples and cinnamon. Cook for a few minutes.
3. Heat a nonstick frying pan greased with vegetable oil and pour in one ladleful of batter. Cook the pancake until golden brown.
4. Spoon some caramelised pineapple over the pancake and dust with powdered sugar.

# English Trifle

### Ingredients

- 2 cups castor sugar
- a pinch of salt
- 5 egg yolks
- 3 whole eggs
- 1 cup fresh lemon juice
- 5 tablespoons unsalted butter
- 1 pound cake, 25 cm in diameter*
- 6 cups strawberries, coarsely chopped

whipped cream to serve

### Method

1. Stir together sugar and salt. Add egg yolks and whole eggs one at a time, beating well after each addition. Stir in lemon juice.
2. Place the mixture in a heatproof bowl set over a pan of simmering water. Add butter, stirring constantly until melted. When the mixture is thick enough to coat the back of a spoon, remove the bowl from the heat and cool the mixture completely.
3. To assemble the trifle, spoon a layer of lemon curd thinly in the base of a 2½-litre bowl. Layer with some pound cake and some chopped strawberries. Continue the layering process until all the ingredients are used up.
4. Cover and refrigerate for at least 6 hours or overnight. Serve with a few dollops of whipped cream.

* Refer to recipe for Evelyn Orange Tea Loaf on page 142.

*Opposite: Persimmon Pudding (above) and Pineapple Pancakes (below).*

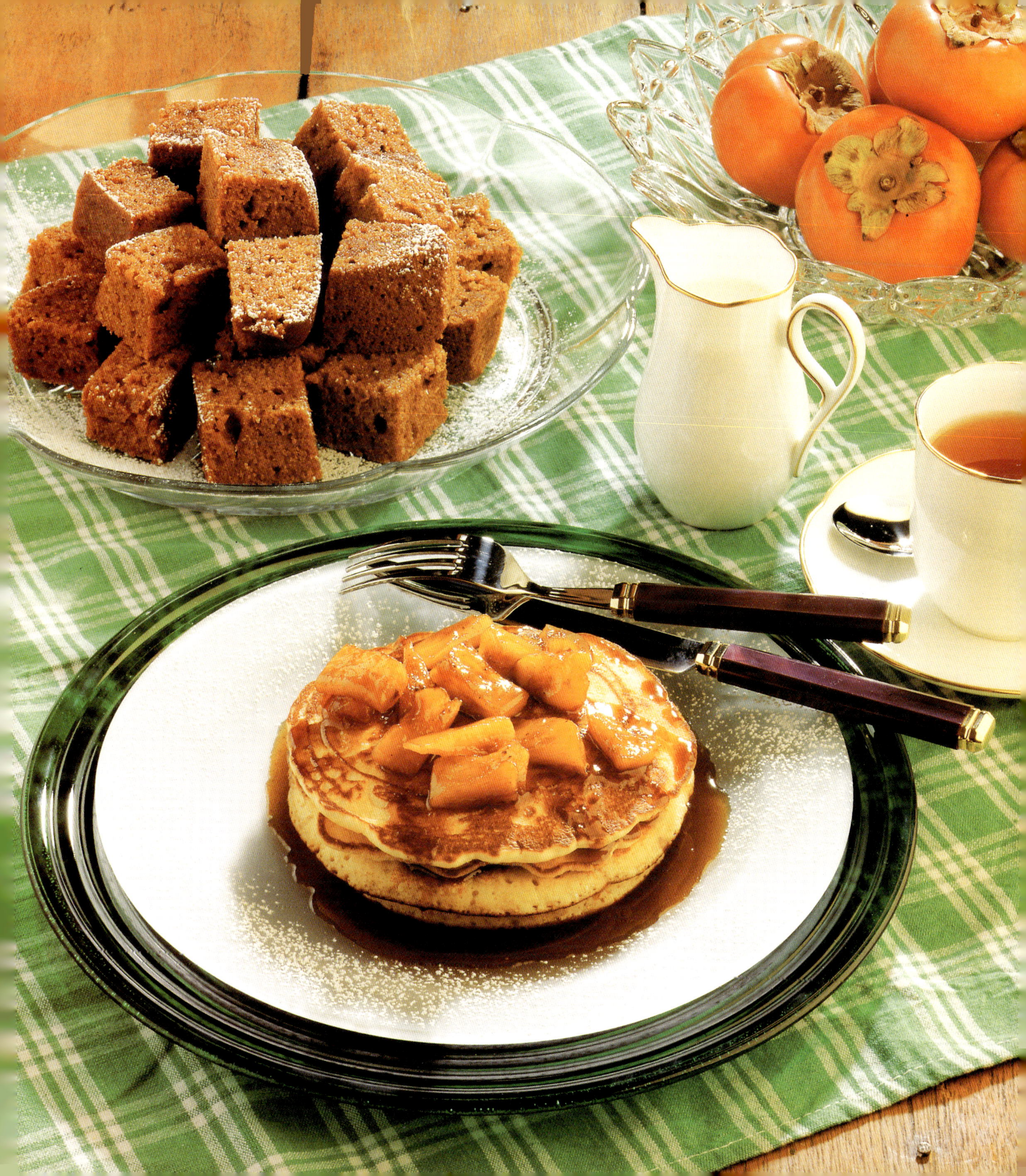

## Strawberry Tea Mousse

### Ingredients

- 4 cups heavy cream, chilled
- 1/2 cup castor sugar
- 1 1/2 cups fresh strawberry puree
- 1 cup fresh strawberries, sliced
- 2 teaspoons vanilla essence
- 2 teaspoons Grand Marnier

### Method

1. Whip cream and sugar until soft peaks form. Gently fold in strawberry puree, sliced strawberries, vanilla essence and Grand Marnier.
2. Spoon into a glass bowl or individual dessert bowls and chill well before serving.

Chef's Note: For an eye-catching presentation, layer the mousse alternately with the puree and sliced fruits.

## Belgian Waffles

### Ingredients

- 1 1/2 teaspoons dried yeast
- 1/4 cup castor sugar
- 1/4 cup warm water
- 2 eggs, separated
- 2 tablespoons vegetable oil
- 1 1/2 cups water
- 1 teaspoon vanilla essence
- 1/4 cup butter, melted
- 2 cups all-purpose flour
- 1/4 teaspoon salt

### Method

1. Dissolve yeast and sugar in the warm water. Set aside. Beat together egg yolks, oil, water, vanilla essence and butter.
2. Combine flour and salt. Stir into the egg mixture. Add the yeast mixture.
3. In a separate bowl beat egg whites until soft peaks form. Add to the batter. Cover with cling wrap and chill in the refrigerator overnight.
4. Stir the batter before spooning onto a greased waffle pan. Cook waffles until golden brown.

## Blackforest Cherry Pudding

### Ingredients

- 1 tablespoon + 4 tablespoons unsalted butter
- 2 tablespoons + 1/2 cup castor sugar
- 6 tablespoons all-purpose flour
- 1 1/4 cups fresh milk
- 3 eggs, separated
- 1 1/2 cups canned black cherries, drained
- a pinch of salt
- powdered sugar for dusting

### Method

1. Grease a souffle dish with 1 tablespoon butter and sprinkle with 2 tablespoons castor sugar.
2. Melt the remaining 4 tablespoons butter and fry the flour. Add the remaining sugar and milk. Whisk quickly until well mixed and boil for 3 to 5 minutes.
3. In a separate bowl beat the egg yolks. Add to the butter mixture and stir in cherries.
4. In another bowl, whisk the egg whites and salt until stiff. Fold into the batter. Pour into the greased dish and bake at 180°C/360°F for 40 minutes. Dust with powdered sugar.

## Baked Pineapple Pudding

### Ingredients

- 2 tablespoons butter
- 1/4 cup brown sugar
- 8 pineapple rings
- 6 eggs
- 1 cup castor sugar
- 1 tablespoon vanilla essence
- 1/2 teaspoon ground cinnamon
- 1 cup golden raisins
- 6 tablespoons dark raisins
- 1 cup grated pineapple
- 4 cups coconut milk, from 2 coconuts
- 4 cups pineapple sponge (purchased ready-made), diced

### Method

1. Grease a baking tray with butter. Sprinkle with brown sugar and arrange pineapple rings in the base of the pan.
2. In a separate bowl beat eggs and sugar. Add vanilla essence, cinnamon, raisins, grated pineapple and coconut milk.
3. Arrange the pineapple sponge over the pineapple rings in the baking tray. Pour in the batter. Set aside for 5 minutes.
4. Put the baking tray in a bigger pan half-filled with hot water. Bake at 170°C/340°F for about an hour.

Chef's Note: The centre of the pudding may look a little soft but the pudding will set when it is completely cool.

*Opposite: Black Forest Cherry Pudding.*

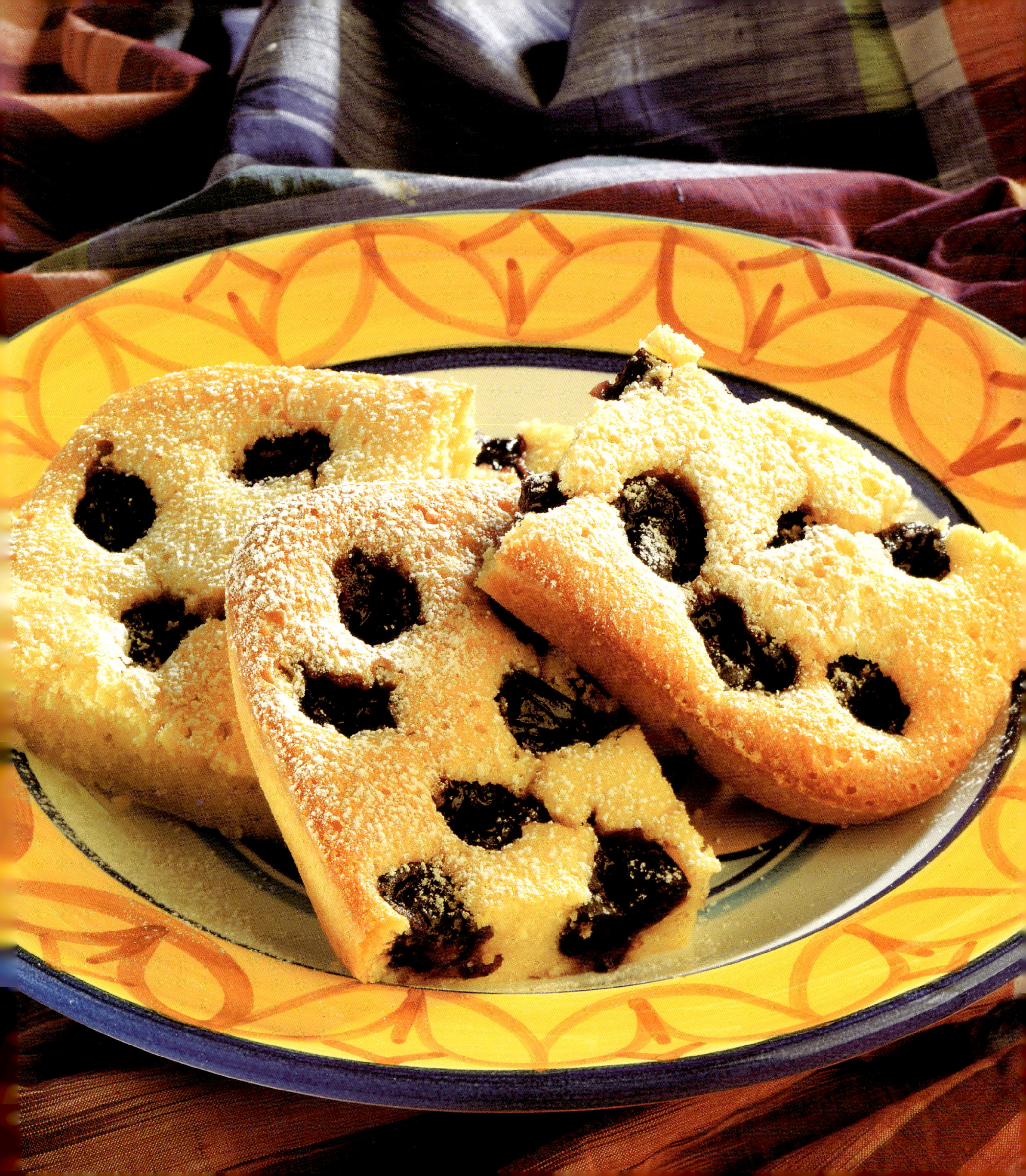

# Index

All-American Apple Pie  18
All-American Chocolate Cake  140
allspice  40, 48, 144, 156, 178
almond  16, 20, 22, 24, 26, 28, 30, 34, 40,
    50, 63, 64, 68, 76, 78, 80, 82, 86, 92, 94,
    96, 100, 102, 104, 106, 108, 110, 114,
    120, 126, 132, 142, 144, 148, 150, 158,
    160, 162, 166, 168
Almond Accidents  92
Almond Apricot Tart  16
Almond Biscuits  114
Almond Bread  120
Almond Crunch Cookies  94
Almond Drops  94
Almond Rings  94
apple  18, 22, 38, 40, 46, 48, 52, 56, 82,
    124, 140, 142, 144, 152, 174, 176
Apple and Date Harvest Cake  140
Apple and Date Princess Cake  140
Apple and Pear Tart with Butterscotch Sauce
    22
Apple Hazelnut Torte  142
Apple and Macadamia Nut Muffins  52
Apple Pecan Muffins  48
Apple Raisin Muffins  48
Apple Yoghurt Pancakes  176
apricot  16, 20, 22, 26, 28, 32, 38, 56, 80,
    98, 100, 102, 106, 110, 114, 122, 126,
    132, 142, 144, 146, 148, 150, 158, 164
Apricot Cake  142
Apricot Coconut Macaroons  100
Apricot Gugelhupf  144
Apricot Jelly Roll  144
Apricot Prune Gugelhupf  146
Apricot Tart  20
Apricot Tea Cake  148

Apricot Walnut Cheesecake  80

Baked Pineapple Pudding  184
banana  28, 46, 56, 58, 122, 132, 142, 146,
    160, 164, 174, 176, 180, 182
Banana Bread Pudding  174
Banana Cake with Cream Cheese Frosting
    146
Banana Chocolate Chip Muffins  58
Banana Pudding  176
Banana Walnut Loaf  122
basil  132, 134
Belgian Waffles  184
Bittersweet Chocolate Date Cake  150
Black Forest Cherry Pudding  184
blueberry  20, 26, 46, 50, 56, 150
Blueberry and Oats Muffin  56
Blueberry Cake  150
Blueberry Custard Tart  26
Blueberry Muffins  50
Boiled Fruitcake  154
Boston Peach Cream Pie  18
bourbon  36, 82, 150, 166
bran  46, 56
brandy  38, 146, 148, 172
Bread Pudding with Apples  174
Brioche  120
Brownie Cheesecake  84
Butter Cookies  106

Cappuccino Chocolate Cheesecake  66
caramel  40, 98, 100, 134, 152, 172, 173,
    178, 182
Caramel Apricot Swirl Cookies  98
Caramelised Apple Cheesecake  82
Caramelised Pineapple Cake  156

cardamom  63, 130
carrot  46, 56, 134, 146, 148, 150
Carrot Cheese Bread  134
Carrot Walnut Cake with Orange Frosting
    146
Cheddar Cheese and Onion Scones  52
Cheddar Cheese Scones  54
cheese  14, 30, 46, 52, 54, 62, 64, 66, 68,
    70, 72, 74, 76, 78, 80, 82, 84, 86, 90, 92,
    96, 98, 110, 120, 128, 134, 146, 156,
    164, 168
Cheesy Coin Cookies  98
cherry  20, 30, 50, 74, 76, 102, 106, 108,
    130, 142, 144, 148, 156, 160, 164, 184
Cherry Almond Cake  144
Cherry Butter Cake  160
chillies  96, 120, 124, 128
chocolate  18, 28, 32, 36, 42, 46, 58, 63, 64,
    66, 70, 72, 76, 82, 84, 86, 90, 92, 96,
    100, 106, 112, 140, 142, 144, 148, 150,
    152, 154, 156, 158, 166, 168, 174, 178,
    180
Chocolate Biscotti  92
Chocolate Bread Pudding  174
Chocolate Cake  152
Chocolate Chip Cookies  92
Chocolate Coconut Strudel  178
Chocolate Gingerbread Cake  144
Chocolate Gugelhupf  152
Chocolate Hazelnut Cheesecake  72
Chocolate Mousse Cheesecake  76
Chocolate Oatmeal Cookies  96
Chocolate Orange Bavaroise  158
Chocolate Paradise Cake  158
Chocolate Potato Cake  152
Chocolate Rehrucken  168

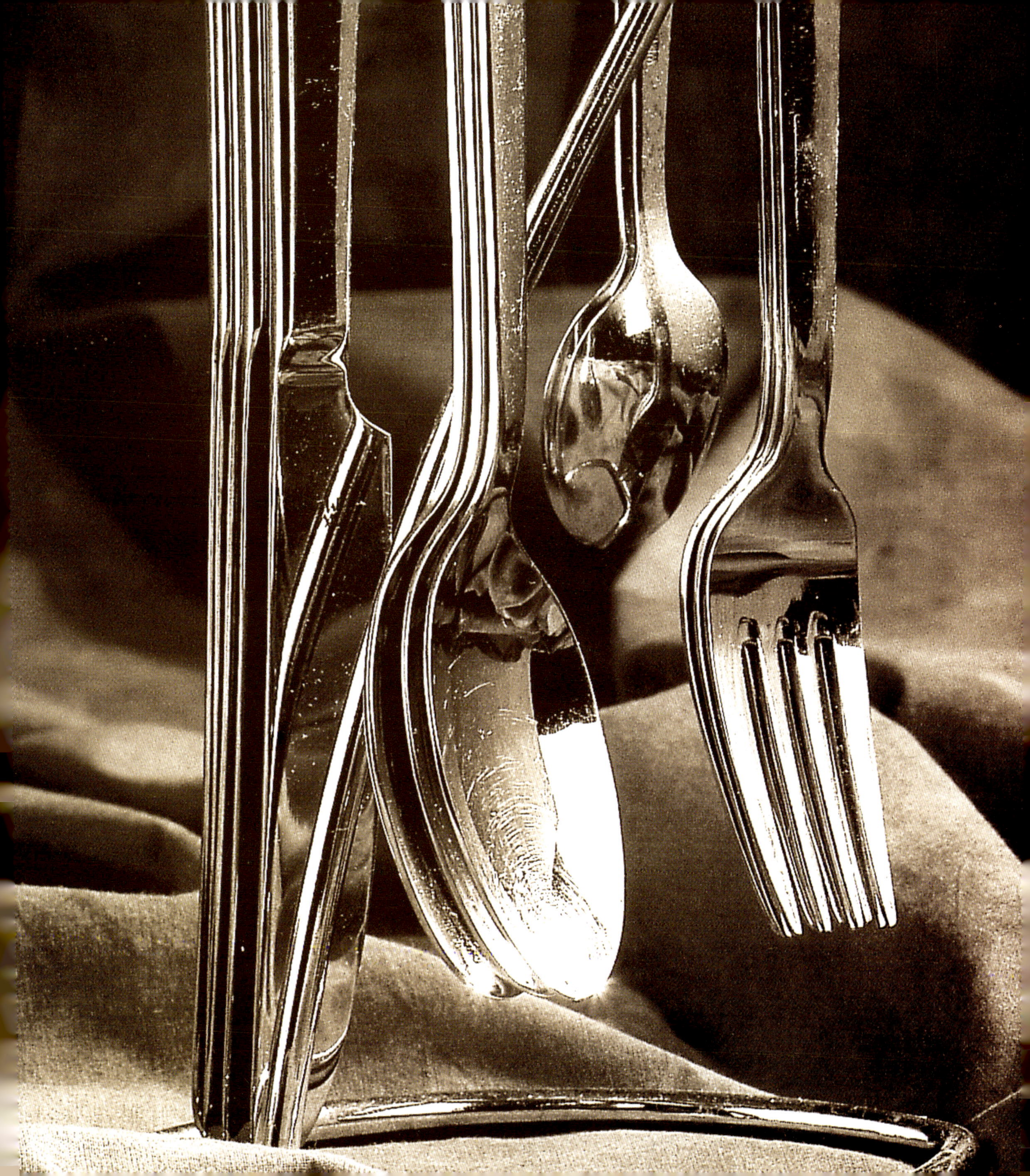

# Index

Chocolate Swirl Espresso Cheesecake 74
Chocolate Valentino 156
Christmas Stollen 126
cinnamon 18, 22, 30, 34, 40, 48, 50, 52, 56, 58, 63, 66, 70, 74, 82, 92, 94, 96, 100, 102, 104, 106, 108, 110, 124, 126, 132, 134, 140, 144, 146, 150, 152, 154, 156, 162, 164, 166, 174, 178, 182, 184
Cinnamon Walnut Coffee Cake 154
Citrus Cheesecake 66
Clafoutis with Cherries 20
Cling Peaches and Almond Tart 22
cloves 18, 24, 30, 34, 50, 58, 63, 78, 92, 100, 106, 124, 150, 152, 158, 162
cocoa 42, 63, 66, 92, 100, 112, 140, 142, 148, 152, 154, 158, 166, 168, 174
coconut 20, 48, 72, 78, 100, 148, 164, 176, 178, 182, 184
Coconut Carrot Cake 148
Coconut Cream Pie 36
Coconut Peach Cheesecake 72
Coconut Pineapple Muffins 48
coffee 42, 63, 64, 66, 72, 84, 100, 144, 154, 166, 168, 176, 180
Coffee Cheesecake 84
Cointreau 22, 80
Cointreau Pear Tart 22
corn 48, 50, 52, 120, 122, 126, 128, 130, 134, 146, 158, 164
Corn and Cheddar Cheese Loaf 128
Cornflake Coffee Kisses 100
Cornflake Crunchies 102
cornflakes 100, 102, 104, 164
cornflour 150
Cream Cheese Gems 96
Crepes 176
Crispy Cornflake Cake 164
Crumpets 52
currant 50, 54, 94, 102, 122, 126, 154, 178
Currant Oat Scones 54
custard 15, 16, 18, 20, 22, 24, 26, 28, 32, 34, 36, 38, 50, 63, 64, 68, 80, 82, 86, 94, 100, 106, 108, 172, 173, 174, 176, 178, 180, 182
Custard Lime Tart 20

Danish Fruit Ring 126
date 28, 48, 56, 70, 92, 100, 104, 122, 140, 148, 150
Date and Pecan Pumpkin Squares 100
Date and Pecan Tartlet 28
Date, Honey and Carrot Muffins 56
Dried Fruit and Apricot Loaf 122

Dried Fruit and Orange Loaf 122
Dried Shrimp Cornflake Cookies 104
Durian Delight Cheesecake 68
Dutch Apple Bread 124
Dutch Country Pear Pie 40
Dutch Kletskoppan 108

English Trifle 182
Evelyn OrangeTea Loaf 142

Farmer's Country Loaf 130
figs 70, 122
Flaming Heart 16
Foccaccia à la Provence 132
Foccaccia with Red Onions and Rosemary 132
Frangipane Pineapple Tart 24
French Orange Biscuits 96
French Peasant Bread 130
Fresh Ginger Cake 162
fruit 16, 18, 20, 22, 26, 32, 34, 50, 54, 63, 104, 122, 126, 130, 132, 154, 164, 182, 184
Fruit Chiffon Cake 142
Fruit Cobbler 164
Fruit Tartlets 32
Fruitcake Cookies 104
Fruitcake Muffins 50
Fruity TangerineTea Cake 148

gelatine 62, 63, 64, 76, 78, 80, 84, 158, 168, 173
German Potato Bread 120
German Sand Biscuits 114
ginger 50, 63, 80, 82, 90, 98, 102, 104, 106, 124, 138, 144, 156, 162
Ginger and Molasses Snaps 104
Ginger, Peaches and Pineapple Cake 162
Ginger Snaps 106
Gingerbread Cookies 102
Gingerbread Raisin Scones 50
Grand Marnier 16, 38, 80, 114, 142, 184
grapes 182
Greek Honey Citrus Cheesecake 70

hazelnut 28, 34, 36, 70, 100, 108
Hazelnut Shortbread 108
honey 30, 32, 52, 56, 62, 68, 70, 78, 102, 104, 110, 112, 154, 182
Honey and Mango Chilled Cheesecake 78
Honey Corn Muffins 52
Honey Pumpkin Tart 30
honeydew 182

Hot Apple Cake with Caramel Pecan Sauce 152
Husarenkrapfert 102

ice-cream 32, 46, 100, 152

Jelly with Coffee Custard 176

Kirsch 74

La Tropicana Cake 164
leavening 46, 91, 119, 138, 139
Lebanese Flat Bread 126
lemon 16, 18, 24, 26, 28, 30, 32, 34, 38, 40, 48, 50, 52, 63, 64, 66, 68, 70, 74, 76, 78, 96, 98, 102, 106, 110, 114, 122, 126, 140, 144, 156, 160, 162, 164, 166, 180, 182
Lemon Custard Cookies 106
Lemon Ginger Tea Cake 156
Lemon Meringue Pie 34
Lemon Poppy Seed Cake 166
Lemon Raspberry Cookies 110
Lemon Tart 34
Lemon Tea Cake 160
lime 20, 24, 50, 56, 114, 148, 154
Lime Tart 24
Linzer Torte 34

Madeleines 162
mango 28, 56, 78, 164, 180
Mango and Banana Custard Pudding 180
Mango and Banana Custard Tart 28
Marble Cheesecake 86
Mexican Wedding Cookies 110
Mississippi Mud Cake 166
Mocha Peach Trifle 180
molasses 28, 36, 46, 50, 91, 102, 104, 106, 144, 162
mousse 172, 173, 184

Nestum Cheesecake 78
New York Cheesecake 74
Noel Nut Balls 112
Norwegian Christmas Bread 130
nougat 76
Nougat Cheesecake 64
nut 48, 50, 52, 58, 63, 64, 66, 70, 72, 76, 90, 92, 94, 96, 100, 102, 104, 106, 108, 110, 112, 122, 124, 126, 128, 132, 140, 142, 146, 148, 152, 154, 158, 164
nutmeg 24, 50, 56, 58, 63, 82, 100, 104, 122, 124, 126, 152, 158, 174, 176, 178

# Index

Oat Bran and Fruit Muffin  56
Oatmeal Biscuits  102
Oatmeal Date Scones  48
oats  46, 48, 54, 56, 63, 90, 96, 102, 104, 112
olive oil  126
onion  52, 120, 124, 128, 132, 134
Onion Walnut Bread  128
orange  20, 22, 24, 48, 50, 54, 56, 63, 64, 66, 68, 70, 80, 96, 98, 100, 102, 104, 106, 112, 114, 122, 126, 132, 142, 144, 146, 148, 152, 154, 158, 162, 164, 166, 182
Orange Ginger Cheesecake  80
Orange Marmalade Biscuits  106
Orange Shortbread Biscuits  98
Orange Shortbread Cookies  104
Orange Sponge Cake  154
Orange Sultana Cheesecake  68
Orange Walnut Shortbread  112

pancakes  176, 182
papaya  64, 182
Papaya Orange Cheesecake  64
parsley  134
peach  15, 18, 22, 30, 72, 162, 180
Peach Cheesecake Pie  30
peanut butter  28, 76, 100, 108
Peanut Butter and Chocolate Chip Pie  28
Peanut Butter Chocolate Chip Cheesecake  76
Peanut Butter Cookies  108
pear  15, 22, 24, 40, 50, 56, 132
Pear Pie  24
pecan  28, 36, 48, 72, 82, 92, 100, 106, 110, 112, 134, 150, 152, 154, 156
Pecan Cookies  106
Pecan Pie with Chocolate Chips  36
persimmon  158, 182
Persimmon Cake  158
Persimmon Pudding  182
Pina Colada Cheesecake  78
pineapple  24, 48, 78, 90, 130, 154, 156, 160, 162, 164, 182, 184
Pineapple Pancakes  182
Pineapple Upside-Down Cake  160
pistachio  42, 108
Pistachio Cantuccini Biscotti  108
Pistachio Lace Cookies  114
Plain Baked Cheesecake  64
plum  20, 26, 164, 166
Plum Tart  26
Plum Tea Cake  166

potato  120, 139, 152, 178
prune  126, 132, 134, 146, 148, 154
Prune and Pecan Sticky Bun  134
Prune and Lemon Cake  154
pudding  172, 174, 182, 184
pumpkin  30, 58, 63, 82, 100, 124, 128
Pumpkin Cheesecake with Pecan Topping  82
Pumpkin Walnut Loaf  124

Raisin Oatmeal Cookies  112
Raisin Pear Muffins  50
Raisin Pumpkin Roll  128
raisins  18, 40, 48, 50, 52, 90, 92, 96, 104, 112, 120, 122, 126, 128, 130, 142, 154, 158, 174, 184
raspberry  16, 32, 34, 110, 160
Raspberry Lemon Tart  32
Rugelash  92
rum  24, 32, 36, 64, 72, 168, 172

Sablé Cookies  112
Savoury Cheese Fingers  96
Scottish Banbury Biscuits  94
shortbread  64, 80, 90, 98, 108, 112
shortening  14, 15, 30, 40, 91, 96, 98, 100, 104, 106, 108, 122, 138, 139, 156
sour cream  14, 48, 64, 66, 68, 70, 72, 74, 76, 80, 82, 160
Spiced Pumpkin Muffins  58
Spicy Corn Bread  120
Strawberries and Cream Cheesecake  84
Strawberries and White Chocolate Cheesecake  86
strawberry  16, 40, 72, 84, 86, 156, 160, 178, 182, 184
Strawberry Almond Tart  40
Strawberry Tea Mousse  184
strudel  178
Sunshine Cheesecake  80
Sweet Corn Bread  122
Sweet Dream Cookies  110
Sweet Potato Flan  178
Swiss Braided Bread  134
Swiss Carrot Cake  150
Swiss Chocolate Rosettes  100

Tarte Alsacienne  38
Tarte Danoise  30
tea  142, 148, 162, 166
Tiramisu  168
trifle  173, 180, 182
Tropical Fruit Loaf  132

Turkish Calzone  124

Upside-Down Apple Tart  40

Vanilla Kipferin  114
Victoria Sponge Sandwich  160
Vienna Walnut Crescents  110
Visitandine  162

walnut  28, 32, 36, 74, 80, 86, 100, 110
Walnut and Honey Tart  32
Walnut Apricot Cookies  102
Walnut Prune Cake  148
Warm Chocolate Tart with Pistachio Sauce  42

yoghurt  46, 56, 63, 68, 70, 84, 128, 144, 146, 152, 156, 162, 176